Writing To Survive

How Teachers and Teens Negotiate the Effects of Abuse, Violence, and Disaster

Deborah M. Alvarez

ROWMAN & LITTLEFIELD EDUCATION

A division of

ROWMAN & LITTLEFIELD PUBLISHERS, INC.

Lanham • New York • Toronto • Plymouth, UK

Published by Rowman & Littlefield Education
A division of Rowman & Littlefield Publishers, Inc.
A wholly owned subsidiary of The Rowman & Littlefield Publishing Group, Inc.
4501 Forbes Boulevard, Suite 200, Lanham, Maryland 20706
www.rowmaneducation.com

Estover Road
Plymouth PL6 7PY
United Kingdom

Copyright © 2011 by Deborah M. Alvarez

British Library Cataloguing in Publication Information Available

Library of Congress Cataloging-in-Publication Data

Alvarez, Deborah M., 1952–
  Writing to survive : how teachers and teens negotiate the effects of abuse, violence, and disaster / Deborah M. Alvarez.
    p. cm.
  Includes bibliographical references and index.
  ISBN 978-1-60709-783-9 (cloth : alk. paper)—ISBN 978-1-60709-784-6 (pbk. : alk. paper)—ISBN 978-1-60709-785-3 (electronic)
  1. Composition (Language arts)—Study and teaching—United States.   2. English language—Composition and exercises—Study and teaching—United States.
3. Youth—Crimes against—United States.   4. Violence in adolescence—United States.   I. Title.
  LB1576.A61576 2011
  808'.0420712—dc22   2010043446

♾™ The paper used in this publication meets the minimum requirements of American National Standard for Information Sciences—Permanence of Paper for Printed Library Materials, ANSI/NISO Z39.48-1992.

Printed in the United States of America

This book is dedicated to Diana, Chase, Danielle, Tommie, Lydia, Tyrone, Ms. Plummer, Ms. Whitson, Mr. Muller, Ms. Jane, and Ms. Martin, without whom this book would not have been possible. I hope that I have kept the truth of your lives and stories. My time with you has had a profound effect upon my teaching and my life.

I want to also dedicate this book to the thousands of adolescents who suffer abuse and experience violence every day, and the teachers who teach them.

May your stories teach us a little more about how to prepare effective instructional strategies and to use writing so that it makes it easier for you to learn, to thrive, but most of all to survive.

I am grateful to the following people who read through this manuscript and helped me to refine its message, stay focused, and catch those pesky errors I became too involved with to see.

Shernise Allen

Jill Ewing Flynn   Mary Mowers   Carol Kerrigan

Sarah Cornwell

Table of Contents

Introduction

Several years ago I attended an International Scholars Forum on literacy and children who have experienced armed conflict and natural disasters. The conference organizer, Dr. Denny Taylor of Hofstra University, brought scholars, photographers, journalists, and teachers from all over the world. Our common purpose was to understand more about how conflict and natural disasters have affected children's literacy and our need to find a way to assist teachers who are presently working with children in affected areas of the world.

One presenter was Adam Shapiro, a photojournalist, who shared his pictures and stories from Ramallah and Darfur. Adam's presentation affected the audience most when he shared his stories about how teachers and children in Darfur built makeshift schoolrooms from the rubble of the desert village. After the armed battle ended, Adam described how these teachers became the community leaders and initiated order by gathering the remaining children together and conducting school. He said that he saw desperate reasons behind these teachers' effort to first establish a literacy environment in the middle of a war zone: the need for safety and security through educational routine, the need to preserve learning, the need to build an identity, and finally, the need to survive.

This manuscript has been coming together for several years. When I heard Adam's presentation along with those of the other speakers at the forum, I knew that I had not been misguided in my research or my conclusions about writing for adolescents and their need to survive. Through a series of uncanny events following Hurricane Katrina, I found the central theme for this book, a theme that had gotten lost in my own struggles with cancer and surviving.

In early October of 2006, I was introduced to a professor from the University of New Orleans, who had found refuge from Katrina in Delaware. When he returned to New Orleans the following spring, he called and asked me if I would be able to talk to New Orleans teachers about adolescents, trauma, and writing. I jumped at the chance to help; however, I had yet to discover whether or not the research I had conducted on writing with abused adolescents would apply to adolescents exposed to critical events surrounding a natural disaster.

At first, it would appear that the effects of abuse and violence upon adolescent literacy habits would have little to do with natural disasters; however, regardless of the initial critical event, violent and critical events create desperate learning conditions for adolescents. When adolescents encounter violence, abuse or the aftermath of a natural disaster like Katrina, they engage in a type of literacy practice constructed for and adapted to their survival needs.

In recent years, we have seen retaliatory violence escalate in places such as Columbine in Colorado, Red Lake in Minnesota, and on a growing number of college campuses, as had happened at Virginia Tech. While the national news media have raised alarms about these violent adolescents, violent events, and the destructive material conditions after natural disasters, the adolescent students and teachers return to the locations now marked by a life changing event. Every teacher or researcher reading this book probably knows of at least one student who has been abused or who has faced unspeakable acts of violence at the hands of some adult or another adolescent. In the broader world community, we add the glaring violence from terrorists, American involvement in terrorism and armed conflict, and finally nature's own fury. This book is about a group of adolescents who encounter or live with violence, abuse, and natural disasters each day and yet learn and practice amazing acts of literacy.

As Adam Shapiro's presentation so poignantly showed, children have a need to learn, in spite of the violence and disasters surrounding them; in fact, it is a necessity that they continue some learning because it assists them in surviving and growing. As teachers, we are confronted each day with a growing number of adolescents who have been affected by violence and disasters. Although these violent acts are different than the armed conflict scenarios presented by the forum's scholars, we intuitively know that any act of violence affects children. I see this book as a study in how these critical life events shape adolescent literacy practices and illustrate for teachers how they can best reach students affected by traumatic conditions and experiences.

In the twenty-five years I have worked with adolescents, I have been frustrated, amazed, and periodically stumped as to how they think and reason. They are creative, clever, and intelligent, yes; they are also impossible, infuriating, and irascible. They are more capable than we allow them to be, and they will learn in spite of whatever we do in the classroom. All of these conditions surround one imperative when it comes to teaching adolescents: I have to believe that there is a learning process at work in every adolescent, a "gnys at wrk."[1]

As a teacher and researcher, I want to understand as much as I can about how adolescents learn so that I can know how to teach them. While I do not intend to essentialize adolescence or any mental process like learning or trauma, I did discover patterns of behavior, material conditions, and other social factors through my research that may influence and direct adolescent learning.

I have come to believe that our search for understanding lies outside the classroom, especially for those so affected by traumatic life events. For some of them, it is a matter of survival just to get to school, to have something to eat and to survive the pressures and influences of peers and adults. Each year continues to bring more complex social problems to adolescents: drugs, violence, abuse, pregnancy, or being surrounded by these attitudes and conditions in or out of school. Those of us who work with adolescents see the personal impact these external forces have upon their ability to learn. The open exposure to violence, drugs, and abuse brings confusion and complication for adolescents, who need to develop healthy sexual identities, academic success, and social behaviors. The issues of poverty, academic inequalities, poor literacy preparation at home, and inadequate teaching in school compound the life and educational stresses adolescents face in acquiring knowledge and literacy skills that will assist them in finding work, relationships, and healing.

I recognize that these conditions are no longer the life reality for only a few students, but the reality for more of the adolescents in high school classrooms than anyone would like to admit or count. In spite of these harsh realities and grim conditions, adolescents show us their personal resiliency to learn and survive through literate practices like the Compensatory Strategies.

I have specialized in teaching adolescents to write and in writing pedagogy and assessments. Over the years, I have changed teaching pedagogies, learning approaches, and theories as often as I have changed my hairstyles. Some of the influences have become the touchstones for change in literacy, writing, and teaching: names like Janet Emig, James Britton, James Moffett, Linda Flower and John Hayes, John Dixon, and Peter Elbow, to name a few.

My readers would probably laugh at the kinds of strategies I used to teach writing in the 1980s. I gave writing assignments like the comparison and contrast essay; I had worksheets for the five-paragraph composition, often correct in form but lacking substance and voice.

In the 1990s, I attempted to develop my high school writing pedagogy using the theories of William Glasser, Nancie Atwell, Shirely Brice Heath, Paolo Freire, Ken Bruffee, Lev Vygotsky, and Lydia Bozhovich. These theories showed the importance of social and cultural literacy heritage that affected the adolesccents' writing products and learning conditions. I am still trying to figure out what I am doing in the twenty-first century. Yes, teaching writing to adolescents is a challenge almost every day. Yet, at the beginning and end of every lesson, there is still the element of magic in their need to learn which may hold the key for understanding how to educate adolescents more effectively.

I think every germ of real understanding is grounded in some event or moment which makes us pause and question what is happening. Like any teacher or researcher, I had hunches about observations in my classroom, but these momentary glimpses into the adolescent mind were fleeting and my explanation for them—just an explanation without evidence. All of this changed for me in one afternoon after I went on a fishing expedition with an adolescent named Randy and his friend Joe. Catching carp in the local stream with them gave me the moment of insight that has since guided my teaching and research work, trying to understand what happened that day, questioning why it happened, how it was possible, and finally seeing it in the stories of Adam Shapiro and all the adolescents who share their stories in this book.

I was in a doctoral program at the University of Wisconsin-Madison and was working on situated literacy practices and adolescent composition. When Randy, a student in my eleventh grade English language arts class, agreed to the research project, I had my first real initiation into what situated literacy practices meant. Randy agreed to let me see all the writing he did in and out of school, and it also meant that I followed him to whatever activities he did after school. To Randy, out of school activities meant fishing. So per our agreement, Randy took me fishing one late autumn afternoon as part of his daily activities.

Randy, his friend, Joe, and I walked to a little stream not far from Randy's home. While the boys talked and fished, I took notes. After catching a few fish and throwing them back into the river, Randy took me back to his home to meet his parents, and here I continued the interview about his writing and his interests. While we were sitting on the porch talking, Randy's mother, who had been listening from a distance, came around the corner and asked me if I had seen Randy's fishing journal. No, I hadn't. In fact, Randy had never mentioned his fishing journal. When I asked him about this, he said, "Well, that isn't writing."

She brought me a two-inch thick three-ring-binder that was filled with pages of charts. These charts contained information about the air temperature, other meteorological data, geographical data related to the condition of the river and surrounding banks, the number of fish, type, weight, length, gender, and any other distinguishing characteristics.

Randy had been keeping this journal since he was in the sixth grade. I asked him how he designed the page on which he wrote the information. He told me he just made it up from bits and pieces he had learned in school, and then he designed the rest to meet his needs for recording data about fishing. Simple! Yet, this was anything but simple! This was an ichthyologist's dream—ten years of consistent and informative data.

What dawned on me at this point was the reason that Randy had not shared his writing outside of school with me; to him, writing was something else. As a participant in this preliminary research project, he knew that I wanted to see everything he was writing in and out of school. When I asked him why he didn't show this to me to test my realization, he said again, "Well, this isn't writing."

What I learned from Randy in his extraordinary project was that adolescents could create their own learning, devise writing strategies, and adapt genre conventions into creative and expressive forms of writing. Because these forms do not resemble traditional school-based writing tasks, Randy didn't consider that it was writing at all. There was something more complex to the writing that Randy had done in his log and the manner in which he had created the fishing matrix for collecting data.

If this was not just an isolated incident, then maybe other students generated written texts like this when they had to know, had to understand, or had to survive in some general way. They did it purposefully and with design and complexity that had not been part of any school lesson or project. This book is a deeper investigation into these compensatory literacy habits that adolescents use when they create written texts. It is about how adolescents use language acts with purpose to educate, and in some cases, to survive the world around them in very literate ways that seem so contrary to the instructional and pedagogical patterns being employed in classrooms.

In the research projects which serve as the foundation for the discussion in this book, the adolescents tell us stories about the way we teach writing in juxtaposition to the way they use it in their private and public lives. Their stories are compelling examples of the disjunction between writing for school and for life, and what intervenes in the process when the academic is detached from real life experiences and their traumatic consequences.

While these issues served as the primary focus for my research, an unexpected element arose: the adolescent informants were all exposed to or victims of violence and abuse. Second, natural disaster circumstances also exposed adolescents to more acts of violence and abuse, as well as the critical life events that the disaster itself imposed. During the research process, the issues with violence emerged early as a strong socio-cultural context for the adolescents' writing. The more I learned about the adolescent informants, the more the violent conditions which surrounded them revealed more about literacy processes and writing than the original research questions asked. While the book investigates the altered and adapted literacy process which the informants used, it does so with a focused lens upon the specific effects that violence and natural disaster have upon writing and learning in respect to the compensations these adolescents develop. These altered and adapted literacy practices visible in the writing practices are called *compensatory strategies.*

At the time, I thought that adolescents who lived in or experienced violent situations were those who lived in predominately urban areas, lived in poverty, and had dysfunctional and unstable family environments. However, I learned that violence, abuse, and the effects of natural disasters do not discriminate by race, economics, or geography. Adolescents witness or experience violent acts in schools, homes, and neighborhood; these are no longer problems that are solely located within urban and poor community schools.

As time has revealed, the violent and abusive experiences our students bring to the classroom are becoming more public than private, more widespread than isolated, and more alarming because of their frequency. These realities force us to focus our teaching lens upon how these conditions affect the learning of adolescents, and then adapt our curricula to ensure they can begin to heal and to regain their ability to learn.

My strategy for presenting these stories and details about teaching is taken from the ethnographic writing research process. I begin each adolescent's story with a vignette, and present the data in a case study format, detailing the adolescent's personal and private history, the English classroom and teacher, his/her process of making compensations under extreme conditions, and the role writing played in an adolescent's ability to deal with the violences.

Each adolescent's story would not be complete without a discussion of the language arts classroom and the adolescent's English language arts teacher. In order to understand the adolescent's use of literacy, I started with the writing tasks adolescents completed for school. Knowing the private, social, and emotional difficulties for each adolescent, I wanted to know what the teacher was offering in terms of writing tasks. What effect would these tasks have upon the adolescent's private or public struggles over time?

Given the amount of time adolescents spend in classrooms, the daily interplay of curricular demands, teacher-selected disciplinary content and pedagogical decisions are important players in each adolescent's story. The classroom writing tasks and assignments had varying effects upon the self-sponsored writing the adolescents completed outside of school.

In order to create a useful book that provides the audience with the richness of the socio-cultural-historical theories and ethnographic reporting underlying this research, each chapter contains the conditions in and out of the classroom, which affected the adolescent's writings. The reader has the circumstances I witnessed, and I describe them in detail. Sometimes, I indulge in lengthy interviews or detailed field notes. In each of these cases, the reader has relevant information in which to contextualize the writing situation, the instructions for the writing or exigency if self-sponsored, and the writing itself and the revisions, if they were required in the school-based writing task.

Furthermore, I describe the teacher's instructional techniques, writing assignment, and assessments that place writing at the center of the adolescent learning and development. These intersections of teaching techniques, writing samples, interview information, and discussions will serve to afford my readers rich instructional materials for discussions in their own classrooms, methods courses, and research examples. I wanted this book to be used for instruction, discussion, and analysis.

As a result, the book is divided into two parts. In part I, chapters 1 through 5, I examine the social, cultural, and educational activities surrounding the private violences in adolescents' lives, and how those conditions shaped their writing as well as how it shaped their uses of writing. In part II, chapters 6 through 9, I examine the public violence a natural disaster introduces and how the shape and use of writing by teachers and adolescents told a similar story about the need for writing, learning, and surviving another horrific crisis event.

Chapter 1 introduces the broader issues of literacy, writing, and the compensatory strategies along with explanations about adolescent crisis, the language concept theories of Vygotsky and Bozhovich as they relate to adolescents, modern brain theory, and writing and trauma. Chapter 2 outlines the ethnographic narrative, which the book uses to detail the case studies and the data. Chapters 3, 4, and 5 narrate the case study data for each adolescent's story of writing, literacy, and the compensatory strategies.

Chapter 6 presents the research on natural disasters, writing, and trauma relative to the traumatic reactions of violence and abuse. Chapters 7 and 8 narrate the teaching strategies and writing after Katrina completed by three adolescents. These chapters are individual case studies that expose adolescent writing composed in response to the critical events they faced after Katrina.

Chapter 9 serves to synthesize the lessons from the case studies and present a program for changing the writing pedagogy for middle and high school adolescents. This chapter argues for a Neo-Expressivist writing program, defined by the four principles of the compensatory strategies and written evidence from research subjects and the needs of those who bring such traumatic experiences to our classrooms.

In our present world, understanding how critical events affect adolescent development and literacy is of immediate importance. My hope is that the adolescents who have shared their life stories and literate practices will show us their "gnys" and help us to teach so that literacy is more about continuing to learn rather than just to survive.

NOTES

1. The reference is to Glenda Bissex's work *A Child Learns to Read and Write*. The "gnys" was written on a piece of paper and hung outside her son's bedroom door one day when she came to check on him. It said, "Gnys at Wrk. Do Not Dstrb."

Part I

Finding a Purpose for Writing in a Violent and Troubled World

Chapter 1

Writing to Survive

"We are, however, arguing what we know to be true—stories about painful, traumatic events in the lives of students do appear in our classrooms, they have always appeared, and they will continue to appear, not because we want or don't want them to, but because writing is quite simply the medium in which, for many people, the deepest, most effective, and most profound healing can take place."

(Anderson and MacCurdy, 2000, p. 9)

When Diana arrived home on Christmas Eve, she found her mother lying outside their apartment complex, surrounded by EMT personnel. During the afternoon, Diana's mother and her latest male companion had gotten drunk. In that drunken stupor, Diana's mother jumped off the roof of their second-floor apartment building so she could fly with Santa's reindeer. Diana arrived home that afternoon to find the paramedics attending to her mother's broken back. Diana consequently spent Christmas Eve and Christmas Day sitting in a hospital waiting room. Then she spent the next few weeks helping her mother recuperate from a broken back.

At the same time that she was experiencing this, Diana had suspicions that she was pregnant—for the fourth time. She had already miscarried or aborted three times. Diana was fifteen. These traumatic personal events resulted in some unevenness in her schoolwork. Diana avoided assignments in her computer class and failed to submit a required essay on *Julius Caesar* in her English class. The only writing I saw her complete was a fire-escape plan for herself and her mother, in her freshman health class.

Diana and the other adolescents in this book are survivors. As survivors, they daily negotiate critical life events alongside the academic schedule of high school. Can you imagine trying to learn and do homework if the story above were your reality? As teachers, we see that stories like Diana's are becoming the personal realities of more and more adolescents in our classrooms. English language arts secondary teachers are prepared to deliver lessons and assess learning about English language, literacy, and literature and to address general behavior problems, which disrupt the engagement with and delivery of this knowledge. The more intense personally troubled history and conditions adolescents bring to the classroom are suppressed, even avoided, beneath a curricular focus on more immediate goals: to teach the curriculum and prepare for federal and state-mandated testing.

In the writing community, the affective domain has been marginalized to favor the cognitive (Brand, 1989), but the research and daily experiences of adolescents like Diana ask us to reconsider how we can educate the children who have been traumatized by life experiences, and to realize that they cannot learn until they have found a way to connect learning with living and surviving. Every day some news report reveals the enormity and frequency of violence perpetrated upon children and adolescents. How do we help them heal and learn amid the violent conditions surrounding their lives?

In the research for this book, I discovered that adolescents used writing in strategic ways to ensure their survival, whether for the classroom or for life. This very type of writing is at the center of healing and surviving for adolescents. Writing was about the immediacy of surviving and healing, especially when the language arts curriculum was writing-centered and topics were personally engaging and relevant to some immediate or past crisis. The writing-centered pedagogy allowed students to select the topics for composing, encouraged writing in multiple genres, pursued a consistent process of journaling, writing, and revising over time, with complementary mini-lessons on issues of establishing clarity and grammatical correctness.

By maintaining a consistent and singular focus, the teacher addressed the learning needs of the students, including those whose daily lives involved some violent act. In traditional English language arts classrooms, the opportunities for personally expressive writing limited the avenues adolescents had to reveal their truths, so they made adjustments. In the private and public spaces between classroom writing assignments, adolescents used writing. When I visited the private and public spaces in these adolescents' social and cultural worlds, I witnessed the violence and saw the resulting behaviors and responses that affected their writing and learning.

Our personal experiences with violence, abuse, and natural disasters vary, but we have all seen it, heard it, watched it, or unfortunately, may have experienced it. Violence surrounds us in so many arenas, that for our discussion in this book, I need to place limits on this powerful term: I use the word violence in part I of this book to refer to the physical, emotional, and psychological harm adolescents are subjected to by any adult, family member, or peer. These include unhealthy and perverted uses of alcohol, drugs, sex, beatings, neglect, deprivations of food, clothing, and stable housing. Adolescents can suffer these violences in private or within a small circle of persons connected to their social world. These are the private violences that silently deprive aggrieved adolescents of fully participating in learning.

In part II of this book, violence occurs at the whim of nature's fury. In a natural disaster, we have a situation in which the traumatic images and experiences are as powerful as those committed by human hands. Katrina's fury exposed layers of historical incompetence in the schools, a racially and economically divided city, and a long history of neglect and inattention to problems. The immense diaspora that followed the flooding and hurricane added another layer of violence to this story. For those who returned to the city, a criminal element also returned and took advantage of vacated drug dealing territory. As a result, a lethal record of gun violence began in those areas hit hardest by the flooding.

Therefore, violence is not only the name given to nature's destruction of personal property, but to the living conditions that drove many adolescents and their parents into survival measures: finding shelter, safety, nourishment, and employment. Sometimes these conditions occur where the other violences of physical, emotional, and psychological abuse are taking place. Whether it is a private violence or a public disaster, the adolescents who experience one or more of these violent acts are living with trauma, which can have long-term deleterious effects upon that individual's ability to learn, to live, and to heal.

When I designed the initial research study for this book, I wanted to learn about adolescents' writing and literacy strategies. As the evidence grew, more compelling analysis drew the discussion into not only writing and literacy strategies, but also into effects this violence had upon writing and literacy strategies. It seemed the stories and evidence mirrored the growing violence that plagued our world. These growing violent events in the private and public arenas meant that I had to investigate the social, cultural aspects within the developmental responses to the stress and trauma the violence triggered. The violent experience and the resulting stress and trauma impact an adolescent's ability to learn and to develop productive literacy habits: that they create a learning environment for themselves is magic enough.

What separates the adolescents in this book from the normal tribulations adolescents face are the severe conditions and chaos that add enormous stress to their lives. As a result, the mental stresses caused by violence, private or public, natural or man-made, produce mental changes that impair an adolescent's ability to learn.[1] Whether a private violence or public disaster, appropriate writing assignments, tasks, and interventions can address an adolescent's trauma and provide a recuperative learning environment. With writing activities that allow connections between the emotions associated with the experience and the images captured in words, an adolescent can write her/his way through these traumatic events. They literally can write their way to understanding and some relief from the stress.

Understanding the writing compensations that adolescents are making can be useful to teachers to encourage and facilitate healing for those adolescents who are affected by violence. This is not to say that this book is about adding another responsibility to teachers to engage in therapy, but instead addresses how to use writing about traumatic events to complement the learning and writing tasks these adolescents need. As Wendy Bishop has so clearly stated, "Therapy is a process that takes place with another person . . . Processes can be therapeutic; they can make you feel healthy and facilitate change, but the processes themselves are not 'therapy'" (Bishop, 1993, p. 503).

The private and public violences adolescents experience have changed the way adolescents learn. Primarily, the trauma producing stresses from the experience divert the direction of thinking and turn it to managing the immediate environmental conditions. Mental processing in this atmosphere is dependent upon memory and emotion. The diversion of brain energy to the limbic functions act as a block or a filter through which the adolescent thinks, reacts and learns in traumatic conditions. Because of the trauma and stress, classroom learning and writing activities need to allow the release of these emotions and be connected to immediate and relevant personal matters. In the narrative discourses of telling and relating, adolescents can process the images and experiences related to the trauma and stress. This process, however subtle and simple, offers stress release.

If the classroom instruction does not provide the relationship between learning activities and relevancy, adolescents will deflect, adapt, convert, subvert, or divert what they are learning into meaning, sometimes far removed from the content knowledge required of classroom assignments and readings. Because of the traumatic stresses the violence has placed upon them, adolescents use specific learning strategies to guide them when they produce school assignments and use writing to facilitate their own survival out of the classroom. These *compensatory strategies* are most evident in the writing adolescents engage in, whether self-sponsored or school-sponsored.

I found evidence of these compensations in my ethnographic research at Prairie High School and in the New Orleans public schools. By asking adolescents and teachers about their private and public writing, I found that both parties were making strategic compensations due to their own public or private trauma. What is most relevant in these two situations is that the trauma, whether public or private, affected the ability of both groups to learn and to recover from their experiences. Writing in both instances was the common thread necessary to their recovery, healing, and a returning ability to learn. When they give voice to their experiences through story and narratives, they experience a type of transformation that can be a link in their healing and learning process. This book is an illustration of how that occurs.

In order to understand how trauma and violence affect an adolescent's learning and to explain the compensatory strategies, I begin by examining Vygotskian perspectives on the "crisis" in adolescent psychological development. This information introduces the role of language and emotional and cognitive processes as they are occurring in adolescents. Then, I will discuss how trauma from the violent critical life events influences those roles. At this juncture, I suggest that the normal psychological processes of crisis occurring internally are parallel to their external counterpart; that is, violence destabilizes an adolescent's development and creates a different learning zone built from a patchwork of existing learning strategies from life and the classroom.

At every turn, language use is the key element through which we can examine these phases and functions in literacy events. Modern brain research and trauma and writing theorists have revealed that language use in the production of oral and written texts assists individuals in recovery and in learning after a traumatic event. In terms of capturing the emotional responses to violence, its images, and its effects, the adolescent brain processes differently than the adult brain.

Through this discussion, I will describe the role of writing as a tool for effective intervention in classrooms for attending to the private violence and how it works with all adolescents, not just those affected by violence. This will lead to the thesis for this book: that the private violences and public disasters affect adolescents' ability to learn, and the trauma and stresses alter the ways in which adolescents construct literacy, which I call the *compensatory strategies*.

Writing tasks are the primary means of affecting traumatic stresses and the primary way of showing how adolescents are making compensations when classroom tasks do not address their needs. In order to create effective lessons and learning environments for these adolescents, classroom instruction and pedagogies must link personally relevant choices in writing tasks with long-term revision processes, offer parallel and varied genre readings, repeated opportunities to tell and investigate the traumatic experience. These classroom strategies can have a positive effect upon an adolescent's ability to learn and to gain resiliency.

CRISIS IN ADOLESCENCE

Crisis has two meanings in this book. The first meaning refers to the psychological state between adolescent developmental stages as an adolescent moves from childhood to adulthood. Various theorists have used this term to refer to the behavior adolescents display during the adolescent growth phase: loud and aggressive verbal confrontations with parents, siblings, and other adults; and general issues with rebellion and behavior displays contrary to the family's accepted norms. Specifically, what drives these behaviors is the biological growth and development that manifests itself in the adolescent's need for separation, in the search and establishment of an individual personal identity. Adolescent psychologist Erik Erikson explains the crisis in adolescence as part of this search for an identity that is driven by physical and mental development (1968).

Vygotsky and his followers examined adolescent crisis as part of the socio-cultural-historical psychology of mind. One of these followers, Lydia Bozhovich, was a student and then a colleague of Vygotsky. Bozhovich conducted research and wrote about adolescent crisis and adolescent psychological development. Her theories and Vygotsky's allowed the expansion of early "inner" speech and language processes beyond childhood and included the role of education in language development and higher psychological functions[2].

> A central theme in Vygotsky's development theory is that cognitive development can be understood as the transformation of basic, biologically determined processes into higher psychological function. According to the theory, the human child is endowed by nature with a wide range of perceptual, attentional and memory capacities, such as the capacity to perceive contrast and movements, the capacity for eidetic[3] memory, and arousal/habitation responses to environmental stimuli, to name a few. Such basic processes (also referred to by Vygotsky as "biological," "natural," or "elementary"), however, are substantially transformed in the context of socialization and education, particularly through the use of language, to constitute the high psychological functions or the unique forms of human cognition. (Diaz et al in Moll, 1999, p. 127)

We see here that Vygotsky's development theory places emphasis on the continuing role of language to direct socialization and education in mediating development.

This is relevant to understanding crisis in adolescence and the effects that trauma stress has upon literacy development. An adolescent's growing need to self-regulate and gain identity are more desperate processes for those adolescents subjected to violence because the violence can take away their sense of power over their lives and their future. The biologically driven forces provide opportunities for adolescents to indeed create unique learning strategies and adaptations of literacy processes in their own survival instincts.

Specifically, crisis in adolescents within the Vygotskian tradition describes the nebulous zone between developmental phases, where the developing adolescent is confronted with an irresolvable situation beyond her/his present understanding. This situation may be a combination of emotional, social, or situational factors that cause the adolescent to be without a course of action. They search outside of their known spheres for answers because the adolescent is without a specific knowledge or course of action. According to L. Bozhovich,

> we believe that the crisis of adolescence is related to the new level of self-awareness that occurs at this period, a characteristic feature of which is the emergence of the capacity and the need to know oneself as an individual with unique qualities, different from everyone else. This engenders in the adolescent the desire for self-affirmation, self-expression (i.e. the desire to display those qualities of personality considered of value), and self-education. Lack of satisfaction of the needs described above is one of the foundations of the crisis of adolescence. (p.65)

This explanation defines crisis in adolescence as a search for a new level of self-awareness and self-education.

The second definition of crisis embodies the most common understanding: a situation in which an individual is in need of immediate assistance, or the intersection of various conditions which threaten the health, safety, or welfare of an individual. These external crisis conditions have parallels to the psychological crisis. The internal crisis driven by biological forces activate psychological operations. Traumatic stresses due to life crises events force adolescents to address issues of safety, health, and survival rather than attend to the development of identity. For purposes of clarity, in this book, trauma will be defined as "an escapably stressful event that overwhelms people's existing coping mechanisms" (van der Kolk, 1996, p. 279).

The stresses and trauma from violence redirect psychological energies into a survival mode. Yet, this drive toward survival engages the adolescents in creative problem solving strategies in alternate literacy acts. In these compensatory strategies, the adolescent has to attend to the intellectual resources while serving to meet an immediate personal crisis. What is important for our discussion is that we have a means and a tool to use in redirecting and reconnecting intellectual energies in times of crisis.

The mental transformations and reconnections can take place with writing and other language intensive activities; the stresses and trauma can be relieved while reestablishing learning through the writing activities that engage the traumatic stresses. The construction of stories and narratives giving voice to the traumatic images and emotions allows the adolescent to observe, reflect, and arrive at a new level of self-awareness and self-expression.

If, as Bozhovich states, adolescence is in part a psychological state that involves the adolescent in a search for self-affirmation, self-expression, and self-education, the conditions surrounding violence, both public and private, only increase the need to problem solve. Learning for adolescents becomes driven by the need for self-affirmation, self-expression, self-education, and self-preservation. When learning and experiences do not challenge or complement these processes, or when the adolescent faces stress from traumatic events, we have adolescents who will deviate and redirect learning, sometimes with negative consequences both in and out of the classroom.

The Adolescent Brain, Learning, and Violence

Because the affective or the emotional plays an important role in how adolescents process experience and information, it is an important piece of the developing picture of how adolescents attempt to respond to moments of trauma or crisis. How do adolescents process emotions, memory, and images? Both in sociocultural theories of language acquisition and in brain research, emotion has been recognized for its position in thought production. Vygotsky (1986) states,

> behind every thought there is an affective-volitional tendency, which holds the answer to the last "why" in the analysis of thinking. A true and full understanding of another's thought is possible only when we understand its affective-volitional basis. (p.150)

In recent brain research on adolescents, there is evidence that adolescents "think" from the amygdala and the mid-brain region, the emotional and memory centers of the limbic brain (Brand in Anderson & MacCurdy, 2000, p.203; Rico, 2008, p.83). Any person teaching or raising or working with adolescents knows of their often volatile emotional eruptions that defy impulse control and reasoning.[4] There is good reason for this: the adolescent brain is growing and pruning cells. The pruning process means that connections established in childhood have to be reorganized and reconnected through the new neural pathways because the childhood connections are being disconnected physically.

At this developmental stage, an adolescent relies more upon the emotional centers for thought than the frontal cortex, the mature adult's seat of reason and impulse control. In Alice Brand's chapter in Anderson and MacCurdy (2000), "Healing and the Brain," she states that

> the amygdala gives affective significance to events. Events passing through the amygdala are rapidly learned and long-lasting. What's more, once our emotional system learns something, we may never let it go completely. This means that in any given situation, fundamental feelings may be more immediate than the intellect, however crucial, both are for learning and remembering. (pp.208–209)

What is more fascinating in the brain chemistry is that the amygdala can circumvent the neural cortex, but the brain cannot function without the amygdala. Understanding the normal function of the limbic brain in adolescent development provides us with additional information about how we might regard the emotional memory and images from traumatic experiences and events.

Another part of the limbic brain, the hippocampus, is a strategic complement to the amygdala and information processing. "The right hippocampus is responsible for physical and spatial maps—including the visual forms of words. The left side is responsible for semantic maps" (Brand in Anderson and MacCurdy, 2000, pp. 205–206). According to Brand, "the hippocampus is best known for its participation in the conscious, declarative, explicit recollection of events—the key to intellectual functioning" (p.206).

While I have not investigated every undergraduate teaching preparation and methods course presented in colleges and universities, I can say that student teachers and in-service teachers do not often have adequate understanding about the emotional brain processes of adolescents. This extends to preparatory courses in the teaching of writing to adolescents. Alice Brand explains how the brain biological/psychological operations are important to teaching:

> We make a serious mistake by not helping students to address their psychological lives, to continually humanize themselves. Some adaptation for education of the learning process that takes place in psychotherapy seems like a promising possibility. Students make peace with themselves by writing about their experiences; they understand what is happening around them.

If learning and memory are denied by the capacity to make changes and remember them, then learning through language has evolved from the ability of the brain to modify thoughts, feelings, and behavior. It is nothing short of astonishing that in some way my words alter the neurons in my brain, the impulses of my motor cortex, the contraction of my muscles, and the design of my activities. In a word, thoughts change behavior. As central as cognition is, without emotion memory and learning could not occur. And what is healing if not learning? (Anderson & MacCurdy, 2000, p.217)

This information about emotional processes reaffirms the need to attend to these processes which are affected more dramatically in adolescents experiencing trauma. Failing to recognize and attend to the natural developmental process as teachers, we stifle the natural way adolescents learn and deprive them of the very system which would help us to reach them more effectively.

I want to draw attention now to what traumatic stress is and how adolescents and children react. The following list provides a brief description of behaviors exhibited by adolescents who experience traumatic stress:

1. Maladaptive patterns of thinking about self, others and situations;
2. Difficulty with getting along with peers;
3. Impaired trust issues with peers and adults;
4. Sadness, fear, anxiety, inability to self-soothe;
5. Avoidance of trauma reminders;
6. Aggressive behaviors including risky sexual and oppositional behaviors;
7. Trouble sleeping, hypervigilance;
8. Anger, poor ability to tolerate regular or negative thoughts. (Cohen, Mannarino, A. & Deblinger, 2006, p.23)

These descriptors correspond to the conclusions of a research study that examines violence in urban settings (Thompson Jr. & Massat, 2005). "Adolescents react with feelings similar to adults: rage, shame and betrayal. It is characteristic of this age group to 'post-traumatic acting out' periods. Teenagers may engage in school truancy, precocious sexual activities, substance abuse, and delinquency. Academic difficulties are a common problem for adolescents exposed to violence" (Thompson Jr. & Massat, 2005, p. 378).

There is a growing body of research that examines the effects of armed conflict on children and adolescents in countries where wars have been raging for extended periods. These studies reveal that the effects of violence on adolescents in our peaceful cities, homes, and schools does not differ from those who experience traumatic stress from armed conflict. Of course, there are subtle differences in the experiences and long-term problems, but the studies indicate again that traumatic stress from being a victim of or witness to violence affects the mental processes and behaviors of adolescents.

One particular study (Barenbaum, Vladislaw, & Schwab-Stone, 2004) confirms the detrimental effects of armed conflict and violence upon the mental and developmental health of children and adolescents. Another detail of this study reveals that there are means through which these detrimental effects can be mitigated. Barenbaum's review of policies suggests that "teachers play a crucial role in creating a therapeutic environment" in the classroom (p. 51). This research study of adolescents and children exposed to violence confirms and grounds the position that violence has a detrimental effect upon adolescents' mental abilities and their abilities to survive and thrive in the world, especially in a world where education and intelligence have extraordinary capital. Violence is all too real, and our children are suffering, some of them quietly and shamefully, in our classrooms.

In terms of trauma, memory, and the brain, traumatic events or critical life events of violence and disaster effectively "freeze" the brain's ability to process information, a term coined by psychiatrist Bessel van der Kolk. MacCurdy's research explains the reasons for this freeze:

> Traumatic memories are sensory, that is, the body reacts to them even when the conscious mind is not aware of the cause of such reactions. This is because these iconic memories are stored in the amygdala, a part of the limbic system which not only retains these images but gives them their emotional weight. It is these images which must be accessed if a story about the trauma is to be told. (Anderson & MacCurdy, 2000, p.162)

These research theories about trauma and brain functioning illustrate how powerful an adolescent's emotional responses are in terms of an adolescent's ability to "think" and process information. Teachers will attest to the power of personal choice and interest in writing to lead to more sophisticated work that comes from the personally motivated production of written texts.

An adolescent's social world is the arena in which the affective directs cognition. The difficulty is, of course, in gaining access to the emotional situation, the writing process and the cognitive/affective interactions. Eric Jensen (1999) has also shown that educators can assume that some students will arrive at class distressed and even threatened. Therefore, investing in the emotional safety of students at the beginning of class will allow students to get into a positive learning state (p.2). If the affective are the primary drives in adolescents and are connected to cognitive development, to avoid at least a consideration of the role of affect eliminates a very effective tool for considering learning and literacy strategies. In many ways, to address the emotional and survival needs of adolescents is to ensure healing, learning, and recovery.

UNDERSTANDING LANGUAGE CONCEPTS IN THE WHOLE SOCIAL CONTEXT

> Learning to direct one's own mental processes with the aid of words or sign is an integral part of the process of concept formation. The ability to regulate one's actions by using auxiliary means reaches its full development only in adolescence. (Vygotsky, 1983, p. 108)

In order to figure out how to survive, adolescents use language to build a plan or a system in order to get their needs met. They articulate this plan in what they do and in what they say, as well as in what they write. So, in order to address how adolescents cope with violence and trauma, we have to understand how language use and acquisition occur in adolescence. Concept formation is central to the way adolescents are building language skills, and it is also where they build their compensatory strategies. In the strategies, adolescents are using written language to form adaptive processes which help them formulate concepts about survival.

According to Vygotsky, concepts are formed through and with language. Concepts themselves are ideas, thoughts, realizations, theories, and in some ways a truth about life and its operations. A concept is a mental construct that allows an individual to make meaning personally, professionally, and privately in relation to the social world he/she lives in. It is our formation of concepts about nature, facts, our experiences in relation to the world that supply us with the operating schemes for thinking and cognitive development.

Creating concepts requires language in the building of ideas. Because language is also semiotic, it carries levels of understanding/meaning that help us create ideas and understanding about the world and our place in it. The most important aspect regarding the discussion of the compensatory strategies is the way in which the adolescents use their English language knowledge to create meaning, make concepts about life and learning. Following this line of thinking, the way teachers employ language use through classroom tasks has a dramatic effect upon an adolescent's ability to use language as a functional tool through which to think and perform.

The language tool is much like the garden shovel: useless, unless it is being employed in the service of some function that builds and creates a new form that didn't exist before. When we employ or manipulate these word tools to arrive at generalizations and formative ideas about how the world operates and operationalize beyond the one instance in which we learned it, then we are using language to build a concept. Vygotsky is saying that words need to be used as tools, much like garden implements, to push development and also to structure it.

The tool image of language means that we are digging around and manipulating thinking by design. According to Wilma Bucci,

> The verbal system is a single channel processor operating primarily within the focus of awareness. We can produce only one message at a time, and can listen to and understand only one. Language is the code of communication and reflections, in which private, subjective experiences, including emotional

experiences, may be shared, and through which the knowledge of the culture and the constraints of logic may be brought to bear upon the contents of individual thought. It is also the code that we may call upon, explicitly or intentionally, to direct and regulate ourselves, to activate internal representations of imagery and emotion, to stimulate action, and to control it. (Pennebaker, 1995, p. 99)

Written language choices mark the strategic difference between what the adolescents in this research do with the current traditional modes of imparting information that dominates classroom instruction. The adolescents dealing with traumatic stresses use language and literacy to access information or create resolutions that will ensure their survival each day. They are not concerned with the future; in some cases, they are unable to envision a future and engage in very risky behavior. Therefore, in classrooms adolescents need to encounter opportunities that allow them to examine and discuss their traumatic stresses in order to reclaim meaningful purpose and direction in life.

In the research, I found that adolescents are still internalizing vocabulary, but not as sponges or as imitative acts like small children, but within specific contexts and for specific purposes. This new vocabulary becomes situated within a personal purpose and exigency. These uses of language serve to build systems for self-education, self-affirmation, and self-fulfillment.

Modern brain theory and Vygotskian theories of language state that cognitive processes evaluate stimuli. "Most obvious, as feelings ascend the biochemical pathways and arrive in consciousness, one way to express, and/or communicate them is by naming them" (Brand in MacCurdy and Anderson, 2000, p. 204). When we give language to the emotions and images, the pathway through the cognitive processes creates the possibility for self-awareness and self-discovery that is vital to healing and learning.

THEORIES OF ADOLESCENT REASONING RELATED TO WRITING AND LANGUAGE USE

The work of Rodriguez-Tomé and Jackson (1983) suggest that an adolescent's social world has three central features: cognition, values, and effects (p.24). Cognition is related to a series of values or schema that are determined in part by prior and present social contexts and interactions. In Figure 1.1, Jackson and Rodriguez-Tomé (p.24) graphically illustrate the general operation of adolescent thinking and reasoning:

Figure 1.1. Model of Adolescent Social Reasoning
Source: Jackson, S. & Rodriguez-Tomé, H. (1983) Adolescence and its social world. Sussex, UK: Erlbaum Press.

Figure 1.1 includes the affect, or emotional factor, as part of the schema of an adolescent's reasoning. The model, however, makes the movement linear which makes adolescent thinking and learning dependent upon each of these sequential factors. According to Jackson and Rodrigues-Tomé, "[their] findings show that minor events or everyday problems may remain psychologically salient over time and require continuing adaptive efforts which may ultimately be more taxing than efforts aimed at coping with major events" (p.177).

Even though adolescents develop coping strategies that assist them in their daily functioning, "one of the strong coping strategies applied after a problem had taken place was to work through the emotions aroused by the event" (p.183). One of the dramatic coping strategies applied by adolescents and relevant to this research is journal writing and diary keeping. In the case studies presented, the more dysfunctional the home environment and stressful survival needs, the more writing became a function of the need to cope with the emotions that surrounded the traumatic event.

The adolescents living with violent environments have the same needs as adolescents in stable environments, but without the surrogate adult or model to stabilize or influence concept formation, the adolescents create another kind of surrogate through which they can learn the skills and satisfy their crisis needs. The traumatic stresses from violence impose additional complications to feeling and thinking through a crisis event. The need for the adolescent in the classroom is not only to handle processing the lingering life crisis but also to "think" through the changing classroom lesson, which may or may not have direct application to solving the need. Instead, the adolescents develop compensatory strategies, perhaps as coping strategies, as unique and individual as the zone of proximal development, but necessary for learning and developing.

The stronger adolescent developmental urge is toward independence and self-education, but most adolescents do not possess all the tools with which to address their changing biological, emotional, and environmental conditions (Csikszentmihalyi & Larson 1984; Erikson 1968; Nunley 2003). In their research on adolescents, Csikszentmihalyi and Larson specifically point to a passionate drive in adolescents, which they label "flow." When an adolescent finds a vehicle through which to steer her energy and interest, she/he establishes a flow, an energy, which allows her to produce. I understand this to be similar to a runner who needs several miles of running to achieve a stable pattern where the body works together effortlessly, similar to being "in the groove." I think this research points to a drive within adolescents who want to learn, grow, and develop. Many are thwarted by various factors, but there is evidence that every adolescent has the need to create, develop, and self-express that is essential to their healthy intellectual development.

In *Reconceptualizing the Literacies in Adolescents' Lives* (Alverman, 1998), Peter Mosenthal suggests that we move from seeing research and discussions about adolescence as problem identification and solution to something he calls dilemma management. The dilemma management allows adolescents to approach problems within their life spheres and create solutions. Mosenthal specifically outlines how the literacy practices of the school reinforce a thinking paralysis that does not allow the adolescent to develop life skills. Instead, students build self-schemata, which are imprinted often with patterns of academic failure, hence life failure (p. 332).

Not all present pedagogy and knowledge-making in classrooms enhance the adolescent's ability to develop life-framing skills. Instead of thinkers, adolescents have become reporters in school. What is most interesting in Mosenthal's article related to this issue is the 6-step process which allows adolescents to identify their own dilemmas, recognize the political or social agenda behind the problem, and then to create a process to solve the dilemma. This process is woven into the classroom pedagogy as more than just problem based learning, but as a personal rhetorical action centered around the student's own needs. The dilemma identification is broad enough to include traumatic stresses and critical life events. More importantly, this pedagogy engages language use and conceptualization that is reflective and requires solution. This dilemma solving system provides a healthy and intellectually stimulating way to respond and address their trauma.

These theories direct us toward a realization that we are not educating adolescents in the manner in which they learn most effectively. In understanding how the adolescent brain stores images, memory with emotional connections, teachers now need to create writing tasks that utilize these emotional/affective forces. With adolescents surviving and living with traumatic life conditions, the emotional/affective processes are even more engaged and in need of direction.

WHY WRITING?

I have talked about language acquisition, crisis, the powerful emotional centers in the adolescent brain related to thinking and reasoning, but I have yet to answer why writing is the most powerful tool. The researchers and theorists have given us a useful picture of how emotion, language use, and adolescent psychological states begin to create a picture of the students in our classrooms. For adolescents with critical life experiences like violence, the picture needs to be readjusted. The one common factor in these theories is the importance of language engagement to give voice to the adolescent's experiences.

The works of James Pennebaker, Marian MacCurdy, Judith Harris, and Alice G. Brand have forwarded the use of writing as a means to heal the wounded psyche of people coping with traumatic life events. Their theories about writing and healing are based upon experiments and research into the effects of writing and trauma. What these researchers and educators have introduced into the discussion is the connection of written text production and the emotional/image operation in the brain. The role of the limbic system in memory and language reveals that images are tied to emotions. Writing about the image details as they are connected with the senses and sequence of events is a powerful tool with which to reconnect disconnected neural pathways and activate literacy processes.

Accessing emotional connections to ideas and words allows a writing teacher to use the brain processes in a more natural way. Gabriel Rico's work *Writing the Natural Way* attests to the fact that we all have a connective process that can be utilized, if we allow our classroom inventive practices to complement the brain's way of grasping ideas and language. In Hildy Miller's work "Sites of Inspiration" (Brand & Graves, 1994), images played a role in writing production, and the images can be used to inspire writers to make more word connections with the images.

Various psychoanalytic researchers like Alice Brand and James Pennebaker show us the uses of writing with populations who have been affected by trauma. The "writing therapies" have been a part of psychoanalysis since Freud. However, modern adaptations and uses of writing to heal trauma has expanded the value of emotional and image connection discussed earlier. James Pennebaker reports in *Opening Up* (1990) that "people who wrote about their deepest thoughts and feeling surrounding a trauma evidenced an impressive drop in illness visits. . . . Writing about trauma affected physical health" (p. 45).

For researchers like Hildy Miller, the narrative is the most powerful tool for doing both. Because of the connection between the amygdala, emotions, and images, the limbic brain's capacity to activate and be activated by language (Brand & Graves, 1994, p. 119) is sufficiently powerful for teachers to consider a redesign of the writing classroom. "The referential process, embodied in story telling, is a powerful function that has potentially significant emotional and also bodily impact" (p. 118). The studies echo similar conclusion: writing as telling and story telling have an impact that is beneficial to our thinking processes.

For an unknown number of students in our classrooms, many come not only bearing the natural adolescent emotions and upheavals, but also bearing the scars of violence. The research suggests that writing about trauma over time in various genres, formations, and investigations lessens the power of the original trauma. Putting the story into words removes some of its emotional power, allows us to take control of it, redefine it, learn about ourselves and recover some personal power. What a potentially transforming way to teach writing—connecting our experiences with words and making them powerful tools to self-definition and self-education and self-awareness. These kinds of writing tasks serve a different vision and purpose than our school-sponsored writing. Do we need to change that?

The school system and systematic implementation of process theory has circumvented other pedagogies and theories for teaching writing to adolescents espoused by James Moffett, Donald Murray, Robert Graves, Jimmy Britton, and Peter Elbow. While Expressivist theories of writing have encouraged journaling and free-writing, I still hear from my students that their high schools' writing experiences are "essay" in almost every instance: persuasive essays, narrative essays, critical essays, literary analysis essays, or just writing a generic essay. In this case, personal writing engages that personal story of tragedy that some teachers want to avoid. Yet, writing that embraces these traumas is the most effective tool we have for addressing these traumatic stresses and for healing them.

Popular authors have extolled the heroic stories of schools and traumatized adolescents. Todd De Stiger's text, *Reflections of a Citizen Teacher*, follows the forgotten and lost Latino/Latina students in a high school. He is able to see and illustrate how the private conditions of adolescents' lives influence their literacy habits. Even though he does not make claims for a specific pattern of literacy, he draws pictures of the difficult learning conditions many adolescents face, regardless of ethnicity and learning in the school. In some cases though, the casualty of school is the instructor's failure to adapt and change to meet the needs of the students, or to recognize that abusive and violent conditions alter the pedagogical structure needed for these students to be successful.

In *Letters for the Living: Teaching Writing in a Violent Age*, Hurlbert and Blitz (1998) use letters in their college composition classes as other teachers might use the essay. The letter exchanges give many of their students a real audience and purpose for writing about violence in their lives, and a necessary forum through which to use their experiences for creative and expressive purposes.

Erin Gruwell's *Freedom Writer's Diary* (2006) more recently attests to the positive effects writing has when students are allowed to write about their lives and use their lived experience in the service of what they are learning. All of these authors reveal the power of using writing to assist students in naming their lived experience and using it to empower them to write about the most critical events without using the essay.

So, why is it writing? The power of narrative to capture the traumatic event is the therapeutic pathway. It requires the writer to express the images through words for the first time, thereby engaging the power of the hidden truth. As the quote that opens this chapter states, writing is the most powerful tool with which to address our truth, our hidden truths about pain and crisis in our lives. In telling rather than hiding, we have power and control as we name our hidden truths. Once a word can be assigned to the emotion, image, and experience, we have control. We can see it, and this allows us to transform our lives because we have awareness and conscientization (Freire, 1970).

The information about the adolescent brain and emotional processing and imaging shows us that we store memory in images and record emotions with those images. By writing and telling about the trauma, and by using their stored mental images to assign to words and to assign emotions to words, the adolescent is releasing traumatic stresses and creating control and awareness. This powerful combination is the pathway to healing and opening other areas of the brain, which have been bypassed.

Current research on the adolescent brain and reasoning demonstrates that the natural brain ontogeny is in part related to the processing of images and emotion through the amygdala and hippocampus. The one element we share as humans and through which we communicate our experiences is the ability to give language to our ideas. The power to turn traumatic stress into resiliency and thereby gain greater control lies in the rendering of experience and traumatic images into language.

THE COMPENSATORY STRATEGIES MODEL

I envision a process beginning with the pre-existing conditions of childhood language and literacy patterns and the natural biologically driven forces. When an external or internal need or crisis point arises, the crisis becomes the nexus for development. In Figure 1.2, I place crisis (external and internal) as the central force through which the pre-existing conditions and the exigent situation intersect. The pre-existing conditions are the traumatic events and images that act as the lens through which the adolescent focuses the new crisis situation. The next movement after the exigent situation is to find a means to address the crisis.

As much as I have been discussing the value of writing about the critical life events, there is another component that adds even greater healing and transformative power to the discourse. That component is rhetorical action. While writing tasks capture the emotional force and the imagery behind the event, doing something creative and expressive to address the trauma provides a healthy and positive avenue for the traumatic energy the writing arouses. Using the traumatic memories as an impetus for action can be a force and give more psychological healing than the writing and telling alone can accomplish. The compensatory strategies are in part a self-sponsored rhetorical action.

In Figure 1.2, the chart illustrates this process and allows for some degree of change and reciprocity between the stages. Initially, the exigent situation triggers a need for response, and the "thinking" that is filtered through the emotions, which then leads the adolescent to gather information about how to handle the situation. In the event there is no answer or way to satisfy the need, the adolescent will develop a strategy, a compensation that allows him or her to find solutions. These types of compensations are goal driven because they contain a purpose and an exigency.

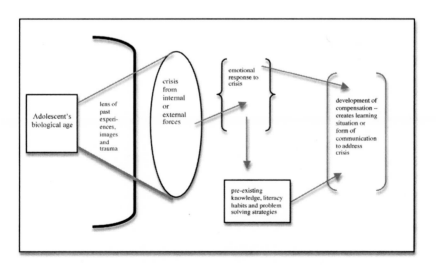

Figure 1.2.   Contemporary Strategies Model of Reasoning

Figure 1.2 illustrates the reasoning processes for making compensations and recognizes the direct influence of the emotional component that is normal in adolescent psychological processes and after traumatic stress. The compensatory writing model, like the model of Rodriguez-Tomé and Jackson, presents a pattern for thinking with more consideration being placed upon the affective role and trauma imagery and experiences. The Compensatory Strategy model diagrams the mental processes of an adolescent affected by traumatic stress and how writing tasks designed to correlate with the process will facilitate a more supportive learning environment. It identifies a descriptive process for addressing traumatic stress as it recognizes the power of experience and emotion to direct thinking and learning and action.

We learn that the type of social precondition varies with each individual. In very dramatic ways, the seven adolescents in this book illustrate the variety of social environments that breed difficulties in school. What can be determined is that adolescents adjust, invent, and compensate in strategic ways for the social instability in their lives and make creative adjustments so that they continue to grow and learn or survive in their social worlds. Writing can provide a way for adolescents to control what otherwise in their worlds can only be described as oppression by social and academic forces.

WHAT WE KNOW ABOUT ADOLESCENT LITERACY THROUGH RESEARCH

The literacy activities of our schools demand a language formulation pattern that is very different from the experiences of many students; again, especially those for whom violence, abuse, and neglect combine with language learning experiences of their early youth (Heath, 1983; O'Connor, 1995; Solsken, 1993). This research investigation suggests that stressed adolescents address their immediate literacy needs by creating their own methods of compensation—often elaborate and adaptive. These two key ingredients, choice and exigency, are missing in many secondary school lessons and classroom activities, especially in English language arts.

It becomes imperative that we look at how adolescents use the compensatory strategies, and when they use them to compensate, adjust, or invent, to stabilize and survive within their worlds. The adolescents may be showing us the best way to adapt as teachers to their unique thinking processes. Bored students display a disregard, inattention, or acquiescence to their learning ennui in order to "play" school. One rule that guides all of nature is the rule of adaptation. As teachers, we cannot keep using the traditional patterns of instruction to reach these students. The students who sit in our classrooms arrive with emotional and experiential conditions that inhibit them from attending to classroom instruction in the traditional lecture, note taking, exam, and reading processes.

However, only the last ten years has provided more evidence about the literacy habits outside the classroom. In a work by Margaret Finders, *Just Girls* (1997), she points to the hidden literacies two distinct groups of adolescent junior high girls practice when their social group is not present. These hidden literacy habits begin to suggest that we know little about what adolescents actually practice in terms of oral and written literacy that influences their learning. Recent work by Elizabeth Moje and David O'Brian (2002) has opened the private processes of adolescent literacy and defined some adolescent writing practices as forms of functional literacy: the literacy practices adolescents use when it serves their purpose or their participation in a particular group.

K. Schultz and G. Hull in *School's Out* (2002) discuss the literacy of adolescents outside of school as a bridge between home and school and a private practice different from hidden literacy and inspired by authentic purposes and audiences. This work is similar to the research project in this book. The researchers report that after school activities, clubs, and reading programs show that literacy is operating in the out of school environments when students are given an opportunity to engage with literacy through interest and rhetorical action. These research activities again reaffirm that we have not done enough to make disciplinary literacy studies relevant and applicable for our students beyond the classroom; it also shows that students want and will develop more sophisticated literacy skills with encouragement and direction.

There is a growing body of research within the last ten years, searching to understand the disparate literate actions of children in and out of schools. The research in this book is conducted within the school day and moves into the private world after school, attempting to see academic and personal literacy acts as they occur in the context of the adolescents' world. Michelle Knoble's work similarly investigates the social contexts of adolescent literate acts in an Australian school (1999). Complementary to her research is work done by Ellen Cushman (1998). Cushman's work reveals the subtle knowledge and literacy of inner city adults who are seeking government assistance. In both of these works, the research subjects demonstrate their adaptive linguistic skills in different social and cultural contexts. These individuals negotiate the non-verbal and verbal discourses of race and economics when they have to survive the governmental assistance process and still maintain an individual identity. In fact, their literacy practices and uses mirror the adaptive and compensatory strategies of the adolescents in this book.

VIOLENCE, WRITING AND THE
COMPENSATORY STRATEGIES

Each of the adolescents who served as informants for this research completed classroom lessons, but behind every classroom assignment, they had another purpose for using what they were learning. In fact, they adjusted, altered, or subverted the classroom information for another strategic purpose that was dependent upon the immediate needs in the adolescent's life; for example, the classroom instruction might be about archeology and how a dig must be recorded, but the adolescent would find an alternate personal use for this classroom information applied to an immediate need.

Their strategies for producing written texts were more than functional literacy (Levine, 1986), but an independent, original process intended to compensate for what was missing in their need to develop or to survive. The adolescents created learning strategies and often used writing and other literacy habits to generate meaning, purpose, and answers.

The entry point for the research began in the classroom, where language and learning tasks abound, but it encompassed the entire social structure including family, friends, religious activities, employment, and other activities and people within the private sphere of the adolescent's life. The evidence began to emerge when the classroom lessons demanded written and oral tasks/assignments, especially when the assignment or writing task had no direct relevance to the adolescent's immediate need.

At times, when there was no pressing dilemma or problem, the adolescents could more easily engage the classroom lesson. When the adolescents could find no relevance, they tended to shape it to their own purposes by altering, adapting, subverting the literacy task given by the teacher. When the adolescent left school and engaged in the private social activities, not school related, the compensatory strategies emerged under different conditions than the academic. In some instances, the specific compensation strategy was a desperate need for survival.

The compensatory strategies begin to identify the hidden working patterns. By understanding the nature of these alternate processes, teachers can use this process to accentuate and complement what is already naturally occurring. If we consider that information and knowledge are being structured for and made by an adolescent during their waking hours, the classroom time becomes an important environment for establishing patterns of literacy that adolescents transfer in exigent situations.

The elaborate and exigent literacy patterns became visible through the public or academic and private/transactional writing the adolescents finished during the years I spent with them. In each adolescent's story, the compensatory literacy strategies she or he develops reaffirm the "genius" of language literacy in adolescents as they attempt to cope with the ever changing demands of the present in three particular areas: (1) the writing instruction in school and what the adolescents do in practice; (2) the process of composing and the literacy compensations they make as efforts in self-education and self-empowerment as a means to survival, and (3) the factors and forces that frame writing for these adolescents.

Studying the writing in these three areas in and out of school uncovers the interrelationships of the social, the academic, and the personal in the relationship to mental or intellectual development of adolescents. Studying the writing of the adolescents showed an underlying series of compensatory strategies for literacy and survival within the interrelationships of the social, academic, and personal.

In the chapters that follow, I present the case studies in the ethnographic tradition. Chapter 2 outlines the research questions and methods along with necessary information about the research location at Prairie High School where the first three case studies took place. Chapters 3, 4, and 5 are the individual case studies of three adolescents who have different experiences with violence. Diana's and Danielle's stories narrate the insidious private violence and abuse. In juxtaposition, Chase's story illustrates the painful experiences of being a second language learner, an immigrant, and a teenager in desperate need to be accepted and loved.

Part II, "Public Disasters," begins with chapter 6, which will introduce the New Literacy Studies theories about language and literacy, which are more relevant to the case studies of a natural disaster and violence. Chapters 7, 8, and 9 will present the three case studies for violence, trauma, and natural disasters. Finally, the last chapter discusses what this research means for teaching adolescents, primarily those who are victims of violence and natural disasters, and how to incorporate these ideas into writing pedagogy and writing assignments. Chapter 10 calls for a different writing pedagogy than the pattern that dominates these case studies. In combining the elements that the case studies illuminate as effective with traumatized students, I arrived at a writing program for secondary students with deep roots in the Expressivist tradition. This Neo-Expressivist writing pedagogy is relevant, consistent, choice-driven, and attentive to narrative storytelling—and always complemented with many levels of re-visioning the text.

NOTES

1. I want to acknowledge that the violence from video games, television, and other visual media are additional factors to be considered but not part of the investigations for this book or discussions of violence and its effect upon adolescents.

2. See Lisbeth Dixon Krauss, *Vygotsky in the Classroom*, and Luis Moll, ed., *Vygotsky and Education*, for a much more detailed discussion of inner speech, activity theory, and literacy acquisition.

3. Eidetic memory is also called photographic memory; it is an individual's ability to recall a memory with visual precision and clarity of detail.

4. In *Time,* May 10, 2004, an article titled "What Makes Teens Tick" summarizes the research findings and includes a diagram picture of the adolescent brain. I refer to it here because it provides general summarized information that some might find more accessible.

Chapter 2

Research Methodology for Prairie High School

INTRODUCTION

Including the research methodology in a book is risky because most readers find the details of conducting research to be tedious and dull. However, I am defying that possible reaction and including this research methodology for specific reasons. In the best of circumstances, there is another educator who wants to replicate this research or conduct research with adolescents beyond the classroom. I wanted this book to be useful for methods instructors, qualitative researchers of adolescent literacy, and teachers of writing: to be able to discuss, analyze, and critique the evidence presented in the stories.

There are guides and manuals that explain how to conduct case study or qualitative research, but these sequential guides do not show what happens between the cracks of observational notes and the data selected for the research report. It also provides a space to discuss the problematic situations that occur in following adolescents throughout an entire day, how the data was collected, and what a researcher using this methodology experiences.

It is not only about the adolescents but the conduct of alcoholic parents, an unexpected bar fight, witnessing deplorable family circumstances, near miss car crashes, and parental neglect that force an ethnographic researcher into difficult positions. Sharing the research methodology also provides a clear and informative process that would be otherwise truncated and generalized, but that is the crucial context for learning and researching about the adolescents.

My intent was to keep the research methodology clear but direct, providing my audience with enough detail that they have access to the sharp turns and twists in conducting this kind of research. So often, research methodologies don't include the ugly and brutal world that becomes the social context for

conducting the research. In the ethnographic tradition, each section is introduced by a vignette, which provides the reader with a lens that details the
cultural world of the informant.

THE RESEARCH ENTRÉE—PART I: A VIGNETTE OF PRAIRIE HIGH SCHOOL

My first research day began at 8:05 in English 11, first block, with Mr. Muller
and Chase, my eleventh-grade informant. While Mr. Muller was advising
students about his attendance policies, I opened my observational notebook,
chose one of my four new pens and wrote down a few bits of information
about Chase's activities. Then, the fire alarm sounded. We all looked at each
other, wondering if this was some kind of joke. Within seconds, the principal
came over the intercom and said that this alarm was not to be ignored and
everyone was to evacuate the building immediately.

Never in my experiences with four different school districts had anyone
ever inflicted a fire drill on the first day of school, in late August, in the heat,
during the first class. Once everyone evacuated the building, a fire truck
pulled up to the school, two police cars blocked off the road in front, and men
in police uniforms raced into the school through the closing automatic doors.

As we stood outside the school on the heated blacktop pavement, I remem-
bered other teaching experiences with practice fire and tornado drills. This
time the situation was entirely different. Noise and complaining voices fell
to a hush as word spread through the crowd—a bomb had been placed inside
the school.

After a long wait, a parade of police dogs, police officers, and school principals, we were given the all clear and summoned back inside to resume class.
Mr. Muller did not attempt to make any reference to the morning's events as
he continued to make up for the lost class time. As the brief class ended, I
gathered my things, said goodbye to Chase and Mr. Muller with a few parting
chuckles about the morning's start, and left for my next English class.

Within a few strides down the long hall, all the lights went out. I and
approximately 1500 other students were standing in darkness with only
patches of light filtering through the doors of rooms with windows. I could
not see my feet or the person next to me. For a few seconds, no one uttered a
sound in the darkness. I knew some sat down because I heard the "plops" onto
the floor. In the distance, familiar voices echoed laughter. A group of English
teachers had gathered in a classroom near where I had stopped. I stumbled
toward them, and we spent the next thirty minutes in darkness looking for the
humor in this absurd situation.

The boiler room had reached such a high temperature that the protective electronics had automatically switched off the electrical system. In a school that covers 460,000 square feet of space, has 4 floors, 5 wings, over 2000 students in grades 9–12, 175 teachers, 5 principals, 5 counselors, 1 school psychologist, 1 full-time nurse, 1 full-time police officer, and over 100 support personnel—there definitely were problems on the first day of school in late August in the heat.

PRAIRIE HIGH SCHOOL AND THE PRAIRIE COMMUNITY: RESEARCH LOCATION #1

Prairie High School sits on the banks of a major river in the northern United States. The town of Prairie itself is located on the state line, making it accessible to people moving between states for reasons of welfare dollars. The difference in welfare allocations in Prairie versus its neighboring state brings with it many problems related to welfare funding and transience among the town population and the students attending the high school. Prairie High School is the only public high school in the city with one very small Catholic high school serving only 100 students to Prairie's 2,000 students, grades nine through twelve.

The town's two main industries were marine engine manufacturing and paper-making machines. Over the last twenty-five years, these industries have continued to decline, making the city governors look for other companies to move into Prairie and rejuvenate its tax base. There have been a few, but the city has trouble attracting larger, more profitable industries.

This is a blue-collar community with inner-city problems brought in part by the history of slavery and movement of many persons from Mississippi to the northern states to work in its marine and paper factories. It is also a pipeline stop for drug transportation due to being situated upon the state line, and the accessibility of major interstates converging nearby.

The ethnic composition of the community is largely German, Italian, and African-American. With World War II and the marine engine plants, many new workers were needed to fill the demands for engines. The plant managers imported many black southerners to fill the assembly line positions.

In order to accommodate this influx of workers, worker-housing units were built like little boxes in barrack military style. Now, these housing units are inhabited by some of the poorer members of the community. The Italian community still maintains roots in the town, even though many have moved to nearby cities and communities, and remains the force behind retaining the lone Catholic high school in town.

Recent immigration has brought Vietnamese, Hmong, and Korean people to the community. Americans of Mexican descent are also moving into the community. Leaving the larger cities of nearby states, they are migrating north into less densely populated areas like Prairie, but still maintain family ties by moving as groups of related family members and friends. The state in which Prairie is located also has a significant number of First Nation peoples: Lac de Flambeau and Ojibwa/Chippewa tribes. The town community is becoming an ethnic representation for the whole United States. Because of these representational demographics, I wanted to set the research within this particular community.

THE NATURE OF THE STUDY

The research methodology came out of a desire to study self-sponsored public and private writing acts of adolescents and to understand how the out-of-school writing is related to the writing skills being taught in secondary English language arts classrooms (Barton, Hamilton & Ivanic, 2000). To investigate literacy acts outside of school means to investigate adolescent culture outside of school; to place the writing moments within a social context; and to understand the interrelationship of social and academic influences in the adolescent's life events, school demands, and writing literacy (Hull & Schultz, 2002). Prairie High School provided an ideal environment for this research agenda.

Specifically, the project focused on how adolescents from 14 to 18 years of age use writing in and out of school for one semester beginning in August and ending the following January. I wanted a cross-age study in order to see if adolescents of different ages responded to different writing tasks, used different genres, and demonstrated visible mental development in the content and detail of the written texts. As a result, the research focused on four separate ages: 14, 15, 16, and 17. This is not to draw conclusions about developmental levels, but to describe and define the writing tasks that adolescents are assigned at different grade levels in English classes versus the writing they produce outside of school. In this book, I present only the case studies of three of the adolescent-informants and their teachers: grades 10, 11, and 12.

THE RESEARCH QUESTIONS AND
QUALITATIVE METHODOLOGY

Five main questions guide this research. The following table gives the major question and then the methodology being used to answer the question.

Table 2.1. **Research Questions and Methodology**

Research Question	Qualitative Method
1. How does an adolescent's social world shape the writing of texts in the adolescent's personal and academic lives?	Participant observer notes Interviews Protocol analysis Researcher's log Cooked notes Comparison of material artifacts Journaling Surveys
2. How do adolescents create written texts? 2a. What characteristics of genre and style distinguish the writing of adolescents?	Participant observer notes Material artifacts consisting of all writings informants do in and out of school Literary analysis/genre analysis Adolescent's log and journal Informant interviews
3. How do an adolescent's life experiences influence the texts she/he writes in and out of school?	Triangulation of participant observer notes with teachers and informants Interviews Literary and genre analysis Parent interviews Teacher logs/lesson plans Material artifacts
4. How does the writing instruction in the language arts classroom affect adolescent writing?	Classroom observational notes Material artifacts with teacher's comments Teacher-informant conferences Teacher lesson plans Teacher interviews Adolescent interviews Final written report by teachers and adolescent informants

SELECTION OF RESEARCH METHODOLOGY

The qualitative design included a variety of qualitative research methods, specifically ethnography and case study, and in general, post-structuralist interpretative research styles (Denzin & Lincoln 1994; Gilmore & Glatthorn, 1982; Spradley, 1979; Stake 1995; Van Maanen 1988; Wolcott 1990; Wolf 1992). The ethnographic research design is based upon similar research investigations into the social construction of literacy and language (Heath 1983; Knobel 1998; Solsken 1996; Voss 1994). Hence, the techniques of collecting data are predominantly ethnographic: participant observer notes, cooked notes, researcher log notes, transcriptions of audio and video interviews and conversations (Denzin & Lincoln, 1994), think-aloud protocols (Emig, 1971), and the collection of relevant material artifacts that had contributed to the student production of writing.

For specific ethnographic techniques in literacy and writing, research articles by Bishop (1999), Heath and Athanases (1995), and Heath and Street (2008) provided the structural foundation. Since few ethnographic studies exist of adolescents (Mead, 1963), their social worlds, and their writing habits, I reviewed texts that used ethnographic methods to study the writing of elementary school children and adapted them to adolescents and my particular study (Finders, 1996; Knobel, 1998; Solsken, 1995; Voss, 1994).

RESEARCHER'S ROLE IN QUALITATIVE RESEARCH WITH ADOLESCENTS

Choosing the role of least adult (Mandell, 1988) placed me as the participant observer in the least restrictive researcher position. The "least adult" position means that the researcher does not deny his/her apparent adult status, but it is a less powerful position in respect to the teacher or parent.

DOCUMENTS REQUIRED WITH ADOLESCENT HUMAN SUBJECTS

Beyond the research permission granted by the school district research office and the high school principal, I collected two required sets of permission forms: the adolescents' assent and their parent or guardian's consent. In addition, the research project often involved other adolescents and friends who had not signed any human subjects permission form. So, I had to carry additional permission forms to be signed by any adolescent who talked to me or gave me information. For students in the classrooms who were not part of the research, I presented another permission form that granted me limited rights to take notes and have access to student writing with permission.

When I was following each adolescent, I kept a separate notebook for notations about questions to ask the student regarding events or conversations, writing process I observed and needed to understand further. These informal interviews and the information I obtained from them were more developed in researcher notes, cooked notes, and observational notes.

TEACHER SELECTION PROCESS

I used the following criteria to select the four teachers: each teacher had to teach writing in an English classroom that was intended for non–college bound students (this meant English courses that were labeled "regular" English); represent grade levels 9, 10, 11, and 12; agree to the research project and become an informant; have different years of experience; be of different genders and ethnic groups; and have proven success with teaching students at the regular level.

From this point, I approached each of the teachers whom I wanted to include and explained the research project. Four teachers accepted, but one had minimal reservations about the additional work that this research project would require of her. After a second discussion, she accepted.[1] Table 2.2 provides a summative educational background for each of the teacher informants.

ADOLESCENT SELECTION PROCEDURES

Each adolescent represented one grade level and had to be in a teacher informant's non-college bound English class. I would select two boys and two girls, and the combination would reflect the ethnicity of the Prairie High School community.

After selecting the high school teachers, I received a copy of the class list each teacher would have for the fall term. In June, I interviewed English

Table 2.2. Data about Teacher Informants

Teacher informant's pseudonym	Class	Degrees	Yrs. of experience	Fall teaching
Ms. Plummer	English 12	M.A. in counseling	26	3 sections of English 12; cooperating teacher of student teacher in fall
Mr. Muller (dept. chair)	English 11	M.A. in Eng.	33 (retiring after this school year)	2 sections of advanced placement English; 1 section of media/journalism
Ms. Whitson	English 10	B.A. +	7	3 sections of English 10
Ms. Pearce	English 9	B.A. +	23	2 sections of English 9; 1 section of English 12; cooperating teacher for student teacher in fall

teachers who had previously had the students in class and asked these three questions:

1. Did the student attend regularly?
2. Were there specific problems that would prevent the adolescent from being involved in the research?
3. Did the student have intentions of going to college?

By interviewing the teachers and the registrar who provided me with attendance records, I eventually narrowed the number of students who would qualify by eliminating students in the class who were known drug dealers, who had violent records or history of violent behavior, who were non-attendees, and who had severe dysfunctional family situations. From the remaining students, I made a list of those who were enrolled in general English language arts classes, who were regular attendees, and who might welcome this project.

I interviewed each student and conveyed the following information: I explained who I was, what research I would be doing in the fall, what I wanted from them, and what her/his role would be in the project. At this point, I asked the students if they were interested. If not, I said thank you and called for the next student. If the student was interested, I continued to explain the project. I often had to juggle potential informants in order to keep the gender and racial balance as I had originally designed it.

OBSERVATIONAL TIME AND DATE
SCHEDULES FOR THE RESEARCH

The instructional time during the high school day was divided into four periods: each period was 90 minutes in length for a semester. The research project time frame extended from the first day of school in August through the last teacher workday during final exam week in January. In order to acquaint myself with their teachers and begin to get to know the students, I was at

Table 2.3.   Data for Adolescent Informants

Informant's pseudonym	Grade level	Age	English teacher	Block time for English
Danielle	Senior	18	Ms. Plummer	3rd
Chase	Junior	16	Mr. Muller	1st
Diana	Sophomore	16	Ms. Whitson	4th

Prairie High School from 8:05 through 3:10 Monday, Wednesday, and Friday of every week.

On Mondays in the month of September, I met with each adolescent informant only in his/her English class. Then, on Wednesdays and Fridays, I spent the entire day with one student observing his/her school schedule. I found this system allowed me time to get to know each adolescent informant before accompanying each one beyond the school day into the private aspects of his/her life. To build trust in each of the adolescent informants took time.

In October, November, December, and January, I spent the two full days with each adolescent informant. During that whole day, I met them at home before school and accompanied them in whatever transportation method the informant used to get to school. On the first full day session, I asked each adolescent informant to introduce me to his/her parent(s), and I took that opportunity to answer questions or to restate the reason I was accompanying that student to school.

PROCEDURES FOR COLLECTING DATA FROM ADOLESCENT INFORMANTS

On the first day of school I gave each adolescent informant a three-ring notebook with my schedule for August and September. In the notebook, I provided each adolescent informant with a date and hour sheet that accounted for the activities they participated in out of school during the month of September. The entry information the students had to provide included the time, event, and focused thoughts about each day's events and social contexts for the writing the adolescent might do: for example, the adolescent informants recorded time for homework, television, church, talking to parents, play, sports or thinking time, and talking on the phone.

The notebook included a separate spiral notebook for journaling about the project. I encouraged them to write in it, but it was not a requirement of the project. I included a set of instructions for what they might write in the journal, since I was looking for a way to monitor social, emotional, and academic influences when I was not observing each one.

I kept four separate records of notes during this entire process. The first collection of notes involved the day-to-day list of things to be done, notes to myself in the form of a research log, and the classroom observation or event observation notes. I collected all material artifacts given to me or collected as information, including copies of class and informant schedules, and letters to all the informants to update the research agenda. I used this notebook as the working organizer for the other three notebooks.

The contents of the second notebook referred specifically to my impressions as the researcher. In this collection, I reflected and commented on the events of the day. I moved freely in this collection to make connections between events and situations without the constraint of the material artifacts, theory, or observational notes.

The third collection was a spiral pad which I used to record questions that I thought of during the observations in and out of classrooms. At times, these were done after the fact or as I was reviewing my research notes. This almost became too cumbersome once I had established a consistency and coordination with the material artifacts, observational notes, and other data collection vehicles like the teacher research log and student research log.

In the fourth collection, I kept a separate notebook for each adolescent informant, dated all material, and attempted to keep track of the time when something happened. In these notebooks, I collected writing drafts, exams, personal notes passed between the students, grade sheets, teacher lesson plans, and transcriptions, when they were finished along with my cooked notes for the adolescent informant. (Cooking the notes is an additional reflective process to refine and distill the participant observer's daily notes).

When I spent one day with an adolescent informant, I had a single set of cooked notes. On the days that I observed each adolescent in his/her English class, I had another set of cooked notes and a set of classroom/teacher observational notes, even though the observational handwritten notes were part of the materials for the adolescent informant. For these observational notes, I used a style of lined paper with a three-inch left margin line. This allowed me to make comprehensible marginal notes about what I thought was happening and how it related to previous situations, or asked questions of what was happening. (Later in the data analysis process, I used these marginal notes for domain, taxonomical, and thematic analysis.)

I made notations in the research log each day, and after the day ended, I cooked my notes. I wrote the research memos after collecting observations and notes from several days. After interviews, I made a transcription of the interview and maintained two separate files: one for teacher interviews and one for student interviews. The beginning and ending interviews lasted approximately one hour. The informal interviews I conducted during the project varied in length as well as in the questions I asked the adolescent and teacher informants.

I collected video or audiotapes of what adolescents did in the class, even though I was not present for every writing assignment. On the days in which a specific writing lesson of any kind was the class focus, the teachers would video tape the writing lesson or give me advance notice so that I could attend that particular class and witness the assignment.

When I spent an entire day with an adolescent informant, I first met him/ her at home, usually around 7:00 a.m. and accompanied the adolescent to school and all after school activities. The morning connection became important because I had an opportunity to talk to my informant about the day's expectations and capture any events or details that had occurred since I last had seen the adolescent informant. Sometimes they would share the latest dating situation or progress in school, trouble at work, or problems they were having at home.

I considered these morning trips a special time to understand their lives and what they were thinking about as the school day began. I followed them to school, after school places, work locations, religious services, and evenings at home. I usually left the informant around 9:00 p.m.

PROCEDURES FOR COLLECTING DATA FROM TEACHER INFORMANTS

In the summer, I interviewed each teacher informant initially to collect information about the teacher's literacy, education, and philosophy about teaching writing to adolescents. The initial interview generally lasted one hour. I interviewed each teacher three times during the research project, and one final summary interview at the end of the semester. In addition to the interviews, I took observational notes on the teachers only when I was observing English classes with my adolescent informant, usually one day each week for the entire semester.

I asked each of the teacher informants to keep a journal to record three topics: how they were affected by the research presence; what they observed about the writing assignments that they gave to students; and what observations they had about the adolescent informant in their class. I collected this journal at the end of the semester. During the course of the semester, teachers who had established writing patterns found it easier to write periodically in the journal; others who did not write found little time for journaling and often apologetically advised me that they hadn't written anything for a while.

I waited until the last two weeks of the research project to interview the parents of the adolescent informants. I had asked each adolescent informant to introduce me to his/her parents initially at the beginning of the project, and I continued to meet with parents throughout the project at home, church, and in carpooling children. I waited until the end to capture the parents' perspective at the end of the project when they had had time to witness the whole process and see its effects. It also became much easier to speak candidly at the final interview, when the parents and I had already had several discussions during the course of the semester's research.

DATA ANALYSIS

The data analysis system is based upon James Spradley's *Ethnographic Interview* and Lincoln and Guba's *Qualitative Research*. In addition to these basic texts, I adapted Spradley's four-part analysis to accommodate writing research that investigated the social context surrounding writing done by adolescents. In Table 2.4, I present the modified chart that now includes the method of analysis for each research question and data collection method.

Spradley's design for analysis is a four-stage process: domain analysis, taxonomic analysis, componential analysis, and theme analysis. I performed the domain analysis upon the interview transcripts that I conducted with each of the informants throughout the course of the research. For the four adolescents, there were four formal interviews; for the teacher informants, there were two formal interviews at the beginning and end of the research project and two group interviews conducted during October and January.

After the domain analysis was completed upon the interviews, I sequenced chronologically all drafts of the adolescent informant's writing. For each draft, I used a plain sheet of paper and looked for the following information: type of writing genre; specific textual features including grammatical patterns and word choice patterns; paragraph design and sequence; narrator point of views; subject matter information provided; exigent purpose; comparison of changes made after each draft with/without teacher comments.

The taxonomic analysis based upon the domain analysis provided the first opportunity to integrate the interview data with the writing analysis. The taxonomy requires a refinement of the domains identified and a closer look at the relationships within a given domain.

In a strictly ethnographic interview sequence such as the one described by Spradley, each analysis is then followed by another interview that seeks to refine the culture under study. I kept a separate notebook where I daily recorded questions or issues that I wanted to ask my informants during the next interview. I altered Spradley's questioning pattern to allow for the integration of the observational notes and interviews taking place over time. This technique meant that I needed to create a method of analysis that would allow me to sequence events with the writing analysis and with the domain and taxonomic analysis information. In order to organize the various data, I created a material artifacts analysis worksheet.

Using the domain headings and the taxonomic outline, I reviewed my observational notes, researcher's log, and cooked notes for each of the events that

Table 2.4. Questions, Qualitative Method, and Analysis

Research Questions	Qualitative Method	Method of Analysis
How does an adolescent's social world shape the writing of texts in the adolescent's personal and academic life?	Observer notes taken as participant observer Interviews Protocol analysis Researcher's log Cooked notes Comparison of material artifacts Journaling Surveys	Domain analysis on interviews Taxonomic analysis Cultural theme analysis
How do non-college-bound adolescents create written texts?	Participant observer notes Material artifacts consisting of all writings informants do in and out of school	Narrative analysis comparing syntactical and grammatical differences between drafts and sequencing to domain and taxonomic analysis
What characteristics of genre and style distinguish the writing of adolescents?	Literary Analysis/Genre analysis Adolescent's log and journal Informant interviews	Narrative analysis comparing syntactical and grammatical differences between drafts and sequencing to domain and taxonomic analysis
How do an adolescent's life experiences influence the texts they write in and out of school?	Triangulation of participant observer notes with teachers and informants Interviews Literary and genre analysis Parent interviews Teacher logs/lesson plans Material artifacts	Analysis sheet for material artifacts and all other data collected excepting interviews
How does the writing instruction in the language arts classroom affect adolescent writing?	Classroom observational notes Material artifacts with teacher's comments Teacher-informant conferences Teacher lesson plans Teacher interviews Adolescent interviews Final written report by teachers and adolescent informants	Domain analysis; taxonomic analysis; cultural theme analysis coordinated with analysis sheet for material artifacts

were the clearest examples of the domains that answered the research questions. This analysis pattern and the componential analysis combine to produce a picture of the culture, which can be illustrated graphically. Spradley refers to this component and material artifacts analysis as the psychological and structural description of the informant's culture. This step was crucial for this research.

At this point, once the graph or illustration had been made for the componential analysis, I consulted all the other surrounding documents collected during the course of the research. I consulted the adolescent informant research journal, fact sheets of daily activities, classroom handouts and information provided in cooked notes and research log and marked those areas as notes under a specific domain heading. Any artifacts that explained or illustrated some facet of these domains were collected together. At times, the volume of information yielded snippets of details relevant to the domains, but the relevant pieces began to fill in a picture of adolescents and the culture of writing.

ETHICAL REPRESENTATION AND RELATED MATTERS

One unexpected twist occurred in the process of acquiring parental permissions: the parents of one adolescent informant would only let their child participate if I did not make reference or use any analysis based upon race/cultural features and language use. The parents were worried that a mention of racial ethnicity would reflect poorly upon their adolescent. Then, they believed that readers would criticize and judge their child because of existing spoken and written stereotypes surrounding race and language use. I agreed not to include any discussion of racial ethnicity in any analysis or discussion of the data from the informants' written or spoken language.

In the original design of the project, I was not seeking information about race or ethnic origin and writing habits. As a result of my agreement with the parents, I have made every attempt in the rendering of the stories to avoid any mention of race and language patterns for every adolescent informant in this book. It will at times be obvious that a student has particular language use pattern that is characteristic among a certain cultural group; however, I ask that my readers put any such notation into the background of the discussion.

Each teacher and adolescent was given editorial rights over the original manuscript and allowed to change, delete, or alter interpretations. Where these occurred, it is noted in the manuscript. One adolescent informant, Diana, had run away by the time her section of the manuscript was completed. I have not been able to locate her.

NOTES

1. The information regarding Ms. Pearce, the fourth teacher, and Michael J. has been published in *Winning Ways of Coaching Writing: A Practical Guide for Teaching Writing*, Mary L. Warner, ed., Allyn, Bacon, Longman, 2001.

Chapter 3

Danielle—"I'm Safe Now"

DANIELLE'S VIGNETTE

Danielle's speech was punctuated with words like *stuff, kinda, everybody,* and lots of *'cuz.* Her easy manner masked a passion and fire that emerged only when her beliefs or values were challenged.

At first, Danielle appeared to be a quiet, self-assured young woman. She often verbally sparred with two of the young men in her English class, one of whom was also in her Spanish class. As a senior, she held a disciplined and mature composure in classes, especially classes where she was the only upperclassman. In drawing, Spanish, and math, Danielle worked efficiently but kept to herself, only talking when she had a specific purpose. When given a project, she quietly worked with others, maintaining her steady composure.

Outside of school, she enjoyed the love of her family and her Christian faith. Danielle had just become a new aunt. On our first outing, she took me to visit the newborn twins. I held one twin and Danielle the other. We sat in her sister-in-law's apartment with sleeping babies and a big black cat, which didn't know quite what to make of all the fuss but also wanted attention.

When Danielle started to reveal her life's story, I had to compose myself, especially when she described her mother's neglect and abandonment at so early an age. Now, the drugs, abuse, and neglect were experiences of the past, but she still carried unresolved anger and hatred. This smoldered beneath the exterior of this soft-spoken but vibrant young woman.

Living now in a modest, well-kept home, Danielle had the family and the support she had so long desired: to live with her biological father, brothers, and extended family at her side. During the research project, I met Danielle's parents many times when I took Danielle home after family gatherings or church functions. I came to realize that Danielle was indeed surrounded by loving and supportive family. She kept her abusive childhood experiences clearly associated with her biological mother, not with the father who had fought to gain custody of her years before.

All around the home, Danielle's art and family portraits graced the walls of every room. Danielle's proud stepmother showed me an album of Danielle's early drawing and paintings, and more of them decorated the living room walls. The family shared the house with a cat, two large golden retrievers, some very large goldfish, and two singing parakeets

Almost every day at lunchtime, Danielle came home to watch her soap operas while she ate lunch. Then, she returned to school for her fourth block Spanish class and then left school for her job at Burger King.

Danielle's school friends were mostly male, and two stood out in particular, Tom and Boom-Boom. Her female companions consisted only of her brother's latest girlfriend. She seemed to prefer male friends, joking, exchanging quips and light-hearted insults without playing the coquette.

When I first met Danielle, she had just returned from Mexico where her church group had been building homes for the poor. So Mexico was an important part of Danielle's world. Her experiences in Mexico provided a way for her to enrich her spiritual life and learn about living in the world through the word of Christ. Church was another safe place to feel at home.

"I'M SAFE NOW"

Overview

Danielle's life is a testament to an adolescent's ability to survive. Through the artful pedagogy of her senior English class, Danielle's writing[1] illustrates how abuse and neglect affect the learning and literacy of an adolescent long after the abuse/neglect have ceased. In this chapter, we see how Danielle details her survival through the written texts required for her senior English classroom.

Danielle's story held unexpected twists and turns as I learned more about her life, her writing habits, and her violent and abusive history. As researchers and teachers, we need to understand how abuse and violence impact an adolescent's learning. Ms. Plummer's twelfth-grade English curriculum demonstrates how adolescents with traumatic experiences can engage in deep written inquiry and critique of a single self-selected topic to their intellectual and psychological benefit.

In this case study, the effective writing program provided the emotional and intellectual support that Danielle needed to narrate her past history. As I looked for her compensatory strategies, I found them contained within the classroom instruction and writing program that one teacher practiced. Danielle's case study is about that writing program and revision processes that allowed Danielle to address her abusive history without having to turn the classroom lessons into trauma therapy. From the specific writing pedagogy, four characteristics emerged in Danielle's writing process and text construction that allowed this adolescent to academically thrive and heal: connection, consistency, choice, and conflict/challenge.

Danielle shows us how a writing-centered pedagogy can effectively address an adolescent's traumatic experiences and facilitate reconnection and development of literacy skills. It is through the actual rendering of experience into longer discourses through stages of deep revision and analysis that Danielle is able to see herself as mature, empowered to express her ideas beyond the trauma that framed her early life.

In Bozhovich's terms, Danielle's achievement in self-identify and self-esteem was one of the hallmarks of healthy adolescent development. Through her written documents about her past experiences, Danielle illustrated how rendering her experiences allowed her to make progress toward self-awareness, when these same experiences could also block her ability to think and address the emotional memories of abuse. Danielle's writing and revisions gave her control over her past and present with every word she wrote. Eventually, she came to realize that writing about her past helped her see who she was and who she wanted to be.

In her school based writing, Danielle transformed the emotional pain of her life into written texts, which showed how literacy can develop in adolescents despite any damage done by previous neglect and physical abuse. Yes, she would continue to make grammatical errors and misspellings that were part of her early language learning and development, but in the course of a semester's writing, Danielle gained a personal power in telling her stories to address the traumatic violence in her life.

Danielle's narrative telling illustrates Bozhovich's theories of adolescent psychological development and intellectual movement: specifically, self-education, self-esteem, and the development of an emotional maturity. Since the traumatic stresses are connected to emotional memory and images, it is important to examine those learning systems that helped Danielle integrate her past experiences with learning and reinvent herself.

I begin Danielle's case study by introducing her biographical information, her story of abuse and neglect up to the point that I met her and she joined the research project. Originally, the research project was designed to discover the relationship between in school writing and out of school writing, teacher-initiated and self-initiated writing and how classroom lessons transferred to actual practice. However, Ms. Plummer's curriculum became important in regard to what Danielle wrote and how she wrote about her traumatic experiences and memories.

The integral component in Ms. Plummer's writing-centered classroom was the Senior Project. Since I had been looking at the relationship between the writing that adolescents did out of school compared to what they learned in school, I had to refocus Danielle's case study on the relationship between Danielle's writing for Ms. Plummer's Senior Project and her traumatic past as it continued to challenge her learning and literacy. Each new writing task challenged her understanding of her past and provoked her into a new awareness beyond her immediate understanding.

In narrating Danielle's case study, I present a series of writings she completed for the Senior Project. In the early samples, she grappled with the abusive images and emotional reactions to telling her stories through the Senior Project topic. The effect of the writing tasks upon Danielle's learning and language use was exposed more clearly in the revising processes. In these sections, I define, describe, and display examples and how they function to assist Danielle in writing.

Danielle's Socio-Cultural-Historical Background

Danielle was born to a mother and father who already had children from previous marriages: her father had two children and her mother had a two-year-old and was pregnant when she married Danielle's father at the age of twenty-one. Danielle's first writing in her English class narrated the abusive events with chilling detail:

> As the years went by my mother had three children—two brothers and Danielle.
>
> Danielle wished she had never been born because her parents never got along.
>
> Because this was such a traumatic time of her life, she doesn't remember much of anything, only things she's been told when she was a teenager. Her father was a drinker when she was about four or five years old. One time her mother told her that her father grabbed her hair and pulled her across the table in anger. Her mother used to do things to her brothers. She use to beat them and beat them.
>
> They would have bruises all over their bodies. Danielle's parents eventually divorced, forcing Danielle to go back and forth between her mother and father, since her mother was given custody by the courts. (8/28 rough draft from English class)

Danielle described her life with her mother in those years immediately after the divorce:

> She [Danielle] hated living with her mother. She was usually never there; she was always left with the babysitter Nancy while mom was out with guys. A lot of the time Nancy and her brother would make marijuana and cocaine stuff right on the coffee table in front of the world to see. (8/28 rough draft from English class)

In 1986, Danielle's mom found a new male companion, Larry, when Danielle was about seven. In the first grade, Danielle, her mother, and Larry moved almost every month, causing Danielle to attend four different schools. She revealed little bits of information about how her trauma from the abuse began to occur and how it affected her learning: "Danielle was held back her first grade year of school because her mother failed to take her to the emergency room when she had ear infections. Now she was a year behind all the other kids" (8/28 rough draft for English class).

Danielle lived under these conditions until she was fourteen, when she planned an escape from her mother's house. One day, under Larry's ever-watchful eyes, Danielle pretended to be cleaning her closet, when she was actually packing her clothes. The next day after school, she called her father and arranged to meet him at the library. Her mother would never think to look for her there. Her father came for her, and then she told her father that Larry had been sexually assaulting her. A court battle began which eventually granted Danielle's father custody of his fourteen-year-old daughter.

Unfortunately for Danielle, this custody settlement came with the stipulation that she had to visit her mother: She's seen her mother a couple of times but does not want anything to do with her. She doesn't have any feelings for her. She doesn't even love her. She has Charlene, her stepmother, who is the perfect mom for her. To give her a fresh start, Danielle's father enrolled her in a private Christian school until her junior year of high school, when she transferred to Prairie High School.

Danielle's Twelfth-Grade English Class

Ms. Plummer, a veteran teacher with over 25 years of experience, had 18 students (4 girls and 14 boys) in her English 12 class, third block, 11:30 a.m. to 1:00 p.m. Monday through Friday. Ms. Plummer orchestrated the classroom environment to encourage communication and to assist easier conferencing opportunities. In order to facilitate this, she arranged the desks in a circle, a way for Ms. Plummer to see her students and for the students to see each other.

Teaching in a 90-minute block, Ms. Plummer used the first 45 to 60 minutes of each class period to teach the day's literary or writing lesson, including a mini-lesson on grammar problems the students were having. The last 45 to 30 minutes of each class was set aside for conferencing, instructional literary content, writing, and researching. Each student had to be working on a writing task or reading related to their project topic.

Since many of the students in this class worked long hours or participated in the school-to-work program, the homework assignments had to be included in the day's class. Ms. Plummer used the last part of the class period to conference individually with students. It is important to note that she would read and comment upon every draft the students gave her; sometimes this meant reading nine to ten different iterations of a single composition. They quickly learned that they had to work during these periods to meet the goals of the course and meet the graduation requirements.

Of the class members, only two girls, Danielle and Rene, finished the course; two other female students eventually dropped. The 14 male students exhibited a variety of behaviors and academic problems: three students had learning disabilities, so Ms. Plummer had a special education teacher to assist these students during the class with reading and writing assignments; two students were classified as seniors but would not have enough credits to graduate, even if they passed the class; several students were taking the course because they didn't want to jeopardize their grade point averages but were planning on attending college; finally, students who had no intention of attending college were taking the class because it was required for graduation.

The students in Ms. Plummer's class initially regarded me with skepticism. Until they understood what I was doing there and whom I was following, most students were extremely reluctant to converse openly with me. My participant observer position did not guarantee easy access into anyone's writing and life other than Danielle's. Eventually, familiarity, Danielle's personal assurances, and group work allowed me to enter this adolescent world.

A dramatic event changed the class's suspicious attitude toward me when Ms. Plummer scolded me for talking in the hallway during a group writing exercise. My talking earned me a detention from Ms. Plummer and the good-humored laughter of the students. Even though I was an adult, I was no longer regarded as one with the same authority. That was when I *joined* the class and our relationship changed, especially my relationship with a student named Tommie. I will revisit Tommie and his writing at the end of the chapter.

Twelfth-Grade Literature and Writing

Ms. Plummer's senior English language arts curriculum embraced certain pieces of canonical literature. Her program sought to use literature as a place for reflecting and thinking about the possibilities of constructing one's own ideas—as source material, not just examples. Ms. Plummer combined the literary canon with meaningful classroom writing tasks throughout the entire course. Her pedagogical design looped together three phases of study: specific literacy texts from the British canon; contemporary works that complemented the canonical selections and student's readings about their Senior Project topic; and finally, a practical written application of the literary genre to their chosen topic.

The students were given opportunities to develop their literacy skills, to rehearse their knowledge about a literary genre, and then to write in that genre. However, the students were not evaluated on the quality of their genre writing, but were measured by the depth to which it demonstrated their knowledge about literature, which the writing practices encouraged and supported. Immediately following a literary selection, for example, Ms. Plummer had the students reading literature related to their topic choice, followed by a writing project connecting the readings, the literature, and new writing form. "The structure of this course makes it a writing and reading based course, constantly using language, especially written forms, associated language, communication, speaking and then using language in ways that these students have not been able to use it before in academic situations or in their personal situations" (researcher's cooked notes, 9/23).

Ms. Plummer incorporated drawing as an expressive tool for creating understanding and comprehension. Students drew pictures depicting characters or story images that would eventually help them to narrate what they understood. Ms. Plummer arranged the learning strategies to begin with simple visual comprehension of the drawing, followed by a narration of their drawings, reading aloud the texts that the drawings inspired, discussing the meaning and style, and participating through board work. She paralleled the learning strategies in accordance with Vygotsky's language acquisition process: from outside spoken language assisting possible concept formation about the literary study.

Ms. Plummer's classroom was not one in which the teacher routinely dominated classroom discussion through lectures or question-answer sessions. Instead, the students were clearly expected to participate. In this sense, the types of writing assignments in Ms. Plummer's class were most effective when the assignments were compatible with the adolescent's need to build identity and personal independence. These were dependent upon the personal connection and relevancy each student found within the writing tasks and readings.

This constant dialogical curriculum engaged Danielle's traumatic experiences in all phases of the classroom agenda. The course tasks gave these otherwise debilitating memories, experiences, and images a context that could be transformed through revision and altered through reflection. This writing-centered curriculum was designed with the Senior Project as the delivery method.

Table 3.1: Senior Project

The Senior Project is a collection of readings and writings that reflect who you are and how your life has been shaped. It is about important people in your life and things about which you feel passionate. It is about what you hope to become and how you will live your life. It is about how you view societal issues and how you respond to injustices. It is your story. It is also a portfolio that you can show to the world, demonstrating the best work of which you are capable!

Contents: Term 1
Writings
        1 Autobiographical Narrative
        1 Descriptive Piece
        1 Poetry Analysis
        1 Interview Piece
Readings
        3 Magazine Articles
        1 Full-Length Book

Contents: Term 2
Writings
        1 Poetry Analysis
        1 Persuasive Piece
        1 Original Poem
        1 Slogan
        1 Introduction
        1 Conclusion
        2 Pieces of Artwork
        Cover, Table of Contents
Readings
        4 Magazine Articles

Writing the Senior Project: Consistency, Choice, Conflict and Connection

Ms. Plummer's design for the English 12 curriculum was a semester-long project investigating one topic, which the student selected. (See appendix A for the complete semester project syllabus.) She advised each student to choose a personal interest. Using a writing-centered pedagogy, she chronologically paired the writing tasks with a major British canonical text and a popular text, and the student selected expository readings relevant to the topic. She called the written product for this semester's work "The Senior Project." As Ms. Plummer defined it, the project is "a collection of reading and writing which reflect who you are and how your life has been shaped. It is about important people in your life and things about which you feel passionate. It is about what you hope to become and how you will live your life. . . . It is your story."

Stories are more than just narratives; they are in fact expressions of culture framed through discourse (Bomer, *Passion,* 1995; Dyson & Genishi, 1994; Rico, 2008). For some of the students, these narratives are the expressions of our violent culture and reveal the dynamics of how violence is affecting our adolescents. Yet, having students write about their lives does not necessarily turn students into sophisticated writers or provide a one-method-fits-all based writing instruction. What it does do is focus language use for writing and thinking into a realm where the adolescents confront and engage their language skills. Then, through the continuous and consistent revision process, they reflect and reconfigure their prior understandings with their new use of language. This is where the power lies, especially for those students who are struggling to learn through their traumatic experiences, memories, and literacy practices.

Ms. Plummer placed choice and conflict at the center of the Senior Project. The choice of the topic reduced complaints about interest, and the conflict throughout the project turned to a more engaging challenge in finding information about the subject, some of which disrupted long held opinions and beliefs. Ms. Plummer's project offered students an opportunity to investigate a subject deeply, challenged them with an inquiry process that questioned perceptions and caused some conflict, to connect it with other meaningful readings and writings, and to make choices that direct their thinking reflection and analysis toward some resolution.

Adolescents' Views on English Class and School

On Fridays, Ms. Plummer saved 30 minutes of class time for the students to discuss any subject they wished. There were specific rules for engagement in the discussion, but everyone was encouraged to share their ideas and opinions, regardless of the outrageous statements students sometimes made. On this particular Friday (9/10), Ms. Plummer had decided to have the students tell her about their past experiences with English classes and explain why they resisted and complained so much about reading and writing. I include this rather lengthy text because it contains so many elements that are important to students who are just surviving, and the issues that clearly affect their literacy development.[2]

> J: The only thing I really don't like about it and with all the teachers we really haven't learned anything new. Like the facts of all the required readings we have. In ninth grade we read *Of Mice and Men.* I even read the book and I got all the answers off the work there was not a point to that whatsoever. We learned Shakespeare. Whoopeedooo. I didn't care about it to begin with. Last year we were supposed to read *Huck Finn,* but we only read parts of it. He made us

like read certain parts to know what's going on and then the *Scarlet Letter*, we watched the movie.

T: He let us work at our own pace. He let us do anything. He gave it to us and we took our time.

K: Like I don't get it. All these book reports you have to do. I mean, you know, it's just like read a book and write on it. [Laughter from the class.] I read the book; I know what's in it. Why I got to write upon it?

L: I don't understand the senior project. ["Me neither," someone else says.] This—most of this stuff—is dumb. Doing these things. Learn more about yourself and sayin' what you think, goin' to us die, write what you see. I think I. . . . That it is real dumb especially at my age. I think we should be doing something more mature.

Ms. Plummer: Do you have any suggestions?

K: See, I really don't see. I done been through everything. I been sittin' here and I haven't thought of one fucking thing to write.

Ms: Plummer: Watch the language, please. I don't allow that kind of language in this discussion.

Q: You're busted!

C: I like that we had to walk along the river. I like the senior project because we get to choose topics, which is good. We get to do our own thing. It's better than taking that book and reading it. I'm not saying I'm illiterate, but I don't enjoy reading unless it's something that I'm really interested in it.

Tommie: If I'm not interested in it, I'm not gonna to read it, you know, man.

C: That's bad. I need to learn to how to read. [Embarrassing laughter from C.] I like that journal. [Other voices try to interrupt her.] Man, I'm not done. Chill! The journals like when we went outside. It's nice to be able to get outside, you know, and journal outside.

K: Back in grade school, we actually learned something. We learned what a verb was and stuff like that. We already know it all. Can you tell me what the point of this class is?

R: I don't like English because it's like an individual thing. You gotta do it yourself. I don't like it because I am more active and I like to do things, but man, physical things. I don't like to sit down and read a book and write in the journal. I get lazy.

Tommie: If it don't catch your eye, I can't read it. If I don't see it's going to be any good, I just don't read it. What I say about this story [*Beowulf*] is I can't read it. I know I can't.

Ch: The point behind an English class when you get to this level is to teach you to think freely. To think for yourself.

A: You have been knowin' that.

T: You know how to think for yourself. Nobody can teach you how to think for yourself. You supposed to know how to think for yourself.

A: Back in elementary school, that when you really got taught the most. [Class echoes with "Yeahs".]

De: I don't want to read no epics or stuff like that and we—you got to stop me and think about what you did.

K: Yeah, really. You have to think about so many things, stop, after you just started to figure out what that line meant.

Ad: I just don't like reading. I just don't like English.

Ms. Plummer: Can you explain why?

Ad: No. Little things in your head tell you you don't like it. You got it from your parents. My parents didn't like English. My mom still thinks that it shouldn't be required and my dad [mumble unintelligible].

Ra: I don't like reading things that are three or four hundred years old.

Ms. Plummer: What does your high school diploma mean?

M: It's just a piece of paper. They'll give one to anybody. I swear to God.

This classroom discussion exposed well-known complaints about some English language arts classroom content and the pedagogy in the hardened disinterest and purposelessness students find in English literary studies. Their perceptions of what English should teach them and what it is lie in the realms of the quantifiable world of grammatical correctness. As the students so clearly state, they viewed "thinking for yourself" as something that cannot be taught. The lone adolescent voice who articulated the purpose of the course was quickly interrupted and silenced by the majority.

Ms. Plummer's curriculum for English 12 was contained in a single, topic driven project, which involved reading and writing extensively about the student-determined topic and was complemented with limited study of literature. Yet, the students, hardened by their past experiences and difficulties with reading and understanding the literary canon of preceding grade levels, presented Ms. Plummer with a most difficult task.

These students give us a view of adolescents' responses to textual reading and writing and provide us with a context for analyzing the purpose of teaching writing and the process of writing inside and outside the classroom. Moreover, they demonstrate what a difficult task it is for any English teacher to engage students in literate tasks, which they deem useless by being irrelevant to their perceptions of literacy and learning at the twelfth grade year.

Choosing the Topic

On the first day of class, Ms. Plummer introduced the first writing that the students would be doing: an autobiographical narrative about an important life event. In order to accomplish the first writing assignment, Ms. Plummer guided the students through a series of reading and writing tasks. She explained the project, provided the students with time to review examples of written projects from previous years, and then gave them a challenging example of an autobiographical narrative (Alice Walker's "Beauty: When the Other Dancer Is the Self"), which she wanted them to produce. Ms. Plummer then gave the following assignment:

> Choose a person: First write an impression. Write for a few minutes about your very first thoughts and feelings about the person: what happened, who was there, how did they act, what thoughts did you have, what did he/she say, what did you say, what feelings can you remember. Now take your time and draft this into an autobiographical narrative.

This assignment, like the other written assignments in the course, had four necessary elements to engage Danielle: choice in the topic, connection to her personal experience, the conflict she encountered in the rhetorical task and challenge in assimilating the past with present knowledge from objective sources, and the interpretative qualification that each writing assignment required and consistency in revising sessions.

As Brandt (1990) suggests, "the text is better seen as a writer's emerging problem, as it delineates an unfolding social reality through which a writer must continue to try to be understood and in which a writer's decisions (including plans) are taking place" (p. 51). In Danielle's case, I would take this idea one step further by adding that her emerging problem was the past, which she confronted in the present by writing about it; this process transformed her experiences to words and released them. These were the decision points she made as a writer: to tell and to keep telling it until she ultimately writes the one piece that gives her confidence, control, and a clear view of her own transformation and survival. Through the objective inquiry into the topic of divorce, Danielle wrote about her painful experiences with this topic, which grew to encompass the abuse and neglect she had experienced. It also gave her information about the divorce process, which helped her to objectively reflect upon her experiences with her parents' divorce. She described it this way:

> I think it was because of going through that whole divorce and everything and like I couldn't settle it or anything in my mind and just let it sit there and dwell on it. But doing the project, helped you like to think about it and make it go away basically.
>
> You can just let them linger on it, not your mind and everything, you're not gonna accomplish anything from it. They're not gonna grow from it; you're not gonna learn from it. It's gonna sit there in your mind and not do anything.
>
> Writing down on paper really helps see a lot of things I didn't see before when I was in the situation. (Personal Communication, 1/21)

Danielle recognized the value of putting her experiences on paper, and this realization provided a reinforcement to continue writing.

The power to transform the trauma lay in the deep description of her emotions and their related images. She stated the value of truth telling and opening up was connected to transformation that can improve learning and literacy. Danielle's statement showed an awareness that writing about the trauma provided a pathway through the trauma to a place of transformation and intellectual growth through reflection and revelation; this was more than emotional ramblings or script-therapy. Danielle described a process of learning that shows teachers how to teach the way children learn.

Dewey in *Experience and Education* (1938) argued that the experience a child has with the instrument [writing] should prepare that child to deal with the moment in time. Dewey might have been referring to the actual physical experience of doing, but also to making the immediate classroom context relevant to any assignment or learning task. Using the adage "What is past is prologue" to describe the literacy context that traumatized adolescents bring to the classroom, I came to understand that those adolescents who experience trauma need a curriculum that first recognizes the impact trauma has upon their ability to learn.

Teachers can use this understanding to create pedagogy and curricula that is meaningful for all the students, regardless of traumatic history by focusing literacy development through personal relevance and linguistic practice. Traumatized adolescents divert thinking energy to protecting and generating items for their survival. Learning, literacy, and writing are acquired tools that can assist in that survival. For children/adolescents with violent experiences, the immediate need is for reconciliation of the trauma they live with each day, so that their brains can attend to making new connections that foster intellectual development.

According to Bozhovich (1979), Danielle's behavior places her in the second phase of adolescence, the period of young adulthood. In this period, the crisis points are related to the unsatisfied needs of the child, but as Bozhovich states:

In the adolescent crisis, internal factors play an important role: prohibitions imposed by the youth on himself/herself; earlier formed psychological characteristics which frequently interfere with the youth's attaining what she/her desires; the life-style the youth has selected. The crisis occurs when the adolescent arrives at a new level of awareness, a characteristic feature of which is the emergence and the capacity and the need to know oneself as an individual with unique qualities, different from everyone else. (pp. 64–65)

For students who have experienced trauma from violence, abuse, and natural disasters, the memory and images of the experience interfere, perhaps even control, what an adolescent desires and needs. Certainly, the unpredictable living conditions create an unhealthy environment that interferes with the adolescent's ability to search for his/her identity since the mental energy is working to secure basic survival needs.

Searching to achieve that level of awareness and reconciling the traumatic history have to be seen as intricate and related forces in adolescent crises. In some cases, the violence does not allow the adolescent to select a life style or make independent choices because they have other needs to be met. Through making their traumatic truth visible in the writing, the adolescent can see beyond his/her distresses and discover hope and resiliency.

Danielle's Writings

The Senior Project's writing tasks included various genres, not just exposition or essay writing. In Ms. Plummer's English language arts curriculum, the Senior Project focused all the readings and writings the students would complete. In respect to writing, Ms. Plummer joined a literature reading and a writing task, which asked students to imitate the conventions of the literary genre. After each literary selection, the students located a literary sample that demonstrated some aspect of their senior project topic.

Each writing task involved the initial assignment, inventing for the writing, completing drafts, guided revisions and editing sessions, conferences, and finally the publication of the final work. In the 90-minute period, 45 minutes each day was dedicated to working on the latest writing assignment (see appendix B). For her Senior Project topic, Danielle chose "divorce."

Danielle's Writing #1: Life Changing Experience

As the researcher, Danielle's first writing was my initiation into the hidden world of abuse. The first example is taken from the first writing she did for the Senior Project. Her calm narrative manner in the third-person point of view makes it even more disturbing.

When Danielle wrote her first composition about divorce, she spoke as a distant third-person narrator. Writing caused an intersection of images and emotions that Danielle had long kept hidden. This first writing forced her to make the crucial step from the hidden truth about her parents' divorce and the words she used to describe what happened. This information gave her the opportunity to visualize and realize concepts about divorce that she was not able to understand prior to this project. The third-person narrator point of view allowed the author and the narrator separate stages from which to tell.

This was a start of a new nightmare unknown to both. As the years went by my mother had three children. My two brothers and Danielle. Danielle sometimes wished she had never been born. Her parents never got along. Because this was such a traumatic time of her life she doesn't remember much of anything. Just things she has been told when she was a teenager. Her father was a drinker when she was young, about four or five years old. One time her mother told her that her father grabbed her hair and pulled her across the table in anger. She never believed that her father could do such a thing to his little princess. But as days go by, she started getting flashbacks of what her father had done. She was stunned. (8/28 draft of topic for paper; Life-Changing Experience)

Writing in the third person, and Ms. Plummer's nonjudgmental acceptance of her story, helped Danielle to dance around the details of abuse until she learned not to fear or be ashamed of exposing these traumatic events. Danielle wrote one draft of the Life-Changing Experience, and it did not make its way into her final senior project; however, it served to solidify and initiate the topic for the Senior Project and her written acknowledgement of the relationship of her past and present experiences and images.

Shortly after this draft, I asked Danielle to describe her writing process. I expected to find a process-oriented pattern because I assumed that was what she learned to do, and would at least mimic it in her writing for Ms. Plummer's class. However, what I found was a very different process:

D: Right now sometimes, most of the time, I don't [use a process] even though I just write. So, I just write it down. I really don't have a specific way to write. Sometimes I do. This one lady said that she could see me writing a book.
Deb: What goes on in your head before you write the words?
D: Usually I come up with a picture of it. Like divorce, I come up with pictures of the way it was when I was little. Or um we had to do a thing on culture. Like culture, you had to pick things that were in your environment. Like things that make up you, things that you believe in or your morals or whatever. (Personal Communication, 11/13)

This exchange showed the power of the image to drive the search for expression. Danielle often experienced frustrating moments during the semester because she could not remember details from childhood that she needed in order to carry on her writing.

Danielle's Writing #2: Poetry Analysis and Revision

Deb: Does writing help?
D: I guess it does. It makes you look at things differently and in a different way.

Deb: How?

D: Like that poem thing. I really didn't think; I don't think it all went with my topic. Then, a certain thing happened that week and then it's like, oh yeah, I can relate to that.

Deb: Something happened outside of school? Can I ask you what happened?

D: Me and my stepmom haven't been getting along that well because I have been getting irritated with things that she has been saying. And I haven't really realized it that much. I had before, but I really ignored it, but then my sister-in-law said something to me about it, and it made me realize, and I wrote that poem.

Deb: Is it a specific line?

D: I don't think it was a specific line. It was the poem theme of it.

Deb: Was what?

D: That one that we did. [Looking through her notes.] It's that one by Jason Talmadge did. It's basically about how his mom was going to remarry and show she was going to pick a fight with his soon-to-be step-father to see what side his mom would take, and she would obviously take her boyfriend's side over him, and he knew that. It was kinda like that way like my step-mom favors her son over everybody else. So kinda like how I tied it in.

Deb: Does it come across at the time, or was it just in reading the poem that there was a connection for you?

D: It took a while to really think about it, but yeah.

Deb: What yeah?

D: I just have this thing in my craw. Things in life.

Deb: At home?

D: Yeah, just the way I grew up all these years. Chaotic.

Deb: Does it affect you in school?

D: Yeah, it affects everything. The way I grew up affects me the person that I am and the environment that you're in. When I lived with my mom, it was totally different than living with my dad. I've lived with my dad for three years. But then there's like change in school, which affects that much by going through those experiences, which makes me feel like I am totally ahead of everybody else in school, like they're too immature or they can't relate to the things I've gone through or like just the same interests . . . (Personal Communication, 9/25)

In this interview, Danielle revealed the link between her abuse and the permeating influence it had upon her literacy processes, her ability to think and reason. In the transcript, we witnessed Danielle's self-awareness of how her abusive experiences have separated her from other students. She explained that her social cultural world, as it had changed, had also affected the way that she perceived herself.

This psychological precondition, which Bozhovich identified in her theory of adolescent development of mind, is characteristic of the second phase. In reaching for self-awareness and self-education, Danielle has used her traumatic past and named the words that frame them if she was to move beyond them. Writing to survive is not about becoming a sophisticated writer and not about achieving perfect grammatical correctness and expression; it is about writing so deeply and so broadly as to encapsulate personal trauma and release the powerful emotional hold it has over her mental processes.

In the following poetic analysis, Danielle illustrated the connectedness of lived experience to making meaning in literature and writing. She had selected this poem because it was related to her chosen topic on divorce.

> In one situation, "I Picked a Fight" reminds me of one night I came home from youth group, and everyone was in a bad mood. . . . Well, we got to the topic of my step-brother. He was in a bad mood because there was no supper for him. . . . She [step-mother] then started to defend him and she does that all the time. So it's like no matter where I live, there still are problems, which I can understand to a certain extent. I didn't want to live with my mother because she cared more about the welfare money she got for having me there and her boyfriend. . . . "I Picked Fight" reminds me of my life. . . . (Student writing, 9/25)

Being personally referential in every piece of writing and reading forced a conflict, as we see in Danielle's poetry analysis. These personal illuminations about her present life and literary readings were the core of "thinking." Through the contemplation and self-reflection, Danielle was able to understand more about herself and her reactions. Identity development came in the reflective moments of challenge, when internal emotional and cognitive forces met in conflict over a task. In Danielle's case, the channel for such thinking and analysis revolved around her traumatic experiences, as they rise through the present poetic connection, conditions at home and the classroom instruction.

The emotional and psychological depth of trauma is never far away from tasks that present adolescents with a challenge: the need to reconcile the past so that they can move on. In every draft, she refocused her entire abusive history in order to work through the crisis of the moment and the internal crises of growth and development.

The analysis of the poem might not show skillful poetic understanding, but the conditions surrounding it revealed that the actual analysis itself was significant. Through the analysis, Danielle was able to connect and produce a text that did relate to her topic, and she had to confront her own personal distaste and dislike of poetry and make meaning through writing. A sample of her writing process in three separate phases of revision is intended to show this struggle. With each revision, Danielle has to do more than change a few words; she has to reflect upon how she feels about poetry, about what she is saying, and then revise for new meaning and understanding. Again, I present Danielle's writing as she originally drafted it.

Poetry Draft #1

The thought is going through his mind. His parents want a life of their own and it doesn't include him. He feels unwanted and her. He thinks why is he's here in the first place? If his parents ask this way and make him feel unwanted and why did they have him.

In the first set of revisions, Ms. Plummer advised Danielle to tell clearly and directly about the poem's content, and then to reflect in future paragraphs. Ms. Plummer avoided commenting upon the spelling and grammatical correctness until the material content became more clearly expressed.

Poetry Draft #2

Just image how he feels. He feels now that his father doesn't want him either. "You know I tried kid" is telling the kid that he did his best by trying to get custody of him. "They both want a life of their own, a life which doesn't include me." With Jason crying out in his own way to each of his parents and having them not understanding it is making him feel bad. He feels as though his parents don't want him. That they want a life of their own without him. He then ends it by saying "If I am such a burden to both of them, why did they have me in the first place?" He feels down and doesn't know what to do. He thinks his parents don't care about him and with that he ask himself why did they have him in the first place.

After reading the second draft, Ms. Plummer advised Danielle to break apart longer paragraphs and provide headings. She also told her to check on verb tenses, and then suggested that Danielle and Ms. Plummer work together for the next draft.

Poetry Draft #3—final version

He then left to go to his father's house. When he thought to himself that this was silly because he already knew the answer, but he had no other choice. "I'd love to have you here, Jason, but you know how it is." Just imagine how he feels. He feels now that his father doesn't want him either. "You know I tried kid" was telling the that he did his best by trying to get custody of him. "They both want a life of their own, a life which doesn't include me."

With Jason crying out in his own way to each of his parents and having them not understanding it was making him feel bad. He feels as though his parents don't want him. That they want a life of their own without him. He then ends it by saying "If I am such a burden to both of them, why did they have me in the first place?" He feels down and doesn't know what to do. He thinks his parents don't care about him and with that he asks himself why did they have him in the first place.

Each of these revisions reflected Danielle's integration of Ms. Plummer's suggestions. Danielle fixated on one personal event and particular childhood feeling (not being wanted by her mother) and focused her entire summary and analysis through them. After her initial draft on Jason Talmadge's poem, Danielle was very confused about how to continue writing. She had been following Ms. Plummer's format, but as Danielle came to realize, her common habits of writing had been to write all that she knew about the subject.

When she had no more to say, she assumed that she had finished writing, as we witnessed in draft #1. Danielle could not move beyond her summary of the poem in order to find connection to her personal experiences. At Ms. Plummer's prodding, Danielle elaborated in draft #2 to the extent that she has material for analysis. Danielle now had to connect it to her life as the assignment instructed. She began this connection with a recent personal incident about being angry when she came home from school one evening. The bad mood she described drew us into the family clash over household duties and perceived parental favoritism. Here is Danielle's description of the personal incident that helped her to connect to the poem.

> "He was in a bad mood because there was no supper for him when he got home and things were not done. He then talked about how I never do anything and just sit on my butt everyday and watch tv which is a big lie.
>
> So, it's like not matter where I live there still is problems, which I understand, but it goes to a certain extent. I didn't want to live with my mother because she cared more about the welfare money she got for having me there and her boyfriend. I sometimes regret living with my father because I am always stuck in between arguments with my parents.
>
> I am forced to choose between them both." (Poetry analysis, Senior Project)

The writing sample focused how the past traumatic feelings and emotions gave additional background to Danielle's connection between the poem and her life. As Ms. Plummer required revisions, which the drafts have illustrated, Danielle had to re-envision the connection between her personal experiences and the poetic analysis. In her final statement, she made her personal relevancy clear:

> "I Picked a Fight" reminds me of my life. You to go certain degrees to see if your parents love you more than things in there life. Sometimes it's joyful and sometimes it's heartbreaking, but kids are always afraid to lose there parents. I was always afraid to lose my father if he got married. In some ways I did, but other ways we're closer than ever. (Final poetry analysis, Senior Project)

These drafted revisions allowed Danielle to transform these painful memories into something productive and personally meaningful; she learned about poetry analysis, writing, and some grammatical sophistication through these processes. While working with specific writing conventions and the writing assignment, Danielle showed us the thinking progress she was making through the struggle with the poem and her own life experiences; this showed how connection and conflict working in the writing tasks build an awareness of self. When she made progress revising and editing her analysis, she made progress managing and controlling her traumatic past.

Ms. Plummer's consistent conferencing and revising requirements provided a vital link in Danielle's ability to separate her emotional responses and images of her present situation through the objective analysis of a poem. This process allowed Danielle to separate her traumatic past into new awareness that involved language use, poetry content. In the process, she reshaped her past into a new awareness with each step into deep revision and editing. Each writing revision and editing allowed Danielle to push the emotional trauma one step further away from its emotional hold on her because in order to address the comments and make the revisions, Danielle had to "think" differently. We are seeing Danielle write her way to surviving each traumatic ordeal, and we are seeing her make linguistic and literacy progress.

At the writing of the third draft, another family situation intervened and made its way into the revisions. These revisions would continue for weeks, until the students had revised the drafts to show grammatical correctness and to demonstrate the analysis principles Ms. Plummer had set forth. Each time the students revised, another life experience may have worked its way into the analysis.

Opportunities like this poetry analysis accomplished two things: the writing assignment invited students to find ways to connect with forms with which formerly they had difficulty. Second, writing about the same topic in various genres throughout the semester produced evidence of progress and understanding not only about literature but about writing.

Each new writing task required a new story construction about the adolescent's life. By rendering what was so internally and emotionally traumatic into words, Danielle reached a level of self-awareness that she could state in words. The power resided in using words to create the images and emotional realities of story she now wanted to tell. For students like Danielle, learning to use writing as a means to construct, control, and create through her life propels fears and traumatic experiences into a powerful narrative of understanding.

Writing and Thinking to Transform a Life

Ms. Plummer's suggestions empowered and directed Danielle's writing. What is more important to Danielle's development was how her thinking evolved around a writing problem when she became aware of it through

Ms. Plummer's suggestions. In order to change her writing, she had to change the way she perceived the structure of her own language. Changing the way Danielle used language altered the way she thought. We see an example of this process as she reflected upon her writings at the end of her senior year. She evaluated her senior writing experience this way:

> My favorite piece is the poem that I did called "Moments in Time." I wrote that from my own words and ideas. I am going to miss this school and all the memories made in it so I thought I would write a piece on it and I chosed the poem. It means a lot to me because I've learned so much these past two years going to Prairie High School and made great friends with students and teachers that I will miss them all terribly. (Conclusion to Senior Project)

I offer the following series of revisions to illustrate not only the power of consistent revision but also the visible sequence of control Danielle imposes as the author of this poem.

First draft:
    It's cold dreary day with wind rushing through the air. The American flag lopes as the wind ripples through it showing freedom everywhere
    Trees flitter as there freshness lingers amongst the land. Grass lays like water soaken sand.

Second draft after Ms. Plummer's comments:
    It's a cold <u>dreary</u> day with wind rushing through the air.
    The American flag <u>lopes</u> as the wind ripples through it showing freedom everywhere.
    Trees <u>flitter</u> as there freshness lingers <u>amongst</u> the land.
    Grass lays on the horizon like water <u>soakin'</u> sand.
    As I look up in the <u>clear</u> sky of sapphire. . . .
    Yet's there no place like _____ High,
    We leave with future goals and our memories are left lingering behind.

In this second draft, Danielle changes the draft by leaving out a stanza, and changes soaken to soakin'. Ms. Plummer's next revising session pointed out word choice and continuity like dreary and clear; flag lopes and clarity of grass lays like sand.

Third draft:
    It's a cold day with the wind rushing through the air.
    The America flag <u>lopes</u> as the wind ripples through it showing freedom everywhere.
    Trees <u>flitter</u> as there freshness lingers <u>amongst</u> the land.
    <u>Grass lays on the horizon like water soakin' sand.</u>

Danielle in this draft eliminated dreary, but did not make any other significant changes. Ms. Plummer's comments on this draft addressed Danielle's
use of *there*, the *grass*, which Danielle had not clarified, *lopes* as a word,
and *amongst* as appropriate word choice. In its final version, offered below,
Danielle shows us that through the various stages of revisions, she has been
able to create a final draft without the writing mistakes and word miscues that
dominate her early drafts. She has had to relearn spelling and grammar usage
through Ms. Plummer's carefully scaffolded revision assistance.

> Final draft:
>   It's cold day with wind rushing through the air.
>   The American flag stands as the wind ripples through it showing freedom
>   everywhere.
>   Trees flutter as its freshness lingers amongst the land.
>   Grass lays on the horizon as people walk hand in hand.
>   As I look up in the clear sky of sapphire
>   I wonder how this world became like an out of control forest fire.
>   I look down to see cars passing and coming in and out.
>   Possibly skippers
>   \Possibly late comers.
>   The leaves shake in the wind
>   as people scurry in.
>   We're moments in time
>   that change all the time.
>   Student pass on to higher grades as graduation comes near.
>   Leaves grow and die as seasons come and go every year.
>   Yet there's no place like Prairie High School.
>   We graduate with future goals and our memories behind.

Danielle selected this poem for her Senior Project Portfolio. During her revision sessions, I sat next to Danielle and watched her bring up this writing on
the computer screen; read it; read Ms. Plummer's comments on the last draft
she had, and then she edited for each comment. The results were the change
of *flitter* to *flutter*; the *grass* line has a complement after the verb and the sky
images made her think of the world out of control.

   She changed *lopes* to *stands*, which for me lost some of the movement
her made-up words encased. The mixing of word parts is one of Danielle's
unique strategies. In later examples, we see that Danielle does this word-
making, which closely resembles several words that could be the intended
word with an intended meaning.

   These minor changes followed Ms. Plummer's guided suggestions, which
scaffolded for Danielle her ability to change her poem. Between the last draft
and the final copy, Danielle had written two more poems, taken an exam by

writing it as a poem, and had done more poetry analysis in class. I have focused on these revision strategies as integral parts of Danielle's ability to write through her traumatic crisis experiences, and arrive at a place that has given her self-expression and self-awareness. With each word choice, each revision, each new story, Danielle transformed her past and arrived at a new realization.

Not all the writing students completed for the Senior Project was driven by the literary genre study in the curriculum. In some cases, students could use any writing genre they had already learned to take an exam or to write an expressive piece related to the senior project topic. The techniques Danielle learned by redrafting her poem "Moments in Time," she applied to another expressive poem called "Mother Said She Cared."

Danielle's relationship with her mother and the details of the abuse she endured thematically link many of the writing pieces Danielle created for the senior project. This poem had to have ten syllables in each stanza, which was determined by the first full line the students wrote in a free write preceding their rendering into a poem. Ms. Plummer was using this exercise to show syllabification, control over vocabulary, and stanza structure.

My Mother
said she loved
all of us
kids.

My Mother
would leave me
alone with
him.

I told her
and she did
not believe
me.

She kept me
away from
my own
father.

Mom said she
wished she did
not have
any kids.

My mother
said she loved
me: what
happened?

There were only two drafts of this poem, and Danielle elected to include this poem in her Senior Project. The power of revising taught Danielle about using language correctly and effectively to express her ideas, as we see in this more polished poetic writing.

With adolescents, teachers have to deal with a skill and knowledge set brought to the classroom, but the idea that adolescents are still acquiring language use skills is important to consider when witnessing Danielle's development. While these are perhaps minor points of expressing ideas clearly, the process here shows that language acquisition and development in adolescents is tied to their emotional interests, personal images of experiences, and the recursive structure provided by constant revising and editing.

I asked Danielle specifically how her writing process occurred and how Ms. Plummer helped her, since this aspect of her writing was important to her:

> "She helped me out like the way that I would write 'cause I would make a lot of mistakes at first (I interrupted her and asked like what?) Like a whole bunch of different ideas in one paragraph that would really loose the reader's interest or whatever. They wouldn't know what was going on. Basic punctuation errors, she taught me to take my time when I write stuff and not just hurry and write it and get it over with. She taught me to not write. . . . Not to write so much but basically given the point and jot just keep rattling on cause I write a lot. I think she gives students a log of input. . . . I know you do this. You are a good writer. I think a lot of kids need that. It's nice to be appreciated for what I write or what you do. If you say to a somebody, Oh, you're a bad writer, they're not gonna want to do it.
>
> This way you are doing it so that you don't kinda have someone doing it for you but are doing it your own way and so, so learn it better that way when you do it your own. It's not like when you give her something you finish, she gives you ideas how to correct it and you gotta figure out what it is that you have to correct. It's not like she fixes it for you. That's good, and some—a lot of students expect other people to do their own work and tell them what they have to fix. I think it's good this way because they know exactly what it is and they have to figure out what it is. Then they have to figure out what it is and they learn better that way." (Personal Communication, 1/21)

The stage of "think for yourself" recalled the adolescent need for independence, even when they say they can't do it. That "can't do it moment" identified the nebulous zone of proximal development for adult assistance. Ms. Plummer guided Danielle's feelings of insecurity about her writing into an expressive rhetorical composition. The rehearsal and revisions allowed the adolescent to think about the comment, analyze the situation, and make adjustments.

It is the depth of the revising process and the consistent objective attention Ms. Plummer focused on the writing that provided the scaffold for students as traumatized as Danielle. For Danielle, this process of constant revision brought to the surface her problems with the language symbol system in spelling and pronunciation, creating a new awareness of linguistic choices. Constantly working on the mistakes, Danielle learned to "figure out what it is you have to correct."

Writing Her Life and Surviving

During the fall semester, Ms. Plummer's student teacher, Ms. Ferger, took over the responsibility for classroom instruction. As the final writing assignment for the project, Danielle had to create a persuasive document using her topic. The writing lessons for this persuasive writing centered on creating an argument. Ms. Ferger gave the students an outline to follow while the class traced the argument in an article on capital punishment. The whole process was confusing for Danielle, but she eventually produced an outline for her persuasive writing.

During the think-aloud protocol[3] for the persuasive writing, Danielle stated that she was going to make this persuasive piece a letter to her mother. During the protocol, Danielle narrated about what she was writing. She commented about the letter and the words that she was using:

> I here [which Danielle changes to *hear* when she reads it aloud after she has written it] and believe the stories I get told by my family . . . Of the way you treated us when we were really little. You didn't give a dam about any of us. You would just stick a bottle in our mouths and put us in the play pen and hope (she pauses here to search for the right word and asks herself what word can I use?) to entertain ourselves so you can <u>traunt</u> off and do what you liked. (Think-aloud protocol, 11/19 & 11/20)

While completing the first draft of the persuasive piece, Danielle had been learning in class about argument in persuasive writing. The outline, which she wrote originally for class, contained an argument considering the child custody rights. In the protocol draft, she directed the discussion toward her mother and her personal feelings about how the divorce process affected Danielle as a child. Here again, the persuasive writing assignment turned into an opportunity for Danielle to expose and direct her deep anger toward her mother. Danielle finally decided to use a letter to her mother as the framework for her argument.

In the letter draft, Danielle revealed that her knowledge about her past was partially constructed through family stories, which reflected her own memories of neglect and abuse. When she attempted to find a word to describe a memory, she hybridized word pieces that came close to the actual word she wanted to use; for example, "traunt." This same process occurred in her poem "Moments in Time." She made up words that were so close to the actual word. Her vocabulary for the traumatic events in the persuasive writing are captured uniquely in the spelling of idea captured in the hybrid of truant and tramp. Her word closely resembled trot, tramp, trample, tromp, or taunt, and signifies her own coding system for expressing her feelings. When I initially tried to imagine what word she was grasping for, I realized from the words beginning with "t" that closely mirrored her word, that she had created a word whose spelling co-opted many words closely related to her intended meaning. These types of *errors* permeated Danielle's writings, but these mangled spellings and various word combinations carry as many meanings for her as the words she used to construct them.

The persuasive portion of her text reiterated a survival theme—her devotion and need to be with her father and anger at her abusive mother. This persuasive piece of writing was the tool that gave Danielle an opportunity to take control of her feelings. Through the rendering of those emotions into words, she experienced a control that again demonstrated her mental development alongside her emotional development.

In this particular piece, Danielle gained agency over her traumatic past by constructing an authentic and rhetorically expressive writing driven by her conscious and deliberate choices for audience, purpose, and intention. She established an ethos and an exigency that guided and controlled this piece. In order to accomplish this kind of control, Danielle learned and grew through the consistent revision pedagogy that defined this project, the sustained inquiry into a single topic, and the various genre options given to the students for writing. These activities fostered her achievement in this final writing.

I offer a significant portion from her final letter to her mother as an example of Danielle's use of writing to demonstrate the above point:

> I hear and believe the stories I get told by my family of the way you treated us when we were little. Stories like when you would stick a bottle in my mouth and stick me in the playpen and just leave me there while you went to do whatever it was with whomever . . .
>
> What kind of an example are you? You always had different boyfriends every week.
>
> Were you just using them for sex and money? You could never keep a guy for that long, and I always wondered why. I hated it that you always left me with your friend Nancy and at times with her brother. Did you know that he rolled dope right in front of me on the coffee table? What kind of an environment is that for a child to be in. You, as my mother, shouldn't have put me there in that

condition. Sometimes, especially now. I think you had us kids so you could get money for welfare. Where did that money go?

That money was supposed to be used on me. I never got clothes or anything. You always made dad get me clothes and any other things that I needed. Is that why you didn't want me to live with my father, so you could keep getting the money and supporting yourself?

The one thing that I will never forget is the life we had with Larry. I was surprised that he stayed with you so long. I thought that he would've left you a long time ago. He hurt me so much when he was putting the moves on me. My own step-father doing that to me. He even did a lot of it in front of you and you didn't do a thing. Memories of those times still haunt me and always will. I even told you that it was happening, and you believed L over me. What kind of mother are you to believe your own boyfriend over your own flesh and blood! That's when my little of love for you disappeared. You hurt me so much! (Persuasive Letter, Senior Project 1/9)

Every time I read this letter, I have had to pause and breathe for a second. Danielle's writing over the Senior Project fostered her abilities to write this powerful statement of independence and survival. This letter delivered what Danielle had long wanted to say to her mother, and the classroom instruction in argument had given her the space to say it.

My favorite piece that means the most to me is my persuasive piece. I wrote a letter to my mother on how I felt about the way I was raised and the kind of life that I had. I had a lot of emotions to deal with and writing that letter helped out a lot. I also wrote it very good and had a lot of details about my emotions and the life I had growing up. (Conclusion for Senior Project)

In the final paragraph of the letter and her own conclusion for the Senior Project, Danielle acknowledged her transformation. She was now able to claim her identity in a new-found self- awareness. The past, present, and the future converged in this final statement of Danielle's growth and learning. We see the emotional connection, related images, and the writing process and sequence as beneficial to releasing Danielle's long held traumatic story. This is writing to survive.

To eliminate the emotional seed in Danielle's writing would have silenced her and perhaps deprived Danielle of the one healthy pathway through her traumatic life story. This opportunity to write about any topic gave her a place to write about her own cultural, social, and historical world.

On our return to school January 6, Danielle had much to tell me about herself: she was dating a thirty-year-old man, whom her stepmother regarded as too old for Danielle. Without a transition, Danielle casually mentioned that she talked to her biological mother on Christmas Eve, when her mother had called to offer holiday greetings. In my stunned amazement, Danielle told me she read parts of the persuasive letter to her. Danielle said that she was able to tell her biological mother how she really felt about her and how she did not want her mother to be part of her life (Researcher Personal Notes, 1/6).

In my final interview with Danielle's parents, Danielle's stepmother conveyed to me that she was surprised and impressed with the mature and direct manner with which Danielle handled her mother's phone call. As another affirmation of her growth, Danielle gave her letter to her stepmother and father to read when she had finished it (Personal Communication, 1/7). In the following statement, Danielle's self-assessment is complete with self-awareness and self–affirmation at her rhetorical action and her new found abilities.

> When I first heard about this project, I just wanted to give up right away. I thought it was stupid and a waste of my time. I didn't even know what to do it on, but now as look on my finished project, I feel good about myself. I did it!
>
> I wasn't what you would call a good writer. I always made mistakes. Whenever I turned something in and get it back with red marks all over it. It made you hopeless and wanting to give up already.
>
> As time passed and doing some of the pieces that were going to be in my senior project, I could see how much I was improving as a writer. As a person who writes a lot,
>
> I have come a long way. It's true by what they say, the more you do practice something the better you get.
>
> Throughout my senior project, I have gotten really stressed. Divorce is a hard subject to deal with and remembering all the bad stuff that happened makes it difficult to carry on, but I have grown a lot because of it. I've become a better person who can deal with their problems.
>
> Sometimes it wasn't easy doing this particular subject because I forgot about things that had happened. I'm the type of person that it I went through something real bad that I would stuff it in the back of my mind and forget about it. So, it was difficult to do a piece when trying to remember what to put in it. Another thing was that it was an emotional strain on me. There was so much hatred and heartache that I felt about my mother that it would really bring me down.
>
> This project had helped me tremendously. I'm a better writer. It's taught me to be more aware of the way I write. It's taught me to be a stronger person and to deal with my problems when I have them. To never let them sit in the back of my mind. (Personal Communication, 1/21)

Danielle's words delineated how to teach writing and why we should teach it that way. She illustrated how an adolescent's life experiences can coexist with academic work without becoming trauma-therapy.

Even though we as teachers may find these experiences far removed from our own, Danielle's writing illustrated how and why teachers need to connect the academic with the personal. Her interviews and testimonials describe the insider information, including the power of goal setting, repetition, and concentrated revision. This process is not just teaching adolescents about writing, or giving them tasks to demonstrate knowledge, but providing them writing tasks that require them to author their thoughts and ideas into meaningful structures chosen from a repertoire of genres, selected for their appropriateness to the exigent situation. To have control over one's life using words and transform is power, the power to survive.

What We Learn From Danielle

Danielle's case study showed us four elements that guided pedagogy and writing instruction in Ms. Plummer's classroom: connection, choice, consistency, and conflict/challenge. The writing assignments *connect* her life with her learning in a personal way; Danielle had a *choice* of topic reflected within each new reading and writing task. The *challenge/conflict* was provided when Danielle had to do research on her topic for objective information, and then used that information to discuss the topic and make new meanings and find relevancy or controversy. The *consistency* in Ms. Plummer's revision and editing regime, along with her patience and high expectations, made room for Danielle and the other students to address their traumatic situations without fear of reprisal or without fear of peer mockery. This intricate play of the personal nature of her topic, the objectivity attained through reading and library research, the introduction of new genres, and Ms. Plummer's consistent demand for quality written work and oral performances combined to make this English language arts classroom an engaging zone for a traumatized adolescent to retrieve her facilities for learning, growing, and surviving.

Ms. Plummer's Senior Project design and curriculum complemented Danielle's learning situation. In her own description, Danielle told us how her past abusive history and present living conditions affected every aspect of her life, including her learning. We saw in her writing processes how her past interfered with her ability to frame her thoughts and ideas.

Through the carefully designed program, Danielle found avenues to express her feelings, images, and emotions about the past while she was learning. The amazing aspect of this was that the learning was enabled through her writings that included her traumatic life experiences.

TOMMIE'S NARRATIVE: AN OEUVRES[4]

Not every remarkable classroom lesson or curriculum has the power to save or restore what adolescents have lost to violence in their homes and in their social worlds. As a teacher, I felt a weight of responsibility for the students who had troubled lives. I did what I could with the time allotted to each class session, but every teacher deals with limits of learning by the bell. Every teacher has to face the realities that she or he cannot "save" or protect every child from his/her personal hardships. There was one such case in Danielle's class.

Tommie's story is an extreme example of forces within the child's private world that we cannot control as teachers. Despite the factors that limited Tommie's skills with Standard English, his harsh life experiences found a voice in the writing tasks Ms. Plummer assigned.

There are students, sitting quietly in our classrooms, who live in horrendous conditions. Some of these students never complain, never ask for sympathy or help. Others turn angry and resentful at the educational system, which forces them in classrooms with academic expectations and curricula that don't attempt to address their real needs. Students who live in traumatic daily conditions like Tommie and Danielle are not adolescents who will sit and take notes every day and easily comply with reading challenging canonical literature. Their language skills are often unsophisticated and punctuated with errors and misspellings, but in order to see the true "gnys at wrk" in these students, we have to rely upon the language skills and experiences that they bring to the classroom (Heath, 1983) and directly connect them to the classroom content and context.

For Ms. Plummer, Tommie was a tough, resistant learner, hardened by years of failure in a school system unable to provide the academic resources and compensations that Tommie needed for academic success. Tommie had poor grammatical usage, misspelled common words, and yet had managed to succeed enough to reach his senior year.

In tragically dramatic ways, Danielle and Tommie illustrate the need adolescents have for finding purpose and having goals in their lives every day. When crises arise, they can maneuver around them by thinking through the goal and not seizing the immediate urge to end the confusion. Danielle was able to find resolution, gain reconciliation, and transform her past experiences through writing. Danielle's story illustrated how writing pedagogy, invented to complement the emotional and psychological needs of an adolescent, can dramatically employ an adolescent's emotional trauma to engage learning. Tommie was not a reader or a writer, yet Ms. Plummer was able to arrange an agreement with Tommie that helped him to produce writing that was meaningful and expressive.

One particular day Ms. Plummer asked me to work with Tommie and read a piece he had written called "Brother and Sister Love." As I worked that day with Tommie on "Brother and Sister Love," I saw that it was full of grammatical errors even after Ms. Plummer had edited it with him. However, my interest and focus was on the uncomplaining details about a difficult life that he had included in the story. The content and story were so powerful that the errors were a written complement to its power. His story constantly reminded me that as a teacher I cannot look to the correctness of grammar and punctuation to be the only hallmark of critical thought and substantive content.

On another occasion, a Friday discussion in English class led to a heated debate about women and men and how they should treat each other. Tommie so eloquently summed up an idea that Chaucer's Wife of Bath would heartily agree: "You cain't argue with no woman. You might as well say yes 'cause you ain't never gonna win no argument with a woman. I knowed that."

At a later time in the semester, Tommie, Danielle, and I were sitting out in the hallway, and Tommie asked me all about my project—what I was doing. He asked Danielle if she felt funny having me follow her around. He wanted to know what I was going to do next year. I have described this event before, but now I want to reveal the details surrounding Tommie's and my interactions as a result of that event. At last, I had broken through with this very guarded and suspicious student. Tommie, who initially had been hostile toward me, angry, and very disruptive in class, was really curious, funny, and forthcoming with information about his writing and his life.

I saw his frustration with reading and writing things like *Beowulf,* Chaucer, and *1984.* He often refused to read in class or come to class having read the materials. Ms. Plummer's curriculum accommodated this, but the literacy demands for reading were still there. In order to recognize his complaints and language limitations, she and Tommie had a contract regarding his performance with reading and writing activities.

During the final weeks of the class, Tommie, like the others, worked on the Senior Project. He knew that even if he passed this class, he would not graduate in May with the other members of his class; he was credit-deficient since he had not passed enough of the required courses throughout his high school program. Yet, he presented his final project like all the other students in the class.

I had been gone a month from the high school when Ms. Plummer called me about Tommie. She had known that I had also made an effort to get to know him and to include him in my project. Tommie was one of the most colorful characters in the class—disruptive, controlling, and demanding, yet too knowledgeable about hardships in the world. Like Danielle, Tommie had needed to find a way out of the morass of deprivation that had framed his life even now. One survived; one didn't.

A moment of crisis arose in Tommie's life during the month of February. For most adolescents, the severity of a problem is magnified by their inexperience in dealing with relationships, employment, and academics. Even one of these is enough to start a crisis. When all three hit at once, it can become a matter of surviving.

In February, Tommie committed suicide. He had had a fight with his girlfriend; he was about to lose his job; and he knew that he would not graduate. Instead of talking to someone, thinking through the consequences and maybe holding onto a dream or goal, Tommie seized desperation. Without intervention, without guidance, without hope, without self-esteem, he chose.

Ms. Plummer knew that I had tried to work with Tommie, and had tried to get to know him. She asked his sister if she could give me a copy of a poem he had written two weeks before his death. There is the glimmer of hope in the final two lines, but I don't know enough of the facts except for those that I have presented thus far. I would like to think that the strategies and writing lessons Tommie learned in Ms. Plummer's class empowered him to write the poem, although the strategies some adolescents develop to cope with their world of dysfunction do not assure their survival. Yet, a part of Tommie survives with every reading of his poem, and his words resonate in many adolescents who desperately struggle with so many critical life events.

> Searching for something, but what I do not know.
>   Will I ever find it or will it stay
>   hidden in this pale world.
>   Searching for a purpose in life.
>   How to find this I do to know, searching high
>   and low through the dark and the light.
>   Searching in the weary morning at the pale night.
>   I'll use my might and sight till I find that purpose
>   and that light. So, I can smile in the face of those
>   that said I would never find that purpose of life.

So much more is involved in the survival of adolescents than one lesson, or one writing assignment. Tommie's story and his final writing herald one message: as teachers we need to take very seriously the intersection between the tasks we ask students to perform, their approximate development, their unspoken and yet to be written life experiences, and guide them consistently into an acceptable performance of those experiences. I cannot specifically link Tommie's personal hardships with his suicide, or whether the harsh environment he lived in played some role in his academic situation within Ms. Plummer's class.

I do know this: the classroom time we share with students must be filled with purpose and meaning directly related to the adolescents' interests, and not comprised of disconnected assignments and classroom tasks, but challenging and thoughtful interaction with purposeful encounters with written and oral language. It may be the one link in their ability to survive.

NOTES

1. All Danielle's writing and editing are quoted as she wrote them. I did not correct spelling or punctuation in any of her texts. In the cases where I am quoting from transcripts or my own notes, I have attempted to preserve the spelling based upon her pronunciation, and punctuation based upon her pauses and spoken indications of a complete idea.

2. The transcript is presented as closely as possible to the student's use of language and pronunciation.

3. The think-aloud protocols were developed by Janet Emig in her ground breaking work on the *Composing Process of Twelfth Graders*. See reference list for the complete citation.

4. This heading is taken from Foucault's use of the term in *The Archeology of Knowledge*. This term means an artist's body of work as well as the artist's unique expression found in one work.

Chapter 4

Chase—"When I Am Happy, I Have No Problems Thinking"

CHASE'S VIGNETTE

Reaching into his pocket, Chase pulled out a new pack of gum. "Hey, can I have a piece?" another student asked when he saw the gum. Before long, five more students surrounded Chase, and he passed out gum to all who asked for a piece. In these few precious moments before the bell rang to begin English class, Chase found ways to interact with his peers.

As the bell rang to end his class, he abruptly left the classroom and raced to locate the young woman who was the sole object of his adoration and his reason for being happy. Yet, she was totally unaware of his quiet yearning for her. I wondered if she even knew his name or had spoken to him outside of the classroom. He knew her class schedule, her locker number, and he looked for signs in the four months between November and February when she might have her birthday. He was curious about the ring she sometimes wore, which might be a guy's class ring. In this consuming attention, he remained shy, quiet, and clearly at odds with his feelings and his ability to tell her.

Chase had a very difficult time reading any content material in English, especially worksheets. He was still learning the rudiments of written and spoken English, even though he had a basic grasp of everyday exchanges. He had only been in the United States for five years.

At home, at school, and at work, Chase was alert, quiet, and determined. He drove to town, to work, and to school at breakneck speeds with the music so loud that it was difficult to even think. At his work in the restaurant, he washed dishes and seemed perfectly content with his surroundings. In a respectful but obsequious manner, Chase listened to and learned from the older Chinese men and women who worked with him in the restaurant kitchen. At home, he silently listened as his father lectured him on what to do. Then he did it quickly because he wanted to be free to return to his computer collection and begin writing about his one interest; Brenda 1; Brenda 2; Brenda 3; Brenda 4; Brenda 5.

In high school classes, he distanced himself in the classroom by sitting in the back or the far ends of the classroom. Then, in a sudden turn and without warning, he quickly found me and started to ask me questions. One day in biology class in one of these abrupt moves, he asked me what were the most important things in life. I responded, and he abruptly corrected me by saying, "No. Love and rich are the most important."

I asked him why he considered these the most important, and his answer became a gateway into his driving work ethic and desperate need to be loved and valued. At sixteen, he was struggling to understand women, life, his place in the world, while he negotiated through a still-unfamiliar language without sounding "stupid."

"WHEN I AM HAPPY, I HAVE NO PROBLEMS THINKING"

Overview

Of all the adolescents in this study, Chase had the most dramatic system of compensatory strategies. When neither school nor his social and family life provided Chase with learning, he manufactured scenarios, created literacy sequences, and copied linguistic models from electronic sources. These were more than a functional practice; they were elaborate and deliberate patterns of compensation for learning lessons, sometimes unrelated to academics, and evident through the process Chase used to author texts in and out of school.

Unlike Danielle, Chase did not face physical and emotional abuse; his traumatic experiences were associated with his immigrant status, limited English skills, and his desperate need to assimilate into the American culture and have a social life like every other teenager. Chase's story of writing literacy and compensations was more reflective of the struggles and changes that adolescent development brought to bear upon classroom behavior and issues, but his new immigrant status presented him with language barriers that complicated his entrée into the classroom and into a social circle.

In order to find a place within the existing social structure at school, Chase used various media, teen magazines, Internet sources of texts, and films both in Chinese and English. When English words failed to express his feelings, he watched movies in Chinese to gather clues for conduct codes and for understanding about relationships. On the other hand, movies would not give him the words to use; in this case, he looked through female teen magazines in an attempt to learn what he could about adolescent females and dating.

To complete his writing assignments in school, he paraphrased or changed and copied existing sentences from magazines and American movies, sometimes in order to write love poems to the girl he longed to date, and to learn to operate within the broader adolescent social world. Chase's whole experience with language, and the literacy sources he used to learn English, made every encounter with language a challenge for personal expression. In other situations, he would deliberately make mistakes or break the law in order to gather more information about relating to his peers and learning about the social systems. Overall, he created these compensations when he needed to learn the rules for his survival in a new world.

Chase's Socio-Cultural-Historical Background

Chase's family came to the United States to find work, which, a cousin informed them, was plentiful and available. In their native country, Chase's mom and dad owned a restaurant, which did not support the family. In their United States home, Chase's dad worked as a cook and his mother was a dishwasher every day but Monday. Chase followed his parents' occupation: he washed dishes in a restaurant. His parents worked in another franchise restaurant with the same owner.

Chase had only been immersed in the English language for five years. At home, the family spoke their native language, since neither of Chase's parents spoke English. Yet, when I interviewed his parents, Chase's father proudly displayed the English certificate he had earned at the immigration camp. After spending two months in an immigrant location camp in Delaware, Chase and his family moved to their present home. On the first day he attended school in the United States, he told me he talked to no one. The second day he asked one of his peers to help him with his English homework.

> "The next day he come and help me, and later, we go over to his house and we play and start knowing each other. And we play video games. I just learn English from him." (Interview 8/30)

If we look at this scenario as Chase's initial language-acquisition process with English, it served as the foundation for his compensatory strategies. Using other English speakers as resources, playing video games with an English language speaker, or as his vocabulary grew, he could independently read for information and knowledge using computer sources.

Surviving in a New Language

For this sixteen-year-old, writing was for expressing his feelings when he needed to negotiate with adults, the legal system, or school-based assignments. In school, he wrote to fulfill a culturally based work ethic about learning, but wanted to perform well because of his affection for a young woman in his class. He told me he didn't like to write because he kept his feelings in his heart; he didn't need to state them. In his academic writing throughout the semester, writing was an imitative process, disconnected from his life in most cases.

In order to fulfill the course requirements, he created compositions by consulting various visual media (magazines, movies, and CD programs like Encarta) and then co-opting the words and patterns of expression. School based writing was driven by his respect of learning, but his personal writing was about his affection for one young woman. His affection for her was the force behind his learning, writing, and literacy process.

> Deb: What do you see as the role of writing for you?
> Chase: Nothing, nothing unless it is something important.
> Deb: What makes you happy to write?
> Chase: [Laughs]
> Deb: Like what?
> Chase: Having a girlfriend. Being rich.

After a brief exchange about writing something right or wrong, he told me that the students need to know right and wrong.

> Deb: Writing is for correction? Telling the students?
> Chase: Writing is just like the way to express your feelings to the people. Usually people cannot express their feelings, express their feelings to them when they say out loud.
> When you write, you just like tell the basically. You tell the basic of it; what you want to say.
> Deb: Did anything about the project affect you or change you?
> Chase: Nothing in the project changed me. The only thing that changed me was Brenda. (Personal Communication, 1/17)

Throughout the semester, Chase identified his affection for Brenda as the most important thing in his life. While adults might snicker and ignore these intense responses as antithetical to thinking, these kinds of emotions are pathways to learning. Chase told us that socializing and writing or authoring texts were directly related to his feelings for her. For an adolescent, Chase's conflict/challenge began with a personal desire for a girlfriend. Through this desire, he struggled with self-identification and self-fulfillment in order to find an identity that would make him desirable to a female adolescent. When the classroom and home environments did not provide him with the pathways to meet his desires, he created the learning compensations that gave him the knowledge and access he needed.

Chase's English Classroom

Mr. Muller arranged Chase's eleventh-grade English class around the study of American Literature. His long career in teaching provided him with numerous stories, which he told in an attempt to build interest and show the possibility of personal connection with the literature. He regaled the students with these stories, and then proceeded to make literary and personal connections through the newspaper. Mr. Muller was the advisor and faculty editor for the school newspaper, one of the oldest high school newspapers in the United States.

Chase was one of twenty-four students in Mr. Muller's English 11 class, which met from 8:00 to 9:30 every day for one semester. Chase asked to be placed in the back row of the classroom, more to accommodate his need for privacy in the packed classroom. He sat next to a bulletin board covered with posters from the latest movies taken from British classics like *Emma, Hamlet,* and *Romeo and Juliet.* The other twenty-three students provided Mr. Muller with behavioral and learning challenges he was not prepared to address.

Mr. Muller had two young female students who had recently had babies, three students who were on juvenile probation, and two students who were repeating the class because they had failed the course the previous year. One young man was a senior taking English 9, 10, 11, and 12 to cover failures of one or more semesters in each of these courses. Mr. Muller had three students who were non-native speakers and two foreign exchange students: one from Brazil and one from Germany. He also had one young man who was a known drug dealer in the school and slept through the class most days. Two other individuals completed any assignment Mr. Muller gave but remained silent during the class unless Mr. Muller called upon them.

Mr. Muller attempted to engage this colorful group in conversation by telling interesting biographical details about the American authors whom the class was studying. He used visual media like newspapers and movies in an attempt to draw upon student knowledge, but the lecture delivery method and the question, answer, evaluation method for discussion did not reach these students. The dissonance between Ms. Muller's teaching style and the students' responses, or lack thereof, created a tension in the class, making it a difficult learning environment for all. In this environment, Chase was reluctant to speak, complicating his writing and learning to communicate in English.

The eleventh-grade English language arts curriculum was designed to survey canonical pieces of American literature with a writing curriculum loosely based upon personal narrative and newspaper editorials. Each morning, Mr. Muller passed out the local newspaper. The students read it and wrote a summary in their journals on one article they found interesting, and then the class lecture explained the literary material for the day.

Chase's limited English vocabulary placed his reading of American literature well below the level in which the literature was written—for example, the *Scarlet Letter*, "Fall of the House of Usher," and finally *Native Son*. In order to have a general summary of these texts, Chase depended upon Mr. Muller's summary of the material when the class would not participate in a question and answer over the reading material. In frustration, Mr. Muller provided the students with a summary of the important point of the readings. Chase and the class members had knowledge about the readings without ever having to "read" the text and to acquire new vocabulary.

Chase described the course and classroom events this way:

> Deb: What do you learn in English class?
> Chase: I guess I have to learn from Mr. Muller, if I can pay attention. But I don't have time to pay attention. Nobody pays attention in class. Usually if we don't give the answer, he just tells us the answer. Everybody is silent that's all in there. (Interview 11/20)
> Deb: What do you think of the way Mr. Muller taught you?
> Chase: He should make it something more interesting, but I guess for his age, he don't know how to make it something interesting. (Personal Communication, 1/17)

Two situations influenced Mr. Muller's curriculum for this class: he was the department chair and had taught AP English for the last seventeen years. In spite of his expertise, the high school administration had assigned Mr. Muller this class in eleventh-grade English.

To his dismay, Mr. Muller had not taught eleventh-grade English in twenty years. He admitted that this was a real trial for him, since it was the penultimate year before his retirement from high school teaching. The question-and-answer method so effective for AP English students proved less so with the English 11 class. Throughout the semester, I saw both Mr. Muller and Chase struggle with the course materials and disconnected methods of delivery.

I interject this biographical information about Mr. Muller because Chase's statement may be seen as an indictment. That is not the intention. Teaching students who are reluctant learners, who bring experiences with repeated failures in English classes, who have previous poor English skills and a classroom history of ineffective teachers, is a problem for which no teacher has the answer. Mr. Muller confided in me throughout the semester about his struggle to make the English subject matter interesting while he felt unprepared to meet the challenges of teaching non-college bound students, non-native speakers of English and students from such dysfunctional situations.

All of these factors inhibited his teaching of American Literature in the traditional fashion of teacher monologue or teacher-student question-answer. He didn't know what else to do. The minor adjustments Mr. Muller made in order to appeal to student interest areas never strayed far enough away from his own journalistic preferences and question-answer style pedagogy to become effective.

Visual Compensations

Chase's first compensatory strategy was his self-constructed visual vocabulary learning system. His limited but expressive vocabulary meant that to read assignments in most of his classrooms required him to spend hours looking up words in the dictionary, a task he was unwilling to engage in. Instead, Chase managed to process English words as they appeared in American visual media. He used popular visual media, specifically movies and magazines, to provide him with an English vocabulary. He did this by finding a picture or sequence in a movie that expressed what he was trying to say, and then he selected the words that were attached to the picture and incorporated them into his writing. Throughout this process, Chase modeled early language acquisition habits that we would accord with children. He heard the language, saw the pictures and connected meaning to the words, repeated them to himself, and internalized the sound and meanings.

In an elaborate pastiche of visual media, Chase co-opted words, phrases, and the structure of English grammar to write, even when telling a familiar family story. The following sequence occurred at the end of September and was my first view into his visual compensations.

Deb: How do you know what to put down?
   Chase: Like he say you got to tell story like write about time, tell about time. How they change you. Yeah.
   Deb: What do you use for a beginning?
   Chase: One time and then end with the story how they change me.
   Deb: Do you remember hearing any stories when you were a little boy about your native country?

Chase: It's like this monkey. He got a lot of magic. He was first born by a rock like 5,000 years ago, and then he pop out, born out, earth shaking and then when he pop out and he's like a monkey. . . .

He continued this narrative for a long while, and then after the film's heaven-and-hell epic battle, he stopped.

Deb: Somebody told you this?
    Chase: It's a movie.
    Deb: What movie?
    Chase: It's an Asian movie.
    Deb: Is that where you learned to tell stories?
    Chase: Yeah. When you watch a movie, you have story.
    Deb: Mr. Muller gave you another assignment. How are you going to write that one?
    Chase: [He takes out a paper with the assignment and reads it.] You got to tell color, weather, atmosphere. Oh, I probably use one of the magazines to picture how it was.
    Deb: And do what?
    Chase: Like picture some of the image I like to read. Use some of the information from the magazine and write.
    Deb: Why the magazine?
    Chase: Magazines have a lot of things like, all the pictures. It show you and it not boring like when you read a magazine. You got a lot of pictures and work than reading a book. That a lot of words that [make] no sense.
    Deb: How does the magazine help you write?
    Chase: You look in the magazine and they probably write some word in there and then you probably use some part of it. You use a little bit and change a little bit.
    Deb: Here's a magazine. Show me what you mean.
    Chase: See what make it interesting. See it say "I enjoy sex more." Then, you look for the page and then I know what page it's on. Love and probably interesting and probably look that up. And then you find. See the beautiful grass. You don't see from here, then you just keep turning and then you might get some image from here and then you just keep turning then later on you find something good. And then you might think of something good and then you like think of something back.
    Deb: You don't create pictures with words?
    Chase: No. Words like I don't know words. Doesn't come with the pictures when you see a picture you know the words. Like when you advertise something. You got to show the picture. You would buy immediately in the paper. All a bunch of words. (Personal Communication, 9/30)

During the first classes with Chase, we were in the library and he was explaining to me about reading: "I'm a picture guy. I don't read. I hate reading. I like photographs" (Research notes, 8/30). In the visually rich media world, Chase had a variety of visual images from which to patch together a writing. As a visual learner, he had found ways to use the visual media to scaffold for him a vocabulary he had yet to grasp. This included films, CD rom, and magazines, like *Glamour* or *Vogue*. He absorbed the visual images and the words surrounding them and then incorporated them into his collected understanding.

Chase's visual compensatory strategy made visible the brain imaging process discussed in chapter 1. In his case, Chase used the pictures to link the image with words and the feelings he was attempting to express. As he accumulated images that equated word meaning and images, he learned English, especially related to his interests concerning love and female relationships.

During the semester I spent with Chase, I did not witness any adult or teacher including Mr. Muller, use any learning system similar to the one Chase had created for himself, especially when it involved school-centered writing. Since no English was spoken at home, and the walls and print materials in the home were in Chase's native language, he had to find another system.

The Copy and Change System

For the final exam, Mr. Muller asked the students to project their lives into the future and predict what they would be doing and reveal this information as a final essay. Chase's final essay was in part taken from a CD program describing job applications. I do not have any further information about the program, but he described the process he used to answer the essay question this way:

> Deb: Can you show me in here what you are talking about? Where in here does it show what you are talking about?
>
> Chase: [He laughs.] I just get it from sitting 'round and then I just use it and I mean like, when they say it like you, I mean like when they say people I change the person. I say you are them. I change it to me or I. I just started to write things like what I am going to say it. That's how I put it all together.
>
> Deb: So, you get this from CDs?
>
> Chase: No, I just mention the information finder?
>
> Deb: What did you ask it for?
>
> Chase: I just type in college and then come up like, like what is college and how is college. And that's how, read it and do whatever it describes and then put it all together, you know. When they say you, you don't put you in that, you know. You put I.

Deb: Can you give me another example?

Chase: I change it and not on there. I am applying for a job that would advance my career. It's like something other hand over there. I say something (about) my job that would help and then advance in, advance my career, something like that. I take that out and put it there.

Deb: You came up with the next sentence on the CD from what the CD says?

Chase: Yeah, but something a little bit different than then something how to do. It's a long sentence, then a short sentence, then I learn how to contact an employer, an application and keep it shorter.

Deb: This you took from your own life. This is what you want to be? Where did you get this? It wasn't off the CD?

Chase: I just putting down. Every time I think of that name Brenda it's like something in my mind to say. That how I got the other stuff to say.

Deb: When do you stop taking stuff off the CD?

Chase: I look at the page, all that I need to know. Then, I just stop and then I just say "and" you have to answer all the questions down then. So, I just shorten my stuff and answer it down there.

Deb: Is that the way you compose most of your texts?

Chase: Most of my writing is just. . . . Copy and change. Copy and change.

Chase told me that he processed a given assignment by co-opting the information from the CD Rom. If he had to write about the future and what his life will be, he projected that life into applications for college and for jobs. He took the information from the CDs not only in content but in sentence format, replaced the pronoun to "I" as if he had composed this text, broke down the sentences into smaller components and then projected the job in the future as if he were with the young woman, who was the object of his affections. Through his contemplation of her, he anticipated his happiness. Through the fantasy of the essay question, Chase combined the visual plagiarism that marked his composing process, but it also provided visible and attainable goals.

Chase's Use of Story

When teachers taught a lesson using an overhead projector or through a computer and LCD, Chase would ask me what certain words meant, or he would ask me to reinterpret the question, shaking his head negatively until I had used the words he understood to answer his question. Without the visual picture with the words, Chase could not read or interpret the instructions. In our interviews, he would often repeat my question before he would answer it, as if he were translating the vocabulary I was using. When the spoken language did not trigger an understanding or a response, he resorted to telling me a story instead of answering directly. This occurred most often after I asked him a question, and he would be puzzled by the question.

His understanding of story sequences and narrative telling, he stated earlier, came from movies, but movies that are linked to his culture's story paradigm. On one occasion, I was asking Chase about his writing and authoring of texts. When he became frustrated by his inability to use vocabulary to help me understand, he resorted to a story. In the following sequence, Chase narrates a story from his cultural traditions and myths to address my absurd questions about writing.

Deb: What do you mean?

Chase: We learn this thing you have. You don't need to write it out and say what you learned.

Deb: Why not? It doesn't help you to put things down in words?

Chase: I want to tell you a story. When you taught it, people say like when you taught it, you don't want it till you pay out and for it. You start it without paying out.

I don't know how to say it. In Chinese that's how they say it. You don't have to do the stuff to, you don't have to do that stuff, but you do it. That's extra. Like when you . . .

Deb: [I had heard the word "start" but suddenly realized Chase was using another word.] Are you talking about farting?

Chase: Yeah. Farting. You don't need to take your pants off and let the gas come out. You can fart without taking your pant off. That's doing something extra—just taking off your pants and farting.

Deb: What does that have to do with English?

Chase: Yeah, when you read this paper, I mean when you read a paper, you don't have to write it out. When you read a paper like just when you're farting, with a pen arm, when you write it out wrong, sticking your pen out and farting.

(Personal Communication, 1/17)

I had misunderstood the word "farting" for "starting" in this story. Farting was his metaphor to illustrate his concept of writing, which was an unnecessary action when one could just tell it or just know. In this case, Chase's frustration with making me understand how he felt about writing exposed a communication process that depended upon familiar cultural wisdom for which he had English words. During the semester, Chase repeated this cultural story telling and answering my questions. In this compensational strategy, when Chase could not find the English words, he filtered the situation through familiar knowledge and values acquired in his homeland. Then, when he found a story with a message comparable to my question and his intended explanation, he used English to explain it to me.

Writing for English 11—A Clash of Culture and Revision

In an initial writing assignment for English 11, Mr. Muller asked his students to write about something familiar and something personal that would give him an indication of their narrative ability. Chase seized this opportunity to tell a story about his family and their life in his native country. I want to use this first writing as a model to discuss the class of culture, revision, and teaching. In each citation from Chase's writing (Appendix C), I present his spelling, punctuation, and word choice without correction.

> I was six years old. I went to the restaurant with my family. They ordered food and the food took so long. that they started to yell, they said they ordered the food about thirty minutes ago. we were getting hungry, and we wanted the food now! Then they brought the food over to us, other people in the restaurant began looking at us. After we finish the food, my father didn't even tip the waiter at all. Then we walk out to the door, after we leave the restaurant.
>
> Later, we went to the store to buy food. They look at the price of the item, and my father said to the owner, how come your store well the price are higher than other store? Then, the owner said to him, we have to make money to kept the store open. if you like to but it, than we sell it to you, or you could go to other store. After we went to the store, we watch movie at my friend house. we watch from eight to eleven o'clock. after that we went to sleep. (Written draft from first writing assignment)

Chase's use of verb tense, pronouns, and even relative clauses showed that he had the elementary foundations of English syntax. The word choice was simple, and the spelling at times close to the English spelling: "want" instead of "went." His use of commas instead of periods reflected his understanding of the structural units of English. He recognized the cadence that required some stop, but chose to use a comma for such purposes when the discussion involved the same subject.

Chase understood the paragraph unit as a demarcation of one topic or idea being discussed. In his narrative, the three paragraphs separated the restaurant scene, a store scene, and finally a scene at home. In this memory writing, Chase demonstrated he can code his memory into English words; he can read, but his writing vocabulary limited his ability to tell the story. This written text and interviews exhibit the disparities between a reading vocabulary, writing vocabulary, and speaking vocabulary for an English language learner and adolescent.

In the following paragraphs, I present a series of Chase's writings and revisions guided by Mr. Muller. The series portrays a much different process than Ms. Plummer had for writing. In these revisions, we see how Chase responded to the corrections and what impact this had upon building another compensatory strategy for writing.

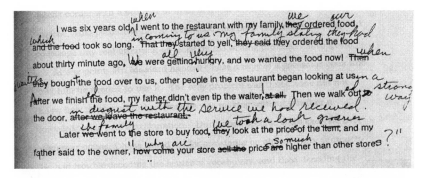

Example 4.1.   Mr. Muller's Revision for First Writing

While this assignment was intended to give Mr. Muller information about his students' abilities with language, the resulting revisions showed the disconnection between Mr. Muller's writing program and his students. Chase could not copy from magazines or other visuals to help him write this story. His limited knowledge of English also limited the depth of expression. This story revealed a series of events without reflection, analysis or comment. When Chase received the first writing back from Mr. Muller, he found a heavily edited text that reflected more about Mr. Muller's expectations and skills as a journalist than about Chase's narrative skills. Mr. Muller transformed the writing into standard English, and by rephrasing many of the sentences, he restructured Chase's story without engaging the author or without attending to Chase's ability to write in English.

This pattern of correction continued throughout the semester for every piece of Chase's writing. Mr. Muller not only corrected Chase's grammar in standard formal usage, he recast the story in more careful vocabulary, words that Chase did not necessarily have available to him in his English vocabulary. This type of revision only had Chase continue a process that he had developed earlier in learning new words with pictures: copy and change. The difference between this type of revision process and Chase's compensatory strategy was that Chase had choices in building pictures and words to construct a composition. He changed his new text to reflect the revisions Mr. Muller had made on his original copy.

Without a verbal conference or instruction to accompany this revision, Mr. Muller's changes did little to help Chase in future writings. Mr. Muller did not hold individual writing conferences other than to briefly confer with a student as he returned papers. This casual accountability permitted Chase to lie about the progress he was making and to escape any real attention or focus on his writing problems in English.

At one point, Mr. Muller handed Chase a copy of a grammar book and told him he needed to use it. The only problem was that Chase did not know how to approach the errors he was making without an adult or a knowledgeable peer's explanation. During one specific class exercise over grammar points, Chase asked me for assistance on almost every sentence. He had trouble decoding the sentence vocabulary, and then understanding the grammatical problem.

The grammar exercises and expected revision were far too complex for him since they required knowledge about the inherent nature of English grammar that Chase had not yet internalized as a second language speaker. He knew syntax, but he could not decipher the deliberate grammar mistakes hidden within the grammar exercise. The generous act proved frustrating for Chase and forced him to rely more heavily upon his own pattern of composing texts.

Chase wanted to learn English well so that he wouldn't sound stupid when he figured out how to ask girls out for a date or be excluded from the social world of his peers. The exigent crisis for this adolescent was the power of language to buy him capital in this new country, to establish friends, and to fulfill the expectations his parents had placed upon his success in this new country. Yet, the faster he acquired the linguistic competence he needed, the faster he would fulfill what he found most meaningful in life: a female companion and money.

Many composition theorists applaud the use of personal stories as a basis for teaching students to write (Bomer, 1995; Dixon & Stratta, 1986; Dyson & Genishi, 1994). What happened in this classroom was that personal writings were permitted but no writing instruction occurred. Mr. Muller alluded to the literature as the impetus for writing, but the students were given a detailed assignment about what to complete. Even after the students turned in the written drafts, Mr. Muller held no writing conferences, no meetings about revision or classroom instruction on how to write. Just writing tasks.

Mr. Muller allowed a choice of personal stories, but little in the way of solid consistent mentoring of grammatical forms, vocabulary, and purpose for writing. His writing instruction and assignments were tangential to the literature study and required no deep revisions. It was often hard to find a connected purpose and personal choice in the writing and literature that students completed. The connection and consistency that proved so beneficial to Danielle's process and healing was absent from Mr. Muller's writing instruction. To sterilize a text of its errors, such as the one Mr. Muller gave to Chase's writing, is to remove some of the socio-cultural-historical expressions, which directed the adolescents' word choices, thus depriving them of voice and authority over the text.

Chase revised only those corrections Mr. Muller had marked. One might make a case for Chase's learning through imitation and rewriting his words into Mr. Muller's recommended standard formal usage, but I found little evidence that Chase made progress through this experience, other than the fact it was a writing exercise and practice. What Chase invented for himself in writing and learning is far more interesting than what he gained through this copy and change process of revision, if we consider what he did to write.

In a second writing assignment, Mr. Muller asked the class to write about a significant person in their lives. This assignment was to mirror the classes' study of early narratives in American Literature. In this writing, Chase candidly wrote about his parents, but Chase did not use visual compensatory strategies to write as he did for other assignments.

I was not proud of my mother and father, and I was embarrassed of their education, because they can't help me doing homework. My mother wanted me to do better in school, They want me finish high school and then go to college. My father work at the restaurant. He was a chef. He work 12 hours a day and 5 ½ days a week. His wages is 5.50 per hour, he got pay every two week. My mother work at the same restaurant, she was a dishwasher, sometime she work 35–40 hours a week.

Sometime I wish they would have a better jobs, like work in the company, they have benefit, and family insurance. I wish I could find a better job, when I grow up.

I would like to the training program, I like to learn how to built car, or fix the car.

My parent wanted me to want in the office, but I told them I don't like to sit in the office to work. I think is more fun to work in the car company, you have benefit, insurance, vacation, sick day, holiday. I think they don't want me to work in the restaurant like them, I don't think they like to work in the restaurant too. That why the(y) are my significant person in my life. (First draft, 9/25)

After Chase handed in this draft, Mr. Muller offered the following revisions:

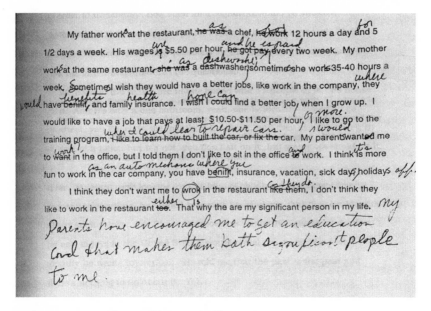

Example 4.2. Mr. Muller's Editing on Significant Person Paper

After Chase received Mr. Muller's comments, Chase revised it by changing the portions of the text that Mr. Muller had corrected. Students may absorb some grammatical correctness through this method, which they can transfer to their own writing, but in Chase's case, he just copied what Mr. Muller gave him without questioning or understanding what he was changing.

Since only Mr. Muller would see these writings, Chase took a chance in communicating candid snippets of his cultural past. These writings were practices for Chase to exercise his English, but their lack of connection and consistency didn't provide the depth of processing that Ms. Plummer's system gave to Danielle. Examining Mr. Muller's editorial corrections and Chase's original sentence, we have to question whether this form of revision really contributed to Chase learning to control his grammatical use of English to express himself. This detached error correction did not guide Chase or offer him advanced understanding of how to use English to express his ideas.

While the writing assignment invited a personal connection, the detachment from the literature and revision process did little to make these writing tasks relevant or purposeful for Chase. For students struggling with various kinds of crises and traumatic events, the writing tasks like Mr. Muller's are well intentioned but not connected enough to provide the assistance Chase needs.

The detail and purpose of a writing assignment involves a choice, a selection that is deliberate. It is not just choice that moves students to author texts, but the deliberate selection from a panorama of stories that will allow them to increase their skills in converting experiences into words that have power.

Writings, which allow Chase to use pictures and to copy verbatim the vocabulary, draw into debate the virtue of copying texts and imitating texts for a second-language learner. If these two processes could be developed consecutively, allowing him to copy and use visual images in the construction of his thoughts and ideas versus the copying of vocabulary to fulfill a writing assignment, Chase developed a way to use modern media to acquire the vocabulary he needed to fulfill writing assignments, imitating but not commanding the structure and message of the words. The writing that required him to use vocabulary without pictures reveals a much different ability, a difficult process for him to do without the visual.

Chase's Writing Compensations and Mr. Muller's Writing Assignments

Mr. Muller's writing assignments asked Chase to produce texts he was not prepared for due to his command of English in contrast to the level of sophistication Mr. Muller expected. In this next writing sample, Chase shows how he interprets the writing assignment to reflect his present situation rather than the past. He presently identifies with his high school as the one place he can write about that has meaning for him.

This writing came from Mr. Muller's assignment after the class had read "The Devil and Tom Walker."

> After discussing Irving's "The Devil and Tom Walker," and the part that setting played in that story, try your hand at a writing that has a particular setting.
>
> Think of a familiar setting that has meaning to you—whether it's a seacoast, the woods, a beautiful autumn, a park, the basketball court when you play, or the school cafeteria—write a description of that place to make a reader "see" it clearly. Focus on the details: colors, weather, atmosphere, dialogue (if any), textures and so on. Try to use as many images as possible, that is, an appeal to the senses.

In class, Chase drafted the following writing based on this assignment.

> The place that mean a lot to me, Prairie High School, is the best School I ever go to. The School is next to the river, the mall, and burger king. The School cafeteria have Taco Bell, Hot lunch, Cousin sub and the School store to get anything you like from there. We have only 10 minutes between block of class

in a day, that let you go to your locker, or talking to your friend in the fall. We have less class, less homework, like other school people have lot of homework, because they have too many class in a day. This school help me make a lot of friend, and teach me lot of thing. I like this school, because you have less class to take, and less homework.

Mr. Muller provided no writing instruction to the students about how they might write a setting for a story. The discussion had been a literary analysis on the Romantic short story, and the students were expected to use this literary understanding to produce a writing.

In this brief setting, Chase revealed more of what was important to him than writing the sensory detail the assignment required. He seized upon the high school cafeteria suggestion in Mr. Muller's assignment, describing the world of food at school. Before coming to the United States, Chase's family owned a restaurant, and Chase and his parents presently work in restaurants. Given these life experiences, Chase brought his expertise about food to his writing. Yet this opportunity to write about a personally relevant topic was missing meaningful connection with language and any challenge to his literacy abilities. Without instructor support and connection, writing assignments like this literary imitation do not empower adolescents to develop more relevant language skills.

Chase's Use of Visual Media

I have already introduced some of the uses Chase made of visual media, primarily film and video games. In creating another visual compensatory strategy, Chase employed the simultaneous visual and oral performances to prepare the foundation for his writing. I found him using this strategy while doing library research on a topic chosen from the daily newspaper readings and journal responses that were routine in his English class. However, what made this sequence so confusing for Chase was the disconnected classroom activities. Mr. Muller showed the film *Native Son* for part of the classroom instruction, followed with a lecture on Marxism, and the class ended after Mr. Muller took the students to the library for independent research on a topic. This sequence of activities had no connection, consistency, or clarity of purpose. Mr. Muller's intention was to provide the students with multiple stimuli, but he was unaware of the confusion he created in these multi-tasked classroom activities. At the beginning of the next class, Mr. Muller reviewed the new writing assignment this way:

> Everyone has chosen a topic that is supposedly argumentative. That will be the basis for the letter to the editor. Marshall evidence to support your stand. Today, get together and sit around and talk about what you plan on writing about. Ideas

from fellow classmates. While in groups of three or four, you're discussing your topics. Your classmates will have good ideas—opposing ideas. In the library, you'll get supporting evidence.

On Monday, the students went to the library to do research on the topic. The letter to the editor would be argumentative and approximately 250–500 words. In Muller's explanations, he used phrases like "What you are doing is getting some appeal to authority, add to your argument, not accept another viewpoint, and handle this deftly. Get the people and audience to read the letter and see an opposing viewpoint." Chase chose sex and violence on TV as his research investigation for this argumentative letter.

After a brief instruction by the librarians, it was clear that Chase didn't understand the issues behind sex and violence on TV, but had opinions about them. Chase sat next to another student and began to ask him questions that expressed his lack of understanding about the assignment and how to search. Mr. Muller and the librarian intervened and guided him into specific search strategies, which proved to be more helpful to Chase. Chase possessed intelligence, but he needed the attention of a skilled adult to constantly monitor and guide his progress through these assignments and tasks—time Mr. Muller does not have to give with 23 other students in the class. With a little guidance and left to his own devices, Chase discovered a book related to his topic called *Plug-in Drug of TV*. This book and article provided pictures from which Chase could construct a narrative. Chase copied the vocabulary from the novel *Plug in TV* and copied the text much like he did when he watched a film: he summarized the pictures while co-opting the words that accompanied the pictures.

> Why people choose to view violence on television, and why there has been an increase in violent programming in spite of periodic outcries from government investigating commissions, educators and parents coalitions, lies as do all the answers to basic questions. . . . But viewers do not choose to watch soothing, relaxing programs on television, though their main purpose in watching is often to be soothed and relaxed.

The last sentence above shows the exact words he copied from the book. In his next draft, Chase wrote, "I believe people choose to watch violence on television, and there has been an increase in violent programming, government investigating commissions, educators, and parents. *Most people do not like to watch relaxing programs on television, because they like to frantic programs willed with the most violent activities, imaginable. . . .* People mind is like a computer, if you put violence on the human mind, people will start to do more violence."

In this revision, Chase edited the first draft by co-opting the film vocabulary, but the sentence structure lapsed into ungrammatical patterns that are characteristic of Chase's previous writings. Chase again compensated for the lack of instruction and assistance by committing acts of plagiarism, which for him were the only process through which he could write. Copy and change as well as the picture associated vocabulary worked when Chase developed this compensatory strategy to help him write.

To illustrate Chase's pervasive dependence upon visual media, which directed his compensatory strategies, Chase had several assignments due in classes that required written reports. On this particular day, Chase was more worried about a history report he did not have finished, and he had less than two hours to get it completed. Chase informed me that he doesn't want me to come home with him for lunch and that he was skipping his third block class, Geometry, because he had to rent the movie *Hiroshima* so that he can write the history report on the novel that day.

In another example of Chase's reliance upon visual media to compose and construct information for classroom writing tasks, Mr. Muller required each student to read a book outside of class, and then write a three part assignment: a summary of the book's plot, one character analysis, and a personal reaction to the novel. Chase avoided completing the assignment until the end of the semester. I asked Chase what he was going to do with this requirement. He told me he would choose a book from the library and rent the movie. Then, he would write the report.

His book report choice—*The Pelican Brief.* Chase could not independently construct the character analysis or personal reaction, since the movie would only supply him with the words necessary to fulfill the first part of the assignment. While this strategy is not uncommon among English language speakers, Chase needed the visual picture and the word pronunciation to even begin to construct writing much less express his ideas in English.

By this compensatory process, Chase did gather knowledge about writing and communicating in English, but how much more effective would his authoring of texts have been if his language learning had more direct adult involvement, and he had more directed contact with his personal writing and word selection. He needed the visual codification of the language symbol system as it related to the auditory pronunciations. Chase's oral language was growing, but he needed more assistance with converting the auditory words into the English symbols.

As Chase informed me, "Writing is boring because no picture." For this adolescent, the visual compensation echoes the importance of the brain processing of the images and emotional associations coded in language symbol systems. Again and again, Chase adapted and adjusted his process to not only read and write but also to construct knowledge. For Chase, this was necessary for his survival.

The Affective in Chase's Authoring of Texts

In this section, emotion "refers to a complex inner or mental condition that has physiological and behavioral properties" (Brand, 1989, p. 57). I use the terms emotions and feeling interchangeably as nouns, and in their verb form as affect. An understanding of how emotions play a role in composing process of adolescents is far from definitive. This section of Chase's case study captures his admitted use of emotional feelings for a female to serve as a type of muse through which to conceptualize ideas for writing.

The next important component in Chase's writing and authoring process existed in his emotional attachment to Brenda. Emotion and desire are linked in his thinking. Adolescence is the time when social identities are formed, and relationships become a part of an adolescent's desires. Bozhovich's second phase of mental development in adolescence characterizes this phase with identity conflicts, biological urges, and earlier formed psychological beliefs. What the adolescent desires, and is prohibited from attaining by his nature as an adolescent, are critical internal factors to defining crisis points and potential zones for learning. As Chase often told me, his most important desire was for an adolescent female student, whom he wanted to date. His lack of English speaking skills and knowledge about dating prohibited him from taking action.

As teachers, we tend to ignore the private squabbles and crises of adolescent relationship angst. Yet, this consuming emotional drive is crucial to development, since the amygdala has such power at this stage of development. The amygdala helps direct memory as it is connected to emotion. It directs first responses to events, situations, and learning because it provides the prior-knowledge base through which learning occurs (Zull, 2002).

To turn on learning, as teachers we need to turn on the emotions and tap their connection to images, memories, and knowledge. Often, we neglect using the emotions because of the personal information and experience, which would be revealed in using the affective thinking processes. Second, without clear assessment criteria related to writing skills, evaluating such traumatic writing can be difficult for some teachers.

The emotional connections we have to images and memory and learning are biologically interrelated. As we internalize the information our senses process, our emotional connections activate before the cognitive. Directing this power and using it to engage learning would take a shift from constructivist teaching pedagogy. For writing, this would mean a shift from the strict applications of process pedagogy, which tend to dominate the teaching of writing in the secondary schools.

I became aware of Brenda's role in Chase's learning and writing process after several odd question and answer events in a biology class that I described earlier. To remind the reader, he told me that love and being rich are the most important things. Then, he proceeded to ask me how to ask out girls, how to talk to girls, what girls want in a guy.

The more I got to know my sixteen-year-old informant, the more I realized how important a female relationship was to him. One late fall day, Chase appeared to be more sullen than usual and avoided meeting my gaze or conversation. When I asked him if he wanted me to go away, he told me he was having a bad day. I pursued the matter. His closest male friend has a girlfriend, and his friend is now spending time with her instead of with Chase. Now, Chase admitted he was lonely and wanted to have a girlfriend.

In an interview, Chase crystallized for me how important his feelings for this young woman were and how his affections for her influenced his schooling and more importantly, his writing.

> Deb: Have you written about other things that are important?
>   Chase: There's nothing more important than that [i.e., Brenda]. I say to myself, why don't you ask her straight out?
>   Deb: Good question.
>   Chase: I know, but I don't know what to say. I am very disappointed in myself [he laughs nervously] all of that simple things, we can't even do it.
>   Deb: What simple things?
>   Chase: All that simple things, like all those easy things that we can't even do. Actually, say to other girls you know, like I can say to Alice [a girl who sits in front of Chase in English class with whom he converses every day], you know that I mean, everybody except her.
>   Deb: Because she is so important?
>   Chase: Yeah.
>   Deb: What are you afraid of?
>   Chase: I am afraid I am going to say something stupid.

More difficult to cull from Chase's description of his process are how emotions affected his writing and authoring. Clearly, Chase used his affection for Brenda as the muse for learning English. In the final essay question in his English class, Chase's thoughts of her and their future life together allowed him to answer the essay question because it presented him with a forum to address his life and emotion for Brenda. This made him happy. Because he was happy or in a positive emotional state, he could think and therefore write. The "emotional" state of being happy allowed him to engage in thinking and writing, and thus, he had a picture of his future. This echoed a statement made by Alice Brand (1989): "If certain emotions precede writing, I am suggesting that particular emotions elicit text" (p. 60).

Chase learned when he can relate his feelings about Brenda into his assignments. Some might dismiss this juvenile emotional reaction as a distraction to learning; however, the evidence shows that by engaging the emotional connection during an invention practice, there is greater possibility that the connections enable students to produce writing. By his own description, Chase engaged in learning when he was emotionally affected by an event in his life; only then could the writing task take on personal purpose and meaningful design. To tap the affective may also be to tap words in the writing discourse like engagement, interest, passion, motivation; all of which stem from a connection that begins with the affective of personal interest.

I need to briefly relate what occurred before another incident with Chase's amorous confusion about women and dating. It was well into the second block of classes, and Chase and I had been to the police station to pay his second speeding ticket. When we started back to the high school, he advised me to wait in the car. He was only going to get a book from his locker and then leave. We were going to his house so that he could finish his assignment for history. At this time, Chase's parents were vacationing in Hawaii for two weeks. His mother and father had left Chase in charge of his brother, a freshman at Prairie High School.

When we arrived at Chase's house, he turned on the television, sat in a chair, opened his textbook and started watching a movie. After 15 or 20 minutes, Chase turned to me and explained the situation in the movie, *Love is Blind*. The movie's story line narrated a love triangle between a woman and two men: one man was a doctor and the other a car mechanic, and both men wanted the same woman. He asked which of the two men I would pick to be with and why. Then, after my response, he said, "If I had someone a woman to love me for what I do, I would be very happy man."

> He asked me about the two girls and we talked about how they resembled girls in school (girls I didn't know). He then said that he wanted to ask some girl out, but he didn't know how. I told him it was easy, just ask her. He said that he couldn't do it. He told me that his horoscope said that he would have to ask someone else out by December or it would be a long time before he would find anyone.
>
> All through the movie, he narrated what they were saying. All the actors are young, beautiful and successful—almost surreal in some ways. A perfect youthful society working through what seemed to me juvenile problems about relationships. Chase saw himself in these characters, much because of the situation as well as the youthfulness of the actors portraying these problems. Also,

the beautiful young woman loved the mechanic not the doctor. (Participant Observer's Notes, 11/20)

From the courtroom (more about this later) to the television room, he plundered the visual world for language. In this brief exchange, the movie became a contact zone of a multitude of images, emotions, and desires mirroring for Chase his life. He reasoned that the pathway to finding love was filtered through a mystical knowledge about learning and life, even in the brief mention of a horoscope, which somehow would predict his fate more than he could. From the courtroom scene, to skipping school, to the movie, and then a brief lunch of chicken and noodles (I passed on the offer of octopus), we returned to school to finish the day.

Wisdom and Learning by Deliberately Making Mistakes

For Chase, authoring texts in and out of school was difficult primarily because of his unfamiliarity with English. In spite of these difficulties, Chase managed the language barrier with specific behavior patterns and beliefs that guided how he responded to the imminent situation when it arrived. All of these factors converged during a day's events in late November. It was the only time that Chase wrote anything out of school for a non-academic purpose to which I had access. He had received a traffic ticket for speeding and reckless driving. The fine for such an offense could be as high as $450.00.

For this adolescent whose job was washing dishes in a restaurant, $450.00 or more and the possible loss of his driver's license presented him with a desperate need to communicate. The day after it happened, Chase told me about it in English class, and that he had to go to court to protest the reckless driving charge. Until the court date in November, this situation would reveal more about Chase's method of authoring texts.

Another compensatory strategy revealed itself through Chase's reckless driving dilemma. Chase created life situations that forced a conflict and challenged his ability to deal with that situation, a type of external crisis. Through the mistake and resulting conflict, Chase had joined two disparate situations through which he learned about life. Chase discussed his trial and error method for learning in a lengthy exchange about the purpose of learning, school, and the real world.

Deb: Why come to school?
Chase: I think school is for purpose to learn something. Then, I think like school, school work got nothing to do with the real world. Like school is like different from getting a job, like work outside a lot different. Outside, you know what I'm talking about, like outside you need skill. In school you need

knowledge. Outside you sometimes needs knowledge. Outside you need more skill than knowledge.

Deb: Do you use anything that you learn [at school] during the day at what you do at work?

Chase: No, but usually I say some stuff not really important but somehow it's funny.

Somehow people may think that's stupid, but sometimes I say some words at work you know like it's really funny, but it's really stupid.

Deb: Can you give me an example?

Chase: Some jokes. Sometimes I cannot say it in English but I say it in Cantonese. I was talking to them [his coworkers at the restaurant] but they know what I am saying and they know what I am saying. We just talk and some people, if they don't know me, they might think I am crazy or stupid.

Deb: You learned something in school and now you use that when you work at [the restaurant] and they teach you?

Chase: I kinda teach. I think that's right. They know like sometimes I do things right and sometimes I do things wrong. Sometimes I show them and sometimes I show them how to do it. That's how I work. If you learn something, you might mess something. If you mess up something then you learn something. It don't matter to me win or lose. In school, it don't matter the A even if I get F. *I learn something, I am happy.*

Deb: Grades don't mean anything to you?

Chase: They don't matter to me but maybe they matter to other people. You can give me a trophy for anything. I really don't like it. I really don't appreciate it. *Only, the thing I appreciate is learning.*

Deb: How do you know when you have learned something?

Chase: *By making a mistake. Anytime you want to learn something, do the opposite. Then you learn something.* (Personal Communication, 10/28)

In this brief interview, Chase painted for me a portrait of his learning values. By doing the opposite of what he knew was right, he set up a deliberate conflict situation which resulted in some reprisal; in this instance, a $450.00 fine for speeding and reckless driving. Chase had a philosophical foundation to his particular pattern of strategies and how they shaped his contexts for learning. He compensated by cleverly testing situations and learning through the consequences. In fact, accepting the consequences of these trial and error situations was part of his learning.

Through the traffic court trial, Chase learned something about the law and its operation. When I asked him if he would change his driving habits after this incident, he said probably not; that his foot just pushes the pedal down harder. What he learned was about the legal justice system; fines and the process of accountability might not change his habits in driving, but it gave him knowledge and that knowledge was self-affirming power. When we arrived

DATE: 10/22/█

Dear: Sir / Madam

To: whom it may concern.

On 10/12/█ at 9:20 P.M. I was looking for my friend's house in █████████ her address was 324 Oakland Ave, ████████████, ██████ That night I needed some money, and I wanted to ask her if she want to buy my Super Nintendo game. I have been go to her house before, but I forgot where's her house, and I remember one day she told me on High way #2 Blackhawk Blvd, either you turn right or left. On High way #2

Blackhawk Blvd I make a right turn, then I make left turn, and another left turn. After too many turn I was lost, then I was afraid and nervous. Later some how I drive in to the dead end, then I stop at the dead end at that time. turn my car off, because I was lost at that time and I needed to think where am I now. After I turn the car off, then I saw the police car pulling over to my car. That night I need the money to go out with my friend, my friend told me he wanted to go to the restaurant. I think I was not guilty to the ticket for reck-less driving.

1. I was unfamiliar with ████████████area, since I was register in Wisconsin.
2. I was lost.
3. Since I was a new student drive, I was afraid, nervous at that time and too busy looking for the Street name.
4. I was in a hurry at that time, and that's why I was speeding.

I wish to **plead not guilty**, because I don't think I was a reck-less driver and I request a fail trial by Judge. I was a good driver all this year, until that night I was in a hurry and that why I speed.

Sincerely

Example 4.3.   Chase's Letter to the Judge

at the court, Chase showed me the letter he had written to the judge. Prior to this trial, Chase had assumed that he would be talking to a judge by himself and that he would have an opportunity to explain what happened. He did not understand the legal procedures that ritualize the process and remove much of the contact between the judge and the defendant. Chase sent the letter to the judge two days after he was stopped. I provide the letter that he wrote to the judge.

In Chase's letter to the judge, he honestly related a series of events surrounding the ticket he received in hopes that this narrative would provide the judge a reason for leniency. Dates, times, and reasons for his behavior exposed a set of motives and rationales that addressed the thinking of a sixteen-year-old adolescent. He reasoned that his driving was not due to any cause related to any malevolent intention, but instead to being lost and desperate.

In the enumeration of the reasons for his behavior, Chase reiterated what the previous paragraph had advised the judge, as if the punctuation of this list would ameliorate the consequences and charges. In the final paragraph, "I wish to plead not guilty" came from the back of the ticket which required him to attend a court appearance and offer a plea. Instead, Chase reasoned that he would provide the plea ahead of time to give the judge ample time to consider Chase's responsibility and punishment.

At moments, Chase made the same grammatical errors that had plagued his writing, but when compared with the classroom-sponsored writings, this text exposed a reasoned explanation for his conduct.

> After too many turn I was lost, then I was afraid and nervous. Later some how I drive into the dead end, then I stop at the dead end at that time, turn my car off because I was lost at that time and I needed to think where am I now.

For many students like Chase who don't write often outside of school, this letter, however simplistic, was complicated, in the effort and reasoning it took for him to produce it. Yet, there is a familiar story pattern present that guided many of Chase's previous writings. The story paradigm that he absorbed from films and narrated through his cultural tales framed the reasoning. These are evident in the sequenced letter to the judge: the story details of what happened; reasons why it happened; conclusion by personal request for a specific action. In a way, this story frame emerged in the expository nature of his letter; expository in the sense that it was a statement and an expanded justification.

Even though his belief that what he learned in school and for life skills were in opposition, the letter demonstrated that Chase had learned enough language to direct their use for a deliberate purpose—to have control over an aspect of his life. These types of compensations help adolescents build learning systems that serve their immediate needs, and by serving their needs, these compensations allow them to gain control and self-educate. These two elements indicate adolescent growth and development and acknowledge their survival literacy.

After the court appearance, we stopped at another police station in another state and city because three nights before Chase had received another speeding ticket. He wanted to check on how much this ticket would cost, whether he had to appear in court and how it would affect his insurance. Through the first trial Chase learned the financial liability of receiving a reckless driving ticket and the effect on his insurance. He was trying to avoid the consequences of a second speeding ticket: losing his license. The harsh realities of the reckless driving encounter created an exemplar through which he would solve the next speeding ticket situation.

In the six months that I spent following Chase, I spent much time explaining what English words meant, translating assignments and textbook vocabulary, and giving advice about girls and dating. My passage into his life was an exchange of information: he let me ask my questions and read his writing in exchange for the little I could provide about females.

What We Learn from Chase

In this chapter, Chase has shown how an adolescent constructed dramatic compensations. In the classroom, the writing tasks and learning English didn't provide the challenge, conflict, choice, and connection as we have seen in Danielle's classroom. As adolescents are moving toward a mature concept of self-knowledge, or at least an operational pathway to self-knowledge when the immediate learning environment doesn't provide it, we witness another case of compensations using writing and literacy processes. What Chase's story invites is more integration of writing and learning lessons that deliberately invite personal reflection, inquiry, and multiple writing experiences with specific goals.

To distinguish this process from other pedagogies, I refer to this as a compensatory curriculum because the students use an alternative pattern or system of learning that is different from the school based instructional process. Chase shows us how an adolescent appropriates various visual and auditory media to communicate with his self-designed learning system through deliberate mistakes and his affective inventive strategies for writing.

When life and the classroom did not provide the systems through which Chase can learn, he devised a compensatory curriculum for himself that involved challenge, conflict, choice, and connection. The source of the connection he wishes to make is language based, since his motive here was to communicate his emotional feelings for a young woman. While his compensatory strategies were not necessarily created because of traumatic stress from violence or abuse, they are nonetheless individual learning adaptations that expose his needs to survive in the adolescent social world in and out of school. Chase's emotional needs provided Chase with a focus and directed purpose for his language learning lessons. As we saw, Chase used an elaborate visual creation to communicate and accomplish academic writing tasks and his attempts to understand the adolescent female. Through that need, he learns or creates learning situations that teach him about language and life, which he may use in his attempts to gain Brenda's affection and gain what he values and desires.

Again, I am reminded of Pratt's statement (1991) that subordinate people will adapt and creatively use dominant culture lessons, and Chase shows us the creative ways in which he adapts modern cultural media for purposes beyond the academic. The lessons are applied to his exigent needs, and Chase shows us how an adolescent will adapt and adjust and subvert the academic lessons into his immediate life and needs. It allows us to ask the question: what is it that we are teaching about concepts of writing synchronized to adolescent development.

Chase showed me intersecting points related to physical, social, and emotional development and exigent situations which foster the compensatory strategies. When Chase authors texts, he is deliberate; the message or content is important, necessary, and really personal. It is through this personal moment and need that the engagement with writing invites an authentic text, but that often describes only the product, not the process that considers the context.

Chase demonstrates four distinct compensatory strategies: process of media plagiarism in the creation of written texts; the ways in which adolescents co-opt language for their personal use in a learning environment; the learning from mistakes scenarios in respect to language acquisition and social rules; and finally the emotional impetus behind composing and learning. Learning something had to have a personal purpose.

In a Vygotskian viewpoint, Chase found visual media would scaffold his learning and written communications. Chase demonstrates what Howard Gardner calls framing. Framing is the creative and purposeful use of a dramatic situation or event in a person's life that may cause them emotional stress or conflict. In this way, Chase invents or purposefully causes conflict in learning situations through mistakes, and then in the conflict that results, he learns something. The mistake is the frame from which Chase forces his own development, a development not often provided with the school-learning environment. Experience is the teacher; and making mistakes purposefully is the experience he needed to frame the learning and writing.

The essential element in the process was the personal relevancy in learning and writing. The important point though is that authoring these texts for purposes other than the academic contained an element that was missing from the work Chase performed within school. Yet, he developed elaborate strategies to learn the language and use visual images to help him create stories, which would address the academic tasks. Rather than seeing these strategies as an intrusion into the personal history of students, we need to use these personal stories and contexts as frames for learning and writing to learn.

As Dewey aptly stated in *Experience and Education*, we need to educate for the moment, not the future. In learning to control and act upon the immediate present and its needs, people have the skills to adapt to whatever the future brings because they have learned how at each moment of their lives to assert themselves and learn in that situation. Adolescents are particularly vulnerable to the ever-changing moment, and to give them a way to assert control and to learn through their lives is to give them, through writing, a way to structure their future as well.

By using the moments of an adolescent's life, which according to Bozhovich can alter and change at any time, teachers can invite the personal connection and let it act as a catalyst for developing writing skills. The process of converting the visual images, emotions, and responses into a story narrative assists development and introduces self-awareness for adolescents who biologically and psychologically are making dramatic changes. In that respect, even the slightest problem, situation or event in an adolescent life can approach the crisis point, another way of identifying the exigent moment that precedes authoring. For Chase, dramatic events happened and were induced purposefully as part of his learning

For Danielle, the dramatic events needed resolution and communication before she could move on to adulthood, even though she considered herself quite mature. Writing her letter to her mother and her poetry gave Danielle a power over her life and through language she was able to control it by giving shape to thoughts in the authored words of her texts. In different ways, Chase and Danielle gained an authority over words through different processes of composing, but they both wrote to survive.

Chapter 5

Diana—"Hell of a Life, Isn't It?"

DIANA'S VIGNETTE

She wanted to be called Diana because she had always liked the name. A beautiful young woman, not unlike images of the goddess Artemis or Diana. Her world, though, was anything but idyllic.

We often walked down to the Quik Mart store during lunchtime. Diana had no money—ever—so I bought lunch for us one day and many days after that. Sitting on the wall outside the school eating lunch, Diana told me about her life as a gang member, the initiation rites, and a new connotation for the word *pharmacist*.

She told me about her short but involved time with the Gangster Disciples. As students walked by, she pointed out GD members, and narrated what *things* they had done. During one of these lunch sessions, three high school boys walked by us with a younger boy, four to six years old. Diana told me that the older boys were teaching the little one how to be a GD. She proceeded to describe how the high school boys found a young kid, held him off the ground and told the other young boy to hit him. They showed him how to strike where it would do the most damage. I asked her where the boys' parents were. No answer.

Then, she quickly spotted another high school boy and informed me of the crush he'd once had on her. As cars drove by, she would be looking for another former or potential admirer. She was always scoping out another admirer, or revisiting her past relationships with a flirtatious wave, if the guy drove by. Her beauty and her physical grace brought her the attention she so desperately sought.

105

Diana lived with her mother in a second-story apartment, which visitors accessed by an outside staircase. The apartment had one small living room, a kitchen, a bathroom, and one bedroom, where Diana's mother and her new boyfriend slept. They had no phone, no car, and only a few pieces of essential furniture. Diana slept on the floor in the living room and studied in the bathroom at night. Her clothes lay folded in the chest that sat in the bathroom closet. Behind the chest, Diana's dream diary hung on a nail.

Diana struggled with money, her health, and her emotions. She told me that she had trouble with her nerves and didn't eat. She would go two days without eating, only drinking an occasional Diet Pepsi because she was addicted to caffeine. Diana had only been alcohol-free for one year. She occasionally indulged in drugs when life became too complicated for her.

Diana's life was unpredictable and dependent upon her mother's moods. On another occasion, Diana's mother kicked her out of the apartment for "whoring around." Diana ended up spending the night with a female police officer who had found her walking the streets late at night.

Diana had been having regular sex at least once a day since she was thirteen. She had painful menstrual cycles and periodic pelvic pain. She had been raped at age three; a family member had tried to kill her when she was two. She still bears the scars of that attempt on her arms. At thirteen, after having sex twice a day regularly, she became pregnant. In a gang fight with another girl, a hard kick to Diana's stomach caused her to miscarry. At fourteen, a doctor told her to stop having sex or she might never be able to have children. In the months that I knew Diana, she was afraid that she was pregnant for the third time and may have had an abortion.

Two months after my research ended, Diana ran away.

"IT'S A HELL OF A LIFE, ISN'T IT?"

Overview

Diana was a beautiful young woman. Her external beauty drew long stares from her male peers, but the only beautiful thing about Diana's story was her will to survive. Her story is about catastrophic abuse and the visible impediments it created for her every day she lived. What makes Diana's story important is that it is not an unusual case or a singular instance among high school adolescents; she, unfortunately, narrates the hidden abuses and silence that keeps them hidden among young female adolescents.

Diana's story continues to be descriptive evidence of survival compensations. Through the compensatory strategies and classroom assignments, we have seen how two adolescents create a type of survival literacy. In Diana's compensatory strategies, I found her writing strategies that led to escape fantasies and visually created compositions. Diana showed how the writing and literacy compensations were directed by her immediate survival conditions.

The central crisis for Diana was maintaining emotional stability. As I reflected back upon my first meeting with her, I understood her immediate acceptance to be an informant in the research. She said that she would like to have an adult female companion, a friend to talk to.

As Diana's story shows, in almost every facet of her life, her mother's uncertain physical and emotional well-being was directly related to Diana's own.

If Diana's mother was drunk, then Diana could not have a peaceful evening at home, because she attended to her mother's state of mind. In a different way, Diana manifested this same need for stability by trying to have or get a male's attention. In every class, she found a male student to notice her, talk to her, or work with her. Then, she moved on to the next class and another male student who flirted with her. She constantly searched for a boyfriend or at least talked about finding one should the present attachment fail. Diana's compensations surrounded this basic need for stability, emotional and environmental.

"Mom, can you come here for a minute?" and then she said, "It sounds like you're the mother and I'm the daughter." It's either, yeah, you're going to come or no you're not.

I mean, hey, I try and that's my mom and I love her and I have to make sure that my mom is going to be OK before I leave her. (Personal Communication, 8/27)

Whatever writing Diana did in or out of school was related to her need for stability and emotional security. When she had a traumatic day or a crisis event, she rejected composing texts that required analysis. When she did have to write a report or an academic essay, she created visual ways to write in much the same manner as Chase, but for very different reasons.

In school, Diana's writings (See appendix D) reflected the immediate need to address the crises in her life; for example, if the writing task asked her to plan an emergency escape from her apartment versus writing a literary analysis on the theme from *Julius Caesar*, Diana chose the first writing task. If passing a class were important to her dream of escape, then Diana found a way to meet the writing requirements.

If the assignment had no direct information or purpose for her survival, she ignored it or refused to complete the task. She participated when classroom assignments and lessons gave her information and room for expression necessary to that day's crisis or crises. These daily crises were inextricably linked to her complicated past history of abuse, neglect, and loss and led the strategic compensations Diana made in writing and literacy.

Goal Setting and Escape

For adolescents who live in circumstances similar to Diana, the traumatic history foregrounded any learning they would do in school. Yet in spite of so much abuse and emotional chaos in her life, Diana fought through these conditions by grasping a happier future. I found this reassuring in the initial interview, but with each day, her ability to accomplish her goal was jeopardized by the instability and neglect she lived. Diana's proclaimed goal was to stay in school, graduate, and leave town for another community. Diana's personal crises each day caused the goal to slip more into wishful fantasy than reality. Under these circumstances, it was almost impossible for Diana to gain the academic skills and knowledge that would ensure her college entrance.

Diana had an adult parent who could not provide basic needs of food, shelter, and security. Initially, her stated goal was an adamant plan for staying in school, but I came to understand that these goals were central to Diana's survival, and that her compensatory writing and literacy acts told the real goal of escape plan for a more secure life. Her goal or reason for staying in school shifted throughout her story and as such delineated her compensatory strategies and her writing to survive. In Diana's own words:

> Right now I am trying to get my grades back up to where they should be. So, I am trying to base myself on each class. That's why I don't want the study hall because I do better at home than I do in a study hall. So, I like to work by myself most of the time. I can work with others, but I get along and I feel more on to what I am doing. I understand more of what I am doing than I do when other people or when I am in a group or something.
>
> I have a plan myself. And um if I have to work with somebody else, they havea plan to what they do and they want to add it on to what I'm doing and right now I am not doin' that.
>
> Right now I am looking forward to graduating high school and looking into certain colleges to which ones I want to go to. I want to try right now. (Personal Communication, 8/15)

Diana wanted to learn, wanted to complete high school, and wanted to be happy, but her goals were constantly thwarted by her mother's drama for male companionship and alcohol and limited financial means. Diana had in a sense become the adult in this mother-daughter relationship. In order to escape her mother's irresponsible neglect, Diana had to raise herself and find avenues for growth and development that helped her achieve her goals and dreams. Yet, in this case, the broad school goals for educating adolescents conflict with Diana's goals. We see Diana weave disciplinary knowledge from the various courses into a survival guide. As Diana progressed through her academic day, her teachers were unaware of her abusive history or the daily instabilities Diana faced and how this would affect her ability to learn, to write, and to survive.

A Traumatic Sequence of Events and Surviving in School

When Diana became worried or frustrated, she would objectify her emotional responses by blaming her nerves. Diana used the word "nerves" to refer to a variety of emotional responses and that these nerves were her way to identify that she was upset. She used the immediate emotional state to engage or block any cognitive exercise that required that she spend more energy in intellectual activities. Unless she accommodated her present emotional state in the activity she was being asked to perform or to focus her attentions on the subject so that it ignited some personal interest, she rejected the task.

In its way, this compensatory strategy was a strategy of disengagement that allowed Diana to focus her mental energies where she needed them most. She compensated for the instability in her life by directing her learning to that which served her immediate needs for survival. What happened at home before school directly affected her behavior and her ability to learn, write, and think. In the following scenarios, I illustrate through an entire school day how a common home disruption directed her learning and her writing throughout that day.

Diana's block schedule of classes began with computer technology, followed by history, Spanish, Health, and then English. I met Diana at home one morning before school, and when she was ready, we walked to school. On the journey, she began to tell me that her mother's boyfriend had gotten another woman pregnant, and her mother had just found out about it. So the previous night, Diana's mother and boyfriend had been fighting long into the night. Diana had no place to hide or run in the small one bedroom apartment, and she had been home to witness the discovery and the ensuing fight.

To make matters worse, her mother and boyfriend were both home sick with the flu. As we made our way to school, Diana finished telling me all the details of her frustrations and that this bothered her nerves. Upon entry to her first period computer class, Diana's computer teacher handed her a stack of assignments to complete, since Diana had missed the previous three days of class.

In the course, Diana was learning HyperCard, browsing, typing, painting, authoring, and scripting. Because of the block construction of the academic day in this high school, Diana had Computer Concepts for ninety minutes each day for nine weeks. While Diana took her seat at the computer, Diana's teacher confided to me her concern over Diana's inability to perform the instructional tasks and the number of Diana's incomplete assignments. The teacher observed that Diana needed individual assistance in order to make up the missed assignments, but her computer teacher's pedagogical style, number of students, and time prevented her from really creating an alternate system in which Diana could actually learn these concepts.

In this classroom, figuring out the detailed sequence to follow, reading the assignment, and translating that information to the computer task required Diana to be her own tutor. She started the task, followed the first few guidelines, but then the detailed and lengthy directions eventually caused her to forsake the assignment and strike up a conversation with the girl next to her. This computer course did not allow Diana to rely upon the patterns for adapting or assimilating the classroom material into her own life. It required her to set aside her conflicted emotional life in order to perform the logical, sequential, and measurable tasks in computer class, which she avoided by talking, or playing with the computer and only minimally doing any work under the teacher's occasional visit.

In her health class, the instructor focused on preparation for crisis in a noncrisis atmosphere. The students had to make an escape plan from their homes and assign responsibilities for all who live in the house, such as considering where parties would meet in a fire emergency. Then, the instructor talked about intervention and enabling as a framework for thinking about being in a fire and talking care of the crisis situation that would follow. Diana took notes, sat quietly, and listened to the instructor. In this case, he had mentioned words like crisis, intervention, and enabling, which attracted her attention and engaged her survival needs. The teacher's delivery called for practical applications based upon each student's living situation. In this case, Diana associated her home safety worries with the classroom discussion.

The assignment for developing a fire escape plan directly affected Diana's perpetual concern for her mother and her health. After outlining her fire escape plan, Diana revealed that her mother has a drinking problem, a problem for her mother's whole family. The connection and protection that the health class initiated for Diana allowed her to focus her present concern into some meaningful action that would protect her mother and provide security for her. Her final class of the day was English 10, the fourth block period of the day. For a short time, we left the class to complete a think-aloud protocol for an essay due in Ms. Whitson's class. We had done the preparation for the protocol, but when we went to the room to complete the protocol, Diana refused to do it. We returned to class where the other students were also working on the essay. Diana never completed this writing assignment. When I asked her why, she said, "I just don't want to do it."

The essay Ms. Whitson had assigned was a literary analysis of a theme from *Julius Caesar*. Diana had read the play only because of her reading group, so I know that she understood rudiments of the story. However, there was little in *Julius Caesar* for Diana to use in solving her problems or addressing her needs. The task of analyzing for theme was too analytical a task for Diana to engage in because she had no direct emotional connection or relevant personal experience she could attach to the essay. In this English class, the teacher provided no direct assistance or discussion since this was a writing day. The teacher's attentions were to keep the students engaged in writing the essay and answering questions briefly, so as not to disturb the quiet writing environment.

In Diana's case, the severe dysfunctional conditions under which she has lived her life limited her ability to "think" about the abstract, irrelevant subject like theme in *Julius Caesar*. This does not mean that such classroom activities are not worthwhile, but for a student with Diana's traumatic living conditions, especially given the circumstances she brought to school on this day, this task was too remote for her to become engaged. The types of strategies she embraced for learning in school were dependent upon an informational application to her survival and problems she faced that day, but as we saw in the classes Diana was taking, there was little opportunity to reveal her "truth" for that day, and little learning that would help her solve her survival needs that day, except for the fire escape plan. I included this sequence to demonstrate the intersection of life and literacy. If one event were not enough, her past life lay as an unresolved foundation for the daily barrage of unpredictable behaviors and experiences with her mother and her own needs for survival.

The English Classroom and Ms. Whitson

In Ms. Whitson's classroom, the walls were filled with posters celebrating African American accomplishments and heritage. Ms. Whitson kept multiple resources on Egyptian history and hieroglyphics, as well as the standard textbooks on language and literature study. The students sat in desks in a horseshoe shaped arrangement, facing the main marker board. During the semester, Ms. Whitson rearranged the students in different desk positions three times, attempting to isolate the talkers into the front of the room where she could have better access to them. Her desk was situated at the side of the classroom. She often lectured from a central podium placed in the middle of the horseshoe formation of desks facing the students.

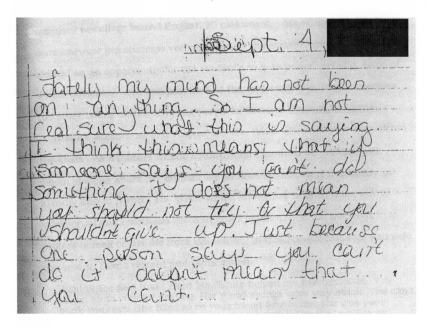

Photo 5.1.

Before the students walked in each class period, Ms. Whitson wrote a daily proverb on the overhead and the students knew that the first fifteen minutes of class was for responding to the proverb in their journals. Class began officially with the discussion of what the students thought about the proverb: some examples include the following:

"If you are patient in a moment of anger, you will escape a hundred days of sorrow."

"I am what I am because of the bridges I have or have not crossed; a person's burden of life is to always try to keep that higher self in command."

"Don't let the lower self take over."

When Ms. Whitson introduced this activity the first day of class, Diana responded with one paragraph of four or five sentences.

By the end of the semester, Diana filled a full page of interpretation and response to these prompts, but because of the similarity in the prompt's message, Diana became bored with them. In spite of her boredom, this type of prompt rehearsal affected Diana's writings later in the semester. She used it as a response formula to address the writing prompts on the state proficiency exams.

After the journal writing, the initiatory opening discussion, Ms. Whitson engaged in a lighthearted and witty exchange with her students, which could last well into the ninety-minute class. Then Ms. Whitson segued into the day's lesson with a comment or idea from the journal prompt discussion. Ms. Whitson relied upon her verbal skills and wit to outmaneuver her students. When she won the verbal exchange that occurred after the prompt, the students allowed the class to continue. She presented each student with an opportunity to gain power verbally, some of whom obviously were well practiced at the art. Diana responded to this teaching style.

> I think the fact that I liked Ms. Whitson helped me like her class. You know, she's very interesting. Her mood swings were very quick. You can't blink your eye. She liked to be your friend first before she was your teacher. I noticed that because the first couple of weeks in class we didn't do too much of anything.
>
> She wanted to better understand her students before she gave out the assignments. (Personal Communication, 1/17)

Diana's view of Ms. Whitson meant that she would be able to write about the personal, private dysfunctions that ruled her life because Ms. Whitson invited it. Ms. Whitson provided Diana with an audience, a much-needed confidant to whom Diana felt she could communicate:

> I guess for them [teachers] to know that I feel myself that I am different from everybody else. . . . Sometimes it depends upon if you can get to know the teacher. Get to know where they are from, and get to know a little bit of what they know. Then, when you write, they'll read what you write and they will be able to understand . . . And it's easier for a student to write if they know who they are writing to. If they know their teacher, if they know the person who is going to read what they write. Even though there are times in your life when you are gonna be writing where you don't know who's gonna be reading it, but if you can tell yourself that you know what you write, and feel that [it] has sense to you, then maybe somebody else will know and understand what you wrote. (Personal Communication, 1/17)

Diana's comments here announce to teachers the power of personal connections and the teacher-student relationship to learning and communicating. For someone who has a lifetime of abusive stories, a teacher like Ms. Whitson would be welcome indeed. I believe that Diana is showing teachers the power of a personal connection and interest that is important for abused adolescents, giving them an audience to whom they can tell. Being able to tell is also part of beginning to heal and to address the intellectual impediments the abusive trauma had caused.

Even though I found Ms. Whitson's first weeks of school slow in covering subject matter content, her instructional method proved important to her students. Writing in Ms. Whitson's classroom was a dialogue between informed parties and contained a reciprocity that took Ms. Whitson time to build. This reciprocal dialogue (Nystrand, 1996), which Diana described as necessary for her to write, determined how her emotions influenced the context of what she wrote about. In Diana's case, the need for the outside adult to whom she revealed personal information was essential for her emotional control, survival, and authoring of texts (Jackson & Rodriguez-Tomé, 1993).

Ms. Whitson's students challenged her values for English language arts study, and this caused her great consternation over the course of the semester. Ms. Whitson wanted to be a writer herself and constantly relied upon the training she had received in her college preparatory classes in Arkansas. When she began giving writing assignments, Ms. Whitson was frustrated with her students and the various stages of language competency in her tenth graders. She recognized the disinterest her students presented when she assigned them the canonical literary works, yet she believed in the academic and intellectual value of literature for study and interpretation.

To interest the students in literature study, Ms. Whitson used the daily journal writing activity referred to earlier, hoping that this practice of writing and interpretation of proverbs would transfer to their ability to interpret the literature and would direct their thinking in the writing she asked them to do. Yet, when Ms. Whitson asked Diana and the class to perform writing tasks, which directly asked for literary analysis, Ms. Whitson's belief in the transfer of interest did not result in more sophisticated writing forms or literary interest.

Compensatory Strategies and Classroom Writing Instruction

In the first official writing assignment for English class, Diana had to compare two myths. These early writings were one-paragraph responses and completed in haste, much like her journal prompt writing, completed at the beginning of class each day.

> It was believed that once Phan Ku died the earth was finnished. It was felt that the people, water, . . . And plants came from his body. I can say that by reading this I can also the religious background of it. I see that the people felt Phan Ku to be as a god and also felt . . .

Diana did not revise this text. As Ms. Whitson's evaluation revealed (Example 5.2), Diana had not completed the assignment as instructed. In her summary of the myths, she merely rephrased the story adding comments to her summary. While the rubric for the assignment offered clear criteria for evaluation, it also provided the student a place for her own assessment. Diana was aware of the poor quality of the assignment, less than she was capable of producing. Often, she accompanied an apology-centered goal with an assurance that she could produce better the next time.

ASSIGNMENT CRITERIA FORM
FOLKTALES, MYTHS, and LEGENDS

Criteria	Points Possible		Teacher Evaluation
Clean loose leaf paper	10		10
Written neatly — black/blue ink	4		10
mechanics — grammar, punct. sent. structure, ¶ form	15		15
Content — what you said	40		25
TOTALS	/100		60

Student's Comments: Not a lot of time.
Misunderstood some things no phone
So I could not get in touch with you.
This type of assignments will not
Teacher's Comments: be handed in again

Will you have, or do you have a phone now?
It seems that you tried to connect the reading with other work and or your previous knowledge — good. etc.
Also work on style and diction. You seemed to also be in a hurry because you left out words in a few places — yes?
Some spots appeared repetitious and wordy. You didn't finish the assignment either.

Example 5.2 Assessment of Myth Writing

On the assignment criteria form, she admitted her need for more time with one important qualification: she had no phone to call Ms. Whitson for help. Even though Ms. Whitson encouraged her students to call her, Diana could only get in touch with her during the school day. I am not sure how significant this detail was, but it suggested to me an unfortunate problem with communicating that Diana might have needed. Throughout the semester, Diana wanted to produce quality work, but something thwarted her from accomplishing that goal.

In the next writing sample completed for history class on 9/11, Diana had been given the thesis statement by the instructor as well as a contract for a grade. In order to get an A on the paper, the students had to include a minimum number of areas. Diana saw the listing of areas in the teacher's directions, and she perceived this as a recipe for getting an A.

Diana's first sentence in the composition began with the teacher's stated criteria: "The ancient Athenians and Spartans were both alike and different in many ways, such as, slavery, education, women, sports, military, culture and laws and punishment." Diana used the teacher's criteria as an organizing principle for her entire paper as she moved from the introduction to the body paragraphs: I would now like to go to education; I would now like to go to slavery, etc. She received a grade of B.

In his assessment comments, the teacher advised her to "refrain from using 1st person references when writing a formal essay." Diana did not use the history paper's organization strategy in any other writing, even when she had to write for the state mandated testing. (I will discuss this later in the chapter.) Because the teacher had provided such explicit instructions for the paper's expectations and organizations, Diana could "plug in" the information.

This kind of formulaic writing has long been questioned (Brannon et al., 2008). Diana might not have been able to write the paper because of the mental energy she would have to direct to figuring out what to say and how to say it. With the formula, she could summarize, copy, and change the formulaic topic sentence and complete the assigned history task. What I question here is what Diana learned. Given her tempestuous living conditions, this formula-driven assignment meant that she did not have to divert crucial mental energies for survival to completing this assignment.

Questions remain: did the formula help her to create an organization and sequence that somehow bypassed the difficulties she had with the Julius Caesar essay? What do these rigid formulas teach students about how to communicate their learning in writing?

We know that format-based writing knowledge does not transfer to other academic writing tasks (McCarthy, 1987). For the college students in McCarthy's study, the genre style required in one academic area did not transfer to other academic writing tasks. In Diana's case, she did not associate the writing form in her history class with any process of composing in English class. She filled in the form without understanding the concept of writing.

At the same time Diana was completing the history task, she was working on a paper in English class, which narrated how she got her name. Ms. Whitson required three drafts of this paper before the final, including a writing workshop session. The writing was produced through a series of classroom lessons on organization: your name, what it means, nicknames, other names the student would like to have. In Ms. Whitson's class, the students were provided with the writing framework, composed a first draft, and then were required to make changes in the drafts. Changes between the first and second drafts occurred minimally.

The following sentence shows how Diana approached revision from first draft to second draft: "This is because I really do not know" became "This is because I really don't know if it does." In her writing, the changes Diana made were indicative of afterthought additions and not necessarily content and communicative clarity in the revision. It was more about the lack of understanding how and what to revise from draft to draft. Diana revised what she knew to revise. Nothing more.

In Diana's writing, the first sentence rephrased the question or topic idea, and then she moved to more personal associations and ideas. Even with suggestions from Ms. Whitson, Diana made minimal changes. Since Ms. Whitson required three revisions, Diana changed the suggested editorial corrections Ms. Whitson had made, but in these corrections, Diana stretched the initial sentence by adding detail to increase the sentence. Here is an example of how she made these additional changes:

> "My aunt decided to spell it the_____ way" became

> "My aunt decided to spell it the_____ way because they felt that I should learn the_____ way of life. Mostly because I lived there at her house till I was two years old."

Her only other major revision to the paper happened in the final two sentences.

> "I picked this because it is cute" became

> "I picked this because it is something new and different. I also found it to be a cute name."

As we have seen in the other student writings, revision is an important process in developing more sophisticated language skills complementary to the adolescent's ability to perceive growth and development. The relationship between the amount of revision and the adolescent's own language skill may be the difference between literacy progress and mimicry. The more skill the adolescent has with using language to express her ideas and tell her stories, the greater her ability to facilitate aspects necessary for their survival in writing. In the consistency of revision, adolescents can reach a level of linguistic control over the traumatic situations and conditions under discussion or related to writing production. Diana was not able to access that depth of revision in Ms. Whitson's system independently.

Diana's Writing Formula as a Compensatory Strategy

Ms. Whitson used writing prompts at the beginning of class to invoke conversation and discussion. Rarely did these journal writings become the inspiration in any other writing tasks. Even so, Diana developed a writing formula from journal responses she completed in Ms. Whitson's class, which she continued to use as her response formula whenever she was given a prompt. She did this without regard for genre, audience, or message.

The example of Diana's writing by this formula can be seen in a writing she did based upon the following prompt: "Destiny is not left to chance; it's a matter of choice." In this one-paragraph format, Diana demonstrated how she struggled with the ideas the prompt inspires. She can't seem to find the right combination of words to express her ideas. Diana's own confusion centered on her need for guidance in finding a way to be happy and take control of her life. This confusion in idea and expression is visible in Diana's entry on destiny. Again, I present Diana's writing as she wrote it.

> We start to see other people who shaart to tell ourselfs we can't do something, We start figuring that if we can't do something so little as actually passing <u>one</u> [her emphasis] class what makes us think we can do something else. You start to actually believe there's no hope for you. You start to feel you can't change your life to whatever you see everybody else having. You feel that you start say there is no since in being [bad] you can't change your life to happy. Other things can add on to making you feel that way. A solution to being able to change your fate is to close your eyes and try see yourself doing something. Try to figure out what you see. . . .—this poem shows that you don't have to only [be] someone [else] because you should know in your heart you can do just what they did maybe even more and even better. (Diana's writing on destiny)

The only detectable difference between the rough draft and the final copy is the neatness of the handwriting. Diana still has one paragraph, and an organizational pattern so common in her writing now: she announces the topic, explains what it means and then moves into anecdote in the disguise of a solution as her final commentary.

In this writing, as in others she produced, Diana found a compensatory format in the paragraph structure that meets the academic requirements for writing, but also served her own personal need to tell her story, or at least some portion of it. Then, after the students wrote their responses, Ms. Whitson asked the students to present their responses orally. Diana did this, and when I asked her about it, she had more connections to this process than I had anticipated:

> D: Another paper it really came out and me and S___ had the same paper. It actually made me feel good that day 'cause it seemed like I was the only

one who actually got an applause that was a little bit louder than anyone. I figure we are listening to a lot of the kids in class, and they would speak their reports. And you could hear that maybe that happened to them, and maybe they know. I feel that if you hear what they are saying, if you can see that they have the knowledge about what they are talking about, then maybe they know.

   Deb: What does that mean to you?

   D: It actually makes me listen. If it is information that they got out of an encyclopedia or workbook or something, it's so you don't want to listen. Maybe if you can get out of it that they actually know, maybe that happened, then it's more interesting to me. (Personal Communication, 1/17)

In the writing sample and interview, Diana described the value of experiential truth telling and literacy practices in the classroom. Diana listened for and learned from the truth in a speaker's presentation when it was grounded in a personal experience, but this personal experience had to resonate with one of Diana's own.

Diana listened for the truth and depth of experience that ignited an emotional connection with the speaker. Adolescents need to tell their stories to an interested audience where their stories and experience have resonance. This personal resonance in genuine narration and depth of experience generated Diana's reason for meaningful written discourse. She reveled in its ability to reach her peers and her teacher, evident in her comment about the applause she received.

Perhaps, these classroom incidents indicate that students with traumatic stresses from violence and abuse needed an outlet to reveal the truth about their lived experiences. When the classroom writing tasks and oral presentations allow, these students found a genuine interest in the literacy lessons they provide. However, in the actual planning and work for this oral presentation, Diana completed the minimum she needed for a grade. In contrast to Diana's exuberance at the class's reception to her speech, Ms. Whitson directed her assessment in areas that illustrated the complexity of the assignment and important personal issues that affected Diana's abilities. (See Appendix E 1, 2, and 3 for the entire persuasive speech assessment.)

Writing and Action—Diana's Compensatory Strategies

As teachers, we attempt to guide students to the specific knowledge within our discipline. In spite of our best efforts, students situate what they learn into a relevant personal application and use our carefully constructed lessons on language arts in other contexts. The following description details Diana's adaptive use of classroom information as a compensatory strategy.

Diana had a course, during the first-quarter block, called Western Civilization. She had failed one quarter earlier, and so she was repeating the quarter she failed. During the lesson, the teacher was lecturing on the archeological process of finding artifacts and how to ask questions to find out information. Diana told me she found this fascinating and gave me an unexpected application for a history lesson in archeological processes.

> Diana later explained that she has learned in his class because he expects them to learn things. Even though Diana does not like [the teacher], she learned from him; she used what he has taught her. She told me about her boyfriend and archeology and digging into [her boyfriend's] past. She found a way to make it into her life. (Participant Observer Notes, 9/18)

Diana explained it this way:

> Well, he [her boyfriend] came looking for me and when he found me I'm like, I started thinking. I started digging. For anything. All kinds of information, anything I wanted to know: How old are you? Birthday? How long have you been working? What's your name? Your mom's name? I wanted to know everything. Now, I do just from digging. (Interview, 9/16)

Diana took this history lesson and used it to gather much-needed information. Her digging, as she called it, occurred at the same time that Diana was worried about being pregnant by the young man whose past she had wanted to explore. She not only learned about archeology, but she creatively found a way to use it to fulfill a need and desire.

As teachers, we cannot always control what students learn in our classroom and what they use that knowledge to do. Diana understood the process of inquiry as an archeologist would use it, but she applied this concept to a desire and a need. I am sure the teacher offering this lesson had no idea that these investigative procedures would be used to acquire personal knowledge from Diana's next male interest. There's a broader issue here about disciplinary content divorced from application. In providing students with content knowledge for its own sake, teachers forsake the very details of learning that Diana's story illustrated.

Writing In and Out of School—The Fantasy Compensation

Diana composed self-sponsored writings out of school. These writings, journal, poems, letters to friends in Oklahoma, belonged to Diana's fantasy escape plan and incident specific romantic writings about love. In one such poem Diana detailed her worries about her boyfriend, Nick. She told me that she was looking for someone to fill a space in her life, a former boyfriend who still haunted her dreams.

> My mind is in a daze.
> So please take my mind out of this daze
> and let me know I'm in your heart
> And I won't be afraid that we're going to fall apart.
> Well, hey I am in this daze and don't know why,
> But I can say I am glad that it is you
> that keeps me in the daze of mine.

The content was thematically important to the writing Diana did throughout the school year: her pursuit of a new boyfriend and the intermittent return of an old boyfriend, Nickey. The word "daze" has resonance in Diana's writings. The next time Diana will write out of school it will be to plan her escape from her mother.

Diana's private journal hung on a nail, secreted behind her dresser in the bathroom. She had concealed it there so that her mother's present boyfriend would not find it. In this private diary, Diana invented a fantasy world, where she was happy and loved. In this written fantasy world, Diana escaped the daily barrage of vulgar name-calling and condescending characterizations among mother, daughter, and live-in boyfriend. By using the secreted diary, Diana rebelled in silence and plotted her escape.

Six months before I had met Diana, she had returned from Oklahoma after she had run away from her mother. Upon her return, she was immediately placed in foster home for the summer and eventually returned to her mother. Diana was constantly worried about her mother's safety. Yet, Diana wanted to escape her mother, her mother's traumatic situation, and have a secure and stable home. Her home journal was her way to fantasize that escape and dream of a future life without trauma, violence, and instability. Diana discussed these issues in an early interview.

> I was afraid to where I don't wanna be here no more. I don't. One time I had got to a point where I busted. I had wrapped something around my hand and busted a frame, took the glass out of it and cut my leg.
>
> And now, I have, I call it my tattoo, a name on my leg because when I cut it I didn't feel anything. I started to see if I could feel anything. I think I was so mad I could feel nothing at all. I didn't care. It was just I had gotten to the point where I would pick up things and throw them across the room, watch them shatter. Now, I know that I can't do that. You have to find other ways to get it out or something, you know.

And now I do. *I write things down.* I would get really mad. I didn't care. I used to want to kill myself because I didn't want to be here anymore. Now I know I can't. (Personal Communication, 8/27)

This interview took place very early in the research project, and its disturbing message and story caught me completely by surprise. After she said this, I struggled to remain unaffected and dispassionate about this candid admission. It was at this point that the focus of the research changed and became a disturbing marker for compensations in this adolescent's life.

Diana was a cutter, a person whose self-mutilation spoke of self-loathing. A psychologist would recognize this adolescent as deeply disturbed due to her long traumatic stresses from abuse, rape, and her mother's alcoholism. Diana was an adolescent who desperately needed help, safety, psychiatric counseling, and healthy parental love. Her journal was the only place she could create a fantasy life—literally writing her way to survival.

As Diana's story unfolded, the fantasy journal as well as selected writing assignments within her classes suggested that she separated school writing from personal writing, even though she employed school based literacy. For an adolescent with Diana's traumatic life, more writing opportunities that allow Diana to tell the ongoing traumatic crises of daily life would be important in providing this adolescent with a healthy avenue to address these crises in juxtaposition to what existed in the hidden journal.

Diana showed us that in the event that learning contexts do not provide specific opportunities to investigate these personal crises, she created them. Desperate circumstances called for desperate learning and literacy strategies. Diana employed the classroom content knowledge, writing opportunities, and journaling as a compensatory strategy ensuring her survival.

Journaling: A Compensatory Strategy

Many teachers use journal writing as a common classroom activity. Journaling activities range from a prompt-driven daily or weekly practice to a spontaneous free write to specific invention strategies as a way to engage students with writing. In Diana's case, the self-sponsored writing she did in her own private journal and the prompt driven writing she did for Ms. Whitson became writing format, which Diana used to shape her writing for other classes and tests.

Ms. Whitson's writing instructions in the journal included copying down the proverb and using the first sentence to address the student's immediate response to the proverb. The students were then instructed to continue writing down their thoughts about the proverb. Diana said that she would often have nothing to say immediately, that she wanted to take the proverbs home and write the response after she had time to think about what it meant to her.

In this delayed response, I suspected that Diana could not attend to the prompts intellectually because she was focused on other emotional issues. To release her "thinking" to engage in more abstract thinking, the prompt would require that she divert emotional thinking to cognitive intellectual energy. Diana needed to focus on the immediate conditions she brought to school. Diana referred to these life situations generally with the word "things" or "never had time to do things." In her writing, Diana's "things" could be concrete items like money or abstract things like fun and play with friends. Diana had never been to a dance, joined a club, seen a play, or eaten in a nice restaurant.

At first, I questioned whether or not the daily journal entries, which Ms. Whitson required, had any transfer to writing (Foertsch, 1995). These journal meanings were discussed in class, but never used by the students for any other writing purposes. Ms. Whitson gave students the opportunity to choose the method of application, each dependent upon the student's need or desire to apply them. However, as Diana demonstrated, these journal prompts provided her with an additional opportunity to construct a meaning for her life beyond her secret journal.

Like many of the proverbs that Ms. Whitson offered to her students for journaling, the message was clearly one of responsibility, strength gained through struggle and the place of power to control one's life. Diana complained that the journal prompts grew boring because they repeated the same message. In her ability to write a response to the prompt, she no longer found inspiration or provocative ideas in the prompt. Without greater variety in the prompt, she could not find different meanings and hidden wisdom she needed to guide her latest crises.

> When I first started writing 'em, when I first started the class, it gave me a chance to express myself. Now, I feel like I'm repeating myself. Every time I write something down. I feel like what I wrote Monday I'm again in different words, you know. (Personal Communication, 11/22)
>
> A lot of my journal entries, even if it didn't sound like it had anything to do with it, it did. That was only because I would sit there and think about it so that when she [Ms. Whitson] did ask me to read, I could always tell her what I was thinking about, even though I didn't have it written down yet. (Personal Communication, 1/17)

Ms. Whitson did not require the students to use the journaling in any other writing experiences. Even though she complained about the prompts' similar meanings, they sparked ideas, emotional connections, and avenues for new wisdom.

As a Vygotskian-inspired activity, these writing prompts were meant to activate language and thought. Ms. Whitson extended the writing into an oral discussion that allowed reflection and analysis, as Diana's comments reveal. Diana would willingly write in the journal and in other writing activities, which prompted personal anecdote and narrative. When the writing tasks turned to essay writing or expository writing, Diana refused to complete the assignment. As we have seen, the exception to this was the one history writing, which followed the precise expository format.

In the following excerpt from her school journal for Ms. Whitson, Diana shows her self-awareness that affects her behavior. Diana's journal captures a recurring theme in her writing—a need for positive identity, actions, and choices. Diana was planning an escape, and this journal writing gave her a private and public place to consider her options.

I provide three journal entries in which Diana comments upon her awareness of a new identity and the rules for her conduct. She sifts through her life experiences and questions their purpose. She treats these aphoristic prompts as a surrogate internal conversation. Diana shows us that it is not enough to write about her personal life, but that she needs to use these wise sayings as guidance for her personal situation or most recent crisis. Journaling encouraged that intersection. Another noticeable element is the word choice. Diana's responses echo the language and tone of the prompt, so that writing from the prompt, using the prompt's language to frame her response provided Diana with a new vocabulary that could complement a new identity, a positive identity, self-awareness, and self-control.

> I know that in myself, it took me a long time for me to know who I was. Why? Well, because I did not know who I was because mostly because I changed myself so much that I never knew what way I was supposed to act. (Journal 10/29)
>
> I now respect myself so that I can now respect others. I find these things [respecting others] is easier for me. (Journal 11/ 5)
>
> I am now able to understand that not everything happens because it was supposed to. Lots of things happen because you let it. (Journal 11/14)

Diana's journals for Ms. Whitson all had a reflective quality about them. Diana did not speculate upon the meaning of the text alone; she interpreted these prompts as wisdom about social conduct which she then translated into personal conduct for her situation. Her journal focus allowed her a place to author her life by reflecting on the past, making sense of it through the hard won experiences of her life, and then projecting a future with security and happiness.

I have often seen journaling being assigned as an initial task so that teachers can take attendance, talk with students who have been absent, or attend to other classroom details, rather than seriously using the journaling time as an invention procedure for further study and writing development. Diana revealed that the extensive use of journaling had helped her both inside and outside the classroom, and gave her a written forum to control her life and survive in and out of school. These types of writing presented her with an opportunity to gain clarity about her life and render her experiences into words, as if this process would give her clues to understanding her life and the meaning in these experiences.

The influence that the journal writing had upon Diana's composing strategies became evident when she took the State Assessment Survey (SAS), a test all tenth graders were required to take if they attend a public school. The test was given in October in two-hour periods over five consecutive days. Diana missed the day on which she had to write a composition. When she returned to school, she was called into a classroom by her counselor, along with other students who had missed phases of the exam, and ushered into a room to begin the written portion of the test.

As I sat in the back of the room, I watched Diana finish the writing in twenty minutes. Each student was given a writing prompt based upon one of Bain's four modes of discourse. Once they selected the prompt, the students had one hour to complete their composition. Diana drew the persuasive mode. In reference to her ability to address the persuasive conventions, Diana had not written a persuasive writing in Ms. Whitson's. When Diana began to answer the writing prompt, she drew her answer from the prompt's vocabulary and the most immediate and dominant immediate emotional and situational event in her life, a process she had been rehearsing all semester in Ms. Whitson's class. Despite this rehearsal writing, Diana's response exposed how the traumatic experiences prior to the test influenced Diana's writing for this test. I present sequentially the events and the writing she completed for the test.

In the week prior to the exam, Diana asked to see her counselor about her schedule for the next two years. This was usually done in the spring of the year, but Diana wanted to adjust her schedule for the spring term because she was just completing her previously failed freshman requirements. Diana had run away once during her freshman year, which explained why she was taking so many freshman level courses.

Diana and her counselor planned Diana's course selection through her senior year. By the end of the planning session, Diana had arranged her courses so that she could enter college to be a teacher or to go to law school, while she focused her remaining high school courses on parenting and child-care. She also wanted to work in the Marketing Co-op program her senior year so that she wouldn't have to be in the high school all day but could be earning money.

Diana shifted from one occupation to another without any real sense of the educational difficulty ahead, let alone the financial and emotional support she would need in order to meet her career goals. Diana left her counselor's office with a two-year plan of her life because graduating high school meant she could leave her mother.

Within a week of this meeting, Diana took a part-time job working in a local restaurant. After she had found this job, she told me that she put a cookie jar on her dresser at home and called it her college fund. She told her mother this was "only for college." Diana told her mother not to touch her money, and her mother commented that Diana would probably use the money and not be able to save it. Diana's prompt on the SAS collided with these life events. It was difficult to trace one factor as primary in explaining Diana's response to the essay prompt, but the factors together began to reveal an understandable picture of her writing process.

Diana's writing subject for the exam was the following: "Persistence paid off for the people described in the passage. Describe a time when persistence paid off in your own life. Explain how you benefited from sticking to something until it was accomplished" (SAS exam for Fall, tenth grade writing assessment). In form, Diana's response repeated the many journal responses that she had written for Ms. Whitson's class. Like the journal entries, Diana's response to the persuasive prompt contained only one paragraph and echoed recent events and the meeting with the counselor.

> When I was younger I never had or at least I felt I did not have the time to do things I often got very frustrated with many things. Now I have gotten a job and I am working towards doing bigger and better things. I really can't pick up a time when I was more persistent then I am now. I am trying to so hard now to get up grades and graduate. That is my biggest goal now. I am getting two freshman classes out of the way and [plan] on with getting my credits. I wish and hope I have a could have a chance to do this essay [again?] so then I could tell what I do or have done when already graduated. This is the only persistent time I can see in my life.

Diana wrote this response without any outline or preparation. When I asked her about preparing to write for the exam, Diana said that she knew what she wanted to say right away, but the teacher proctoring the exam made her wait until all the students taking the exam were present. She said that because of what she had been going through, she could write something about the questions that she was asked (Participant Observer Notes, 10/21). Diana seized every opportunity to plan for her future.

In reality, I now believe she was using school lessons and writing to actually build a plan for her physical escape. Each assignment and classroom learning served her goals to leave her mother, even if that meant she had to endure two more years of high school. She had a plan to leave. In this test prompt, Diana made her goals visible. However unrealistic or fantastical her plans were, with every pen stroke, she made the goal a conceivable reality. Diana never revealed to me any other intention than to finish high school and graduate. However, not long after the SAS test and the meeting with her counselor, I had a conversation with Diana's mother about her daughter.

In stark contrast to the hopeful scenario Diana created in the SAS writing and Diana's personal actions, Diana's mother was a constant focus of the emotional concerns and instability in Diana's life. I offer the following dis-cussion with Diana's mother in direct contrast to Diana's own version of her life as it is constructed through the writings in the school semester:

> Diana's mom: And you know, out of all of them, her family is the only one still in school, and it's because I make her go. They [Diana's girlfriends] were saying something about for the last week, she ain't been going because she ain't had no clean clothes, so I let her wear some of my clothes so she could stay in school. But like I was telling them last night, without a high school education, you are not going to get nowhere in this world. Not nowadays.
>
> Deb: Do you think she understands what will happen to her without a high school diploma?
>
> Diana's mom: I think she does, but for the last few days, she's been saying that she's been wanting to quit school. She's . . . Somebody said that the only way that she can quit school is if she goes to a different state, enroll and then quit then . . .
>
> Deb: This quit school business—can you pinpoint when you began hearing about this?
>
> Diana's mom: Two weeks ago. It's back. Not even two weeks ago.
>
> Deb: Did that coincide with your falling off the house?
>
> Diana's mom: No. M_____ says that he told her last night, because he told me after they left, that he told her she better stay in school and go to school.
>
> Deb: Any speculation on your part why she is talking like this now?
>
> Diana's mom: I don't know. I think it's another phase that she's going through. I mean I went through the phase of, oh my goodness, having a baby, to running away to quitting school now, so what's next?
>
> Deb: You want her to be independent and make choices?
>
> Diana's mom: Right. Nowadays I do. Because if she don't be responsible for her life as a teenager, I feel she won't be responsible for her life as she gets on her own. She won't know responsibility. But I think I'm doing a pretty good job with her, because she's not, I mean, we've done them three phases—
>
> Deb: What three phases?
>
> Diana's mom: Oh, umm, wanting to get pregnant, running away, and trying to quit school. And still more to go. (Personal Communication, 1/10)

In this passage Diana's mom outlined the cycle of adolescence, which defined her own life and now her expectations for her daughter. These parental expectations surrounded Diana's escape plan and hope for a happy future. The desperate and bleak future Diana's mother saw for her daughter mirrored her mom's past and made the vision of a different life and future for her daughter undecided.

Right after the November state exams, Diana missed almost a week of school. Whether or not Diana's absences from school right before Christmas break were really related to her lack of clean clothing or to her idea to quit school, they contradicted the journal messages and the positive benefits of persistence, which her writings recorded. The details surrounding Diana's daily existence were controlled by the unpredictable nature of her mother's moods, drinking, and male companionship. In Diana's written world, there was hope, escape, and a positive self-image; in her mother's world, there was despair, regret, and the traumatic ravages of alcoholism and neglect.

Writing to Survive—Crisis and Conflict

Diana's mother evicted Diana from their shared apartment for offenses Diana supposedly committed. These included Diana's "whoring around," running away, and disobeying her mother's orders during one of her mom's drunken stupors. While these scenes swirl around her, we have seen Diana create an alternate reality in her writing that described her secret plans to escape and graduate from high school.

To have a goal is to have some control, which gives purpose and direction to academic study, perhaps in spite of the outside forces that rise to impede the goal. The goal-driven plans worked for a while to help keep Diana focused on her studies, but life intervened and the adult support she needed to sustain her in achieving those goals was undermined by the home situation and her mother's erratic behavior. Diana could never depend on her mother for economic, emotional, or personal support: Diana's mother never attended a parent-teacher conference at the school, never inquired about Diana's progress, nor visited the school for any purpose.

This lack of visible support silently undermined the goals Diana had adamantly declared. In situations where the adult parent has neglected the adolescent's needs, the adult has the power of the oppressor, and few recourses exist that will allow the adolescent to escape such a position. In Diana's case, this oppressed adolescent wanted to survive, and she used her literacy skills and writings to compensate for what her mother couldn't provide.

In the following conversation, Diana describes why writing is her tool for controlling her emotional life.

A lot of times I don't like with her [Diana's mother]. I don't tell her my feelings all the time. I write it. Put it in my diary or something or write a letter to somebody or something. But that was my problem. I had a real emotional problem. I was a very high tempered person, It would irritate me so bad I would like . . . I would like get really mad. I would snap on that. It all came from me not saying anything, not talking to anybody. And when I went to the foster home, they noticed that. They told me they were going to put me in counseling but they never did.

It's like she said so, how do you feel when you think about my boyfriend?

I'm like . . . It's a mixed feeling. That's the time when I sit down and I'll write it all down, just write it down. How I feel. It's the only time, but when I'm happy, I'll write it down. When I'm said or confused or something I write it down. On sheets of paper or sometimes in a journal or something like in my dream notebook that has my assignments and journal in it. It's just a mixture of how I'm feeling at that moment in time, how I'm thinking about something.

And somebody talking to me. Like today, I'll put September 18, I feeling like, I see here, Oh what did you say? That's how I keep my train of thought. (Personal Communication, 9/18)

Diana wrote when she had emotional tension she couldn't control. Again, we see in this interview that Diana used the writing as a type of self-interview. The most important fact from this interview was the role writing played as the listener. It allowed her to tell and share her experiences, a place to speak when she was silenced, and in desperate need to communicate with someone.

In November, when Ms. Whitson assigned a literary analysis essay, Diana's life crises compounded in her ability to write the analysis. Again, her attention to the academic was diverted by a new crisis with her mother. Diana's mother had threatened to kick Diana out of the house if she refused to have an abortion. Diana had reestablished her relationship with an old boyfriend, who had a similar family background and was a "pharmacist." Diana worried that this boyfriend would be in jail when the baby came, since he would be serving time in jail over Thanksgiving break. To complicate the situation, Diana had left a recent boyfriend, by whom she might be pregnant, and was going to get married to another former boyfriend, and leave her mother in one year and seven months, her probable graduation date. These circumstances surrounded the literary analysis essay assignment on *Julius Caesar*, and Diana refused to write it.

Diana was worried that her "pharmacist" boyfriend would be shot because of his heavy involvement in the local drug and gang organization. She was worried that she would never see him again. He was going to be at her house on Sunday and would take her to see the house he would be buying for her to live in. I never knew how much of these jumbled romantic encounters were fantasy and how much were reality in the twisted turns and conflicts about men. While adolescents naturally seek social and romantic relationships with their peers, Diana's adult drama with men and sex only exacerbated her traumatic life and continuing desperate need to escape. Repeatedly, these personal issues absorbed her mental attention and diverted the attention from classroom tasks and learning.

After the Christmas break, Diana returned to school to finish the semester. She began to tell me about all the crises that had happened during the two-week holiday. I wondered what writing Diana did, since I knew she was keeping the private journal. Who did she talk to about these events? Where did she get advice? At the times these chaotic events occurred, how did Diana deal with them? What role did writing play when Diana experienced one of these crisis events?

> Deb: Do you write outside of school?
> Diana: At times. Besides how I feel, now that I have somebody that I can talk to like a friend, I write letter to people, I write to a certain girl. We write letter to each other. She lives in Michigan. I stopped writing my other friend because I never got a letter in return. So, I'm the type of person, hey, I write you and you don't write me back, you obviously don't want to hear from me. I won't write no more. I don't know. I guess that would be the only way that I wrote now. Letter. Or when I'm confused about something or made or just, I just can't. Mind become clear or something. The only time I write. (Personal Communication, 9/18)

Diana described that writing did serve to help her think, and that she needed to have a receptive audience to whom she authentically was corresponding. The power of the need to tell for adolescents who lived in these kinds of traumatic conditions was paramount. I found out that in addition to the private journal, Diana wrote letters to friends in Oklahoma, who sent her money to leave.

In Diana's writing, the emotional drive framed every decision and habit of reasoning Diana grasped onto for guidance and direction. This evidence suggested that writing to survive for traumatized adolescents like Diana was linked to coping strategies. Diana needed someone to tell the truth to, to share her misery and desire to escape. The letters and journals were in fact pathways to learning. Through the writing expressions, Diana could release her emotional responses to the newest crises, and then gain control over her "nerves." When this occurred, her thought processes become unblocked, as Diana described as writing so that her mind becomes "clear or something."

In these descriptive passages of life events and the intersection of literacy, writing, and crisis, Diana's story gave credence to the two different forces of crisis. In Bozhovitch's terms, Diana was seeking an identity, developing or trying to develop a self, separate from that of her mother and her mother's fate. She set goals for herself that demonstrate a self-awareness that encompasses its own kind of healing strategy. Finally, she created and used, in spite of the horrific life conditions, writing strategies that helped her compensate and survive in the world around her.

The evidence suggested that while the biological crises were progressing, she still had to control the external crises that added turmoil and impediments to her biological development. Traumatic events destabilized the progress of Diana's mental development. She did not engage in tasks that asked her to think abstractly; for example, the history assignment and the essay on *Julius Caesar*. She complied with classroom learning tasks when they were directly related to her present life situation, her traumatic history, her mother's safety, or her own escape.

Compensations in Pictures

In addition to the writing formula, the journaling compensatory strategies, Diana developed a different process for an academic writing assignment when research information was required. Diana's visual compensation process was similar to what we saw with Chase; however, Diana's process involved her ability to create a story from pictures.

After a teacher assigned an essay that required research, she would chose a general text like an encyclopedia, but the text had to have plenty of pictures. Diana viewed the pictures until they gave her a visual frame to tell her story. She searched for pictures that literally spoke to her. She could make up the research evidence by narrating what the pictures told her.

The writing process, which Diana used to write academic texts, differed from the letter and journal writing already described. By its nature, the academic essay or report writing distances the students' personal connection and evidence substitutes for the authorial anecdote. The school-based academic writing texts required a different organization and narrator point of view than Diana regularly used. In the following passage, Diana explains how she organizes her academic writing assignments and relies upon visual media to trigger words and ideas.

Diana: I try to gather all the information I can about what I'm doing. Then, when I feel like I have enough, . . . When I basically feel like I don't wanna write that much. [She laughs.] That's basically when I have enough. Hey, if I gotta have two pages, that's it. It really depends because sometimes I go over, when I do my report.

Deb: Do you take notes?

Diana: Sometimes. I just make visual notes such as pictures or something like that. I'll look at pictures that are in the book that I've gotten.

Deb: Why the pictures?

Diana: Because I feel like the pictures tell a lot more than what the words do. If you can read a picture, you know the story. I've seen that a lot and I didn't know for a long time that's how it was, but if you can read a picture you know the story. Just like if you can read a person' facial features, if you can read they see things in their face, you know who they are.

Deb: What does it have to do with the way you write?

Diana: If I can do that, then I can write down the feelings like the feelings that are in a child, like the homeless children they show on TV in the pictures. You read their feelings just by looking at them. You can tell to an extent they're happy because they have their families; they're not in a cardboard box.

Deb: Have you always done that?

Diana: No. I used to do outlines and the little spider webs where you have the subject right here and put the topic right here and do that. I used to do that in elementary school. Then, I used to do all kinds of different kinds of outlines and stuff.

Deb: What happened?

Diana: Cause I started to really, cause when I heard that thousands of words you know tells the pictures. I didn't believe it. All right. When you start to get older, you start to realize, you start to see things. Just like when M____ told [me] how he feels, this world gonna end soon. You know, I thought about that because I started to see different things happening. I started to actually see people dying and then you think about it and the world is ending and nobody knows when it could be tomorrow. You feel you have to do everything you can up to that point. You never put off, like grandma told when I was little. . . .

Deb: What do you do?

Diana: I look at the cover. And then I mean I pick out main words and stuff like that that's in the story. But I just I write it.

Deb: How do you do it?

Diana: I just write words down, and then I'll do my rough draft from the words I have on the paper and then from what I have in my mind from what I seen in the pictures, I just write it down. Like my Venezuela report. I looked at the pictures of the party and I knew all this and that. Of course, I knew all of the things about already about the quinceanera party and everything else. There's more to everything then just in the books because the book doesn't tell about the . . . It tells about the smaller parts of it. It tells about what they call lower class people. It doesn't really tell. It just says lower class.

Deb: You pick out the words, sorta make an outline, look at the pictures plus what you read and. . . ?

Diana: Then, you can write it into words.

Deb: How do you write your papers?

Diana: I think to me. I think it's how I'm feeling that day. You know, It's like it all depends upon how I am that day; how I'm feeling like I want to write it; what it is I am writing about what I am reading. (Personal Communication, 11/22)

As she clearly related in this interview exchange, she relied upon her emotions and experiences to tell her the story. Diana examined the assignment task and filtered it through a "file" of life experiences until she could select enough ideas to compose the written assignment. Every task she interpreted through her emotional lens, responded through the emotional lens, and defined her progress through that emotional lens.

In this next interview, Diana explains how these experiences determine the thinking process she uses to complete the task. Diana searches for the answer through her self-awareness born through her traumatic knowledge and its emotional counterpoint that will help her understand the work.

> Depending upon what the paper is, I can better understand. If I can understand myself, then to an extent I can understand what the assignment is asking. Then, I will look and kinda find myself and then see maybe I have some experience. It's like maybe a file inside of me, and I just flip through the file and I just start. I don't know. It helps me better understand what I am writing about. (Personal Communication, 1/17)

Diana in this discussion reiterates her dependence upon the emotional status to produce written texts. In her private or academic journals and now in these academic assignments, Diana described how she filtered the writing task through her emotional/affective lens. According to Zull (2002) and other brain researchers, this writing behavior described the "thinking" process for many traumatized individuals. Their access to memories is linked to the emotion functioning of the amygdala and the memory distribution process through the hippocampus. To ignite the emotions is to ignite the memories and experiences associated with the most recent learning task.

Behaviorally, we saw this when Diana recounted how she used her memories to narrate the pictures for the research report. Chase looked at the picture to tell him the context and meaning of the words he could imitate. Then, he adapted them to the writing assignment. Diana looked at the pictures to create a context from within her experience and to describe the picture as it allowed her to reveal her own emotional understanding.

Pictures, which Diana took from a geography/history book about Venezuela in part, wrote the report for her Spanish class on Venezuela. Diana showed me the book she was looking at for the pictures. The picture was a village celebration of a young girl's quinceañera (a Hispanic celebration that occurs on a female's fifteenth birthday, intended to announce her eligibility for marriage and adult status in the community). Given Diana's own story, the reader can understand how this celebration would be important. Diana's own personal knowledge allowed her to "read" words and combine the worlds as if they were saying the same thing. In the passage about Diana's process of reading pictures for writing, she stated that they don't tell, they just "say." She made an important distinction related to her process of composing: telling is prescriptive; saying is instructive.

In part, this language acquisition through reading pictures is a compensatory strategy surrounding Diana's created fantasy. Diana's process of saying and telling was dependent upon a formed language base and emotional coding and imaging that were built with traumatic experiences. At this time, the adolescent brain is pruning cells and needs to establish new neural links. When continued instability forces the adolescent to use her thinking skills to survive in the fight and flight mode, it would be difficult to establish reconnective patterns for developing knowledge except through the contemporary emotional responses and connected images.

In light of this understanding, Ms. Plummer's program was effective because it continued to press challenges to the adolescent's current thinking, and forced them to establish new viewpoints, positions, and values through an evolving written inquiry into a topic. In Diana's schedule of classes, no classroom pedagogy arranged learning the way she needed to learn. Even though Ms. Whitson's instruction included relevant writing and telling activities, these were not consistent, connected, or integrated with conflict and adolescent crises. These occurred by chance not design.

The pictures of familiar cultural activities allowed Diana to project into the picture her own story. The picture "says" because Diana can interject fantasies and the text in the book in a clear and inclusive narrative. Diana can place her invented or real life experiences and desires within her reading of the picture, and then transfer that to her writing about the subject.

Final Crises

Diana wrote three letters during the final days of this research project, when she was looking for someone to communicate with. As a result, a friend in Oklahoma, Jose, sent her $98.00 so that she could buy a ticket to Oklahoma City and leave her mother. One week after the letter arrived, Diana's mother kicked her out of the house. When Diana returned, her mother kicked her out again, and Diana ended up staying with a female police officer.

In the second letter, to her Michigan friend, Diana told her friend that she knew all the answers in her English class about the novel they were reading, *Jane Eyre*. Diana watched the film; she said, "I did not read the book, but I did see the movie." Like Chase, Diana relied upon the visual medium to do the work for her. In Diana's case, the reading time was sacrificed so that she could either work or avoid being at home.

In a third letter to a friend, Diana bounced from subject to subject: her need to find a special guy, the latest novel she had to read in class, her college application hopes in attending either Oklahoma City University or Sonoma State in California and then right back to the movie she had watched. Her letters read like a flight of ideas, disjointedly narrating what she was facing in her life, but with a lightness that betrayed the real tragedy in her life.

On December 24, Diana returned home in the morning to find that her mother had called the police, reported her as a runaway, and was going to kick her out again. When Diana talked to the police officer, he told her that her mother cannot do that. He then instructed Diana to call him if anything happened. Diana retorted by saying that something bad was going to happen that day. After the officer left, Diana's mother and boyfriend began drinking. Diana left. When she returned about 6:00 p.m., she found her mother on the ground surrounded by paramedics and police officers. Her mother had jumped off the roof trying to fly with Santa's reindeer.

What We Learn From Diana

Diana's social world was the most dysfunctional and brutal among adolescents I researched. Within the evidence of her writing and narrations, there were significant psychological issues that I was not qualified to address, but that were nonetheless related to Diana's daily life: the cutting, her mother's alcoholism, and financial neglect. The mother-daughter issues alone were significantly plaguing Diana's ability to learn in school. While these life crises existed as context for every day Diana lived, we saw how the school day and classroom activities only unintentionally addressed any of her traumatic history.

Diana's life situations controlled what she learned and how she applied that learning. We saw her make both visual and literacy compensations to ensure her survival in school so that she could escape out of school. Adolescents will adapt, change, or transform the classroom lessons into life lessons, especially for those students who need to make compensations. To survive in the social world, adolescents like Diana need relevant and personal literacy acts that allow them to build practical life-saving learning.

Since we have examples of a wide range of written texts Diana completed, we are able to see where Diana engaged with writing—when it served her purpose. Even though the writing pedagogy in Ms. Whitson's class offered writing opportunities in multiple genres, the eventual purpose in those writing assignments was to direct them to literary analysis essays. We saw examples of how Diana rejected more abstract composition unless the purpose of the composition was self-serving in a personal and rhetorically exigent way.

Diana's story is an illustration of how important connection and choice are to a student who struggles with her daily life in ways that prevent her from engaging in tasks more expository forms require. Diana may be capable of abstracted thought, but her life writings reveal a reasoning process initiated by her emotional connections. Ms. Whitson's journal writing tasks have purpose and design intended to engage students in thinking and writing that will affect their ability to write more analytical compositions. While Ms. Whitson continues this discussion into the classroom dialogue, Diana relied upon this form of self-expression.

I conclude that Diana relied upon this form not because of its rehearsal with the journal writing, but because it was an easy formula for self-expression. Extending the discussion into more abstract thinking beyond her immediate needs would be limited unless the tension and trauma she carried with her were resolved and eased. Writing with choice and connection that is directly personal provided a type of therapeutic writing forum that made learning and writing relevant.

When Diana engaged in these types of tasks, she made progress in academic subjects through the personal meaning it provided to her daily survival. In terms of adolescent development, the need for identity and self-expression are markers of growth that should be attached to every writing and literacy task in the classroom. This connection and directed personal purpose are especially relevant for students with traumatic histories.

As teachers of language arts, our tools are all matters of language use. Letting Diana or Danielle or Chase write about whatever they want, without a directed purpose related to their traumatic needs, does not facilitate learning. When the classroom doesn't provide or facilitate the needs, these adolescents make compensations. I am not saying that all adolescents don't make these types of compensations, but for adolescents like Diana they are lifelines to survival and success. It is all connected: writing, choice, connection, recovery, resiliency, and learning. For adolescents who live with traumatic stresses like Diana, writing is a pathway to recovery and resiliency. We have seen when the writing pedagogy complements the behavioral manifestations of trauma, then teachers need to connect writing tasks with personal choice in subject, sustained inquiry, and revision. Ms. Whitson' pedagogy contained only part of the formula.

In Ms. Whitson's writing pedagogy, Diana found some personal connections in the journaling and informal writing assignments. Diana specifically told us that what was important in these tasks was her need for an authentic audience to whom she told her story. She also relied upon the story narrative whether in revealing her own life's story or in the construction of a required report. The power to control their worlds with language and use it for purposes they themselves decide was to empower the students. The key resides in the consistency and repetition of editing and shaping that accompany the construction of any writing. It is not just the linear sequence of the writing process model, which had very little effect upon Diana's composing growth, but the expressive need to tell her story to others who could relate to its raw truth with reciprocal understanding.

Even the simplest forms of writing like letters or notes or journal entries carry the essential components of empowerment and control, even though the written products don't become literary examples. The goal is the immediate and productive use of writing in a child's life, not the post secondary employment or college emphasis that often directs writing tasks. That is not the way the adolescents in this research project used writing. They used writing and learning to control vagaries of their lives and traumatic conditions through words and in words. Therefore, writing tasks and instructions have to address the immediate contexts in which the adolescents understand their lives and experiences.

What is especially important here is that the goal for teaching of writing to adolescents has paradigmatically shifted. A teacher now teaches writing to help the adolescents use their lived experiences as prior knowledge upon which to base the writing instruction. These instructional patterns include direct instruction into specific language use and more sophisticated writing skills that give greater power to the adolescents to tell, instead of preparing them to write college essays and write resumes for employment. If a student can express and control their ideas and thoughts, then the forms mentioned are matters of learning a few conventions. In spite of their dysfunctional social world, adolescents can learn in distress when these situations are welcomed into the writing classroom. This would be teaching the way adolescents learn.

Finally, we learn that adolescents use the writing to control what is within their power to control; under the social and educational restrictions they have, the adolescents find ways to use that knowledge in creative ways to take action in their worlds. The more desperate the situation, the more need they have for learning how to use language and writing for empowerment. As a result, we have seen that adolescents transform themselves through the relevant learning and writing that they need to survive.

Part II

Finding a Purpose for Writing
After Disaster Strikes

Chapter 6

Research Methodology for New Orleans Public High Schools

NATURAL DISASTERS AND TRAUMATIC STRESS OVERVIEW

The tsunami in Indonesia, 9/11 in New York, and a hurricane named Katrina present, with unprecedented clarity, the violence man and nature can impose. The world began to wake up to its unpreparedness to handle these public disasters when media viewers saw the pleading cries of hurricane victims left to suffer for days without assistance. Not only was there a lack of communication, resources, and failure of some agencies to provide immediate assistance, there were hesitating responses about how these disasters would affect individuals, neighborhoods, and the larger communities.

Not everyone experienced firsthand the devastation Katrina brought; yet, it touched everyone who depended upon the infrastructure and services in the city, especially those attached to the schools. The educational problems in New Orleans were only compounded and exacerbated by the upheaval Katrina caused. Like violence and abuse, the natural disaster wrecked the stability in education for many adolescents, already just surviving day to day. Whether it was abuse, violence, or the natural disaster, these critical life events caused stress in adolescents' lives. This additional unexpected crisis brought another layer to an already stressed life.

Critical life events are situations, happenings, or occasions that have a shocking or unexpected consequence for an individual. A natural disaster is a critical life event that may cause traumatic stresses. According to the American Psychiatric Association, "Features that distinguish traumatic events include the following: sudden and unexpected events; the shocking nature of such events; death or threat to life or bodily integrity; and/or subjective feeling of intense terror, horror or helplessness" (Cohen, Mannarino, & Deblinger, 2006, p. 3). The hurricane and the resulting natural disaster in Louisiana qualify as a traumatic event. While not everyone who experiences a natural disaster develops traumatic stress disorders, people do experience stress as they attempt to recover their lives in the affected area.

The response to the traumatic event manifests itself in specific ways. Adults may experience sleeplessness, numbness, recurring nightmares and replay of the event, inability to focus, inattentiveness, emotional outbursts, paranoia, more aggressive physical behavior to physical illness, new physical disabilities or debilitating pain. In adults, these symptoms may be light to severe depending upon the depth of the trauma.

Traumatic stress may manifest itself within days of the critical life event or over considerable time. The trauma an individual experiences after a natural disaster may be compounded by other critical life events that have preceded the disaster event. In this case, healing the trauma may depend upon the adult's coping strategies, abilities to communicate or discuss feelings, or release the stress induced by the trauma.

Stress imposes physical damage to the brain and body. "Given that the function and structure of the brain are interactive with our life experiences, thoughts, feelings and behaviors, it would make sense that a return to more adaptive psychological functioning would be associated with corresponding normalization of brain functioning and perhaps structure" (Cohen et al., 2006, p. 14). This description suggests that therapeutic (or other) interventions that result in re-regulation of a person's emotional, cognitive, and behavioral functioning can minimize or reverse the adverse impact of trauma on the brain and body.

In adolescents, "Some professionals believe that only certain types of therapeutic activities can access pathways for brain changes, and that 'talking' therapies that do not include specified, physical activities cannot create meaningful brain or bodily changes in traumatized children" (Cohen et al., 2006, p.15). When we consider the natural pruning and brain development that is normal to adolescent growth, the added stress of a life crisis event adds greater imperative to our understanding of how to academically assist re-regulation of brain functions after a crisis event. This process makes it necessary to reduce an adolescent's stress, and therefore, engage learning and cognitive functions through various types of literacy activities like story telling and writing.

The citations above suggest that physical and vocal activities combined with stress reducing activities can help an adolescent or adult achieve normal brain function and learning potential. In applying the research evidence to classrooms and teaching instruction, the physical and vocal activities may mean a dramatic change in classroom practice, content, and instructional techniques immediately following a natural disaster and possibly for several years after the event.

TRAUMATIC STRESS AND ADOLESCENTS

In the United States, research on how disasters affect the literacy development of adolescents has been growing (Dyregrov & Mitchell, 1992; *English Journal* 96.2., 2006; UNICEF, 2004; Whittaker, 2004). Since Hurricane Katrina and Hurricane Andrew, research investigations into how these natural disasters have affected children and adolescents has revealed that the disaster event is over quickly, but the physical and mental consequences can last months and years beyond the event (Brock, Lazarus, & Jimerson, 2006). In a study of Nicaraguan adolescents (Goenjian et al., 2001), the researchers found that youths in "heavily affected areas experienced chronic and severe levels of post traumatic stress and depressive symptoms" (p. 439).

Three research studies (Dyregrov & Mitchell, 1992; Reijneveid, Crone, & Verhulst, 2003; Warheit et al., 1996) show that adolescents experiencing the stresses from a natural disaster demonstrate behavioral changes that can signal depression, stress, and an increase in risky behaviors. In a study by Vogel and Vernberg (Barrett, Ausbrooks, & Martinez-Cosio, 2008), "[the researchers] noted studies finding high levels of fear, depression, survival guilt, and physical complaints as well as reduction in academic performance and abilities to concentrate" (p. 203). These studies provide much needed information for teachers who have students affected by a natural disaster in the classroom. The research suggests noticeable changes in students' academic performance and abilities to concentrate. As a result, these changes require instructional modifications and accommodations.

Adolescents do not have the same abilities as adults to cope with the stress and trauma of a natural disaster. They learn coping strategies from their parents' responses and behaviors during crises. So not only are their coping strategies different, their obvious physical and emotional responses differ from those of adults. Adolescents can experience emotional numbness, inability to focus or retain attention, angry outbursts, hopelessness, insomnia, feelings of insecurity, recurring nightmares in which they replay the events, and finally make poor decisions by engaging in risky behavior, as reported by the National Institute of Mental Health (http://www.nimh.nih.gov/healthinformation/ptsdmenu.cfm).

The physical and cognitive behaviors associated with trauma and resulting stress in children and adolescents manifest themselves in the following ways: "children may try to avoid any thoughts, people, places or situations that remind them of their traumatic experience" (Cohen et al., 2006, p.9). "These children may avoid healthy age-appropriate peer interactions" (Cohen et al., 2006, p.10). For adolescents, this means that they may engage in more risky behaviors regarding sex, drugs, and alcohol as well as committing petty crimes. Some adolescents withdraw emotionally and become unresponsive; others will act out aggressively, and fighting may become more violent and frequent. Benign challenges in the classroom and in social situations can erupt into intense and violent physical conflicts.

Perhaps most disturbing among adolescents' responses to trauma is that adolescents lose trust in adults. In school, teachers have to work to reestablish trust with their students. Through consistency and established routine, teachers can regain trust; however, the cycle of distress can recur when the possibility of a disaster reappears. This lack of trust and possible disaster recurrence compound the behavioral responses already mentioned and create alternate goals for incorporating adolescent behavior into post-natural disaster classroom pedagogy.

TRAUMA, STRESS, AND LEARNING

Before I could really understand how a natural disaster affected the pedagogical practices of teachers and their students, I needed to understand what stress a natural disaster would cause and how it would affect learning. Our understanding of these conditions prepares us to recognize conditions that affect an adolescent's learning, literacy, and a teacher's ability to teach. The stories in Part II analyze and illustrate how the natural disaster affected adolescents' learning and how teaching these students requires a different academic approach, very similar to the student stories in Part I. These stressed adolescents make similar compensations in their literacy practices as students affected by violence and abuse. Yet, the English language arts teachers and the adolescents they teach both experienced the disaster, and together they negotiate the disruption and irregular cadence to learning in this new disaster situation.

While I do not attempt any diagnosis of Post Traumatic Stress Disorder (PTSD), I think it is important to highlight the possibility that some of the research informants suffered to some degree the effects of PTSD. According to the DSM-IV (Reid & Wise, 1995), the essential features of PTSD for adults follows an event "that is extremely traumatic and experienced with intense fear, terror, and/or helplessness. The event must be directly experienced, observed, or related to a family member or other close associate" (p. 189). Critical features of PTSD in adults are the following (p. 191):

1. Persistent avoidance of stimuli associated with the trauma and numbing of general responsiveness as indicated by three of the following:
   a. efforts to avoid thoughts, feelings, or conversations associated with the trauma;
   b. efforts to avoid activities, places, or people that arouse recollections of the trauma;
   c. inability to recall an important aspect of the trauma;
   d. markedly diminished interest or participation in significant activities;
   e. feeling of detachment or estrangement from others;
   f. restricted range of affect (e.g., unable to have loving feelings);
   g. sense of foreshortened future.
2. Persistent symptoms of increased arousal as indicated by the following:
   a. difficulty falling asleep or staying asleep;
   b. irritability or outburst of anger;
   c. difficulty concentrating;
   d. hyper vigilance;
   e. exaggerated startle response.

These features are relevant to this discussion in terms of the teacher behaviors and changes made within the classroom. In adults, traumatic stress may manifest itself within days of the critical life event or take years. In two of the teacher informants, these symptoms affected their classroom practice and the writing tasks they assigned to adolescents in their classroom.

One concern about the effects of stress and trauma is its ability to interrupt intellectual development in adolescents. The brain's normal processing system is interrupted by the physiological reactions to the stress caused by the trauma. The brain's response to the stress from the traumatic event can be viewed as a "freeze" to cognitive processes (van der Kolk, McFarlane, & Weisaeth, 1996) and "thinking" now becomes reliant upon emotional responses and memory making aspects in the brain, the amygdala and hippocampus. These organs make up part of the limbic system, the system that triggers action to fight or flight when it senses danger or fear.

Alice Brand and van der Kolk have studied neurological functions under stress and have outlined the processes of brain activity. Critical to our understanding of these brain processes is to understand the two important areas in the brain: amygdala and hippocampus, which are directly affected by traumatic stress as well as by biological growth and development in respect to thinking and feeling. Figure 6.1 shows the major cognitive and emotive systems (reprinted with permission from Berger, 2006).

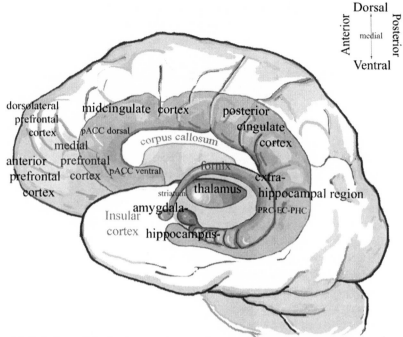

Medial view of the brain superimposed on the lateral view. Abbreviations:
PRC-perirhinal cortex; EC-entorhinal cortex; PHC-parahippocampus;
pACC-perigenual anterior cingulate cortex. Reprinted with permission
from Berger (2006).

Figure 6.1.   Brain Image with Amygdala and Hippocampus

In the schematic view of the brain, we focus on the anatomical segments for
memory. The hippocampus creates the distribution pattern for memory and
the amygdala processes emotions. "Most obvious, as the feelings ascend the
biochemical pathways and arrive in consciousness, one way to express and/
or communicate them is by naming them" (Brand in Anderson & MacCurdy,
2000, p. 204). Thus, by naming something we bring it fully into consciousness and can at that point reflect, direct, and alter its meaning.

What this information reveals to teachers and educators is the importance
of adjusting instruction to provide activities that would encourage the flow
of emotion and memory. Since the abstract thinking processes or higher level
cognitive functions may be frozen, these activities encourage the release of
the block. By inviting learning and literacy activities that complement this
"freeze," teachers can unlock the pathways and reestablish literacy-making
processes.

My readers may understand this process as they can refer to a time in their own lives when a critical life event jolted them. Unexpected as it may have been, we go on living with automatic behaviors and responses. We rely upon our habitual patterns of living when our concentration and ability to think beyond the moment lie in a numb fog. Until we adjust to the crisis and the trauma it brings, we have to have help finding our way out of the fog. This describes the case for many adolescents who have experienced the trauma of disaster conditions.

There is a way out. For teachers, I am not suggesting that we all become psychologists in addition to our teaching credentials, but we recognize that these brain "freezes" are affecting the literacy abilities of students in our classrooms. For adolescents, the amygdala relays sensory information, and may account, along with biological development, for the passionate drives of "flow" discussed by Csikszentmihalyi and Larson (1984). "Events passing through the amygdala are rapidly learned and long lasting. What's more, once our emotional system learns something, we may never let it completely go. This means that in any given situation, fundamental feeling may be more immediate than the intellect, however crucial both are for learning and remembering" (Brand in Anderson & MacCurdy, 2000, p. 209).

Given the psychological effects of trauma and stress from a disaster, memory of the images and the feelings attached to them are stored and processed through the amygdala and the hippocampus. The hippocampus stores and processes the recollection of events, which Alice Brand cites as the key to intellectual functioning (Brand in Anderson & MacCurdy, 2000, p. 206). If we are to accommodate and compensate for the changes in brain function after a natural disaster, understanding how the brain operates is crucial to making the right adjustments. This understanding leads to considerations of how healing can be facilitated.

If we accept the idea that stresses from trauma can inhibit normal brain functioning, then it remains for us to find ways to facilitate and restore learning possibilities since for adolescents and children development continues regardless of the interruptions. In these important biological developments interrupted by life crisis events, precious development time can be lost. As teachers, we have the tools of language to assist us in creating a restorative classroom environment that can accommodate various levels of stress and trauma.

Several recent research articles provide evidence that the stresses from the Katrina disaster trauma affect children and adolescents (Weems & Overstreet, 2008). Left untreated, the effects of the disaster can linger and affect future living conditions (Goenjian et al., 2001). These research studies corroborate reports completed after the Indonesian Tsunami (UNICEF, 2004) and describe the reactions among adolescents. One research study outlines the ways in which adolescents were affected by Katrina and the resulting flooding, but its major point draws attention to the fact that individuals who work with adolescents need to recognize the ways in which they are affected by disasters (Reich & Wadsworth, 2008).

How Writing Works to Heal the Trauma

In the immediate time after a disaster, returning to school can be the safest place for children and adolescents. While there was a need to achieve a normal instructional rhythm, teachers also needed to incorporate more writing and narration into the daily instructional activities, as the adolescent and teacher stories in this section reveal. Yet, an additional complication emerges in a natural disaster context that didn't exist in the first case studies.

Every teacher in the stories from New Orleans was in some way touched by the destruction Katrina wrought. In the first series of case studies, none of the teachers to my knowledge had experienced any form of abuse, neglect, or violence in their personal life histories. In this section, the teachers are as much affected by their need for safety, reestablishment of order and routine, and resiliency, as the adolescents in the case studies.

This is a book about writing to survive the experiences that cause trauma and stress in the lives of adolescents, but the thesis moves beyond just adolescents. The teachers of adolescents also can learn about healing psychological wounds through writing about them. Writing about the critical life events that have shaped and changed our lives can also assist in the healing of those wounds, but the writing teachers did existed with their instructional compensations. Before the reader labels this kind of writing or theory as scripto-therapy and only a technique for psychologists, psychiatrists, and counselors, the information presented in this chapter and in chapter 1 were intended to ground any discussion of writing literacy and the compensatory strategies not just in sociocultural theories of mind, but also within scientific facts of biological processes. Integrating the adolescent brain processing into the ethnographic study of adolescents provides a more powerful understanding of the adolescent discourses and the language they use to shape the world they live in.

In discussions with high school English teachers on the goals of teaching writing to adolescents, I often hear voices that shout the need for more literate, productive, and skilled workers for the market. The subtext I hear is that teaching English language arts is about economics and productivity, not about building learners and skilled users of knowledge, who can use their literacy skills to heal, to inspire to create and express their ideas and emotions, and most of all to survive.

Rather than teaching language to strengthen how one lives in the world, we spend countless hours of teaching English language arts to meet the standardized tests and ever-present classroom mantra of "You are going to need this." I am suggesting that we teach writing and literacy to assist adolescents in naming and making sense of their experiences. In doing that, they will learn to use written literacies to work in the world as well as to make meaning of it. Empowerment is foregrounded in the teaching and in making content decisions.

The work of Paolo Freire (1970) testifies to the power of teaching language to name the world and the transformative power naming provides an individual person. This same consciousness of language is necessary for those who have been hurt by traumatic events and stresses. If we really want our children and students to be successful, then we need to empower them with language skills that can bring them to realizations, reflections, learning, and healing. By extension, these principles for teaching language and literacy also address the pedagogical interventions needed for children who have traumatic stresses and debilitating life crises.

This shift in perspective about the brain, writing, trauma, and healing requires a shift in our teaching and classroom pedagogy. As educators, we can use this knowledge to complement the emotional needs of students in classrooms who have experienced natural disasters and developed various levels of stress from the trauma. Telling stories about the event is the initial way to debrief individuals about what they have experienced (Dyregrov, 1991). According to Dyregrov, the first phase of debriefing is to get the individuals to tell the story attending to the details of sound, sight, smell, and vision without also responding emotionally.

This initial process works to begin the debriefing or healing process by helping the individual recall the event. We know from neurological explanations about brain function and stress, the emotional or limbic brain areas are working. The amygdala and the hippocampus work together to recreate the images and emotional responses that the recollection stirs. By using words to describe the event, the individual now gains some cognitive control over the images and emotions. In following the debriefing pattern, the individual will again tell the story and reflect upon it with emotional detail added to the sensory detail. Each time the individual revisits the story, another layer of detail or attention refocuses the story and provides more psychological distance.

When the oral stories are converted to written texts, the individual has an even greater opportunity to provide a cognitive control over the event. In the revision process of the event, the individual must address sentence structure or logical detail and sequence of the narrative. By "distraction" of the structural and grammatical revisions and added information, the individual gains control over the words, and over the event. This operation needs to continue over time by adding objective information and inquiry to the existing story.

One author, Marian Mesrobian MacCurdy, has detailed the process of writing about trauma not only to describe how to teach writing but the effects such writing has upon the individual who tells. In her book *The Mind's Eye* (2007), she relates the writing process with individuals who have experienced trauma and explains how the brain processes operate with the mediating activity of writing.

> First, by unlocking these traumatic experiences from the parts of the brain that store iconic images and allowing us to put words to our difficult moments, writing is not only cathartic but it also creates understanding; we can realize just how bad we felt, that we are not going crazy, that indeed these traumas were hard to endure. Our emotions are validated. Second, writing can join the cognitive and emotional, resulting in a sense of control over that which we cannot control: the past. Writing produces a sense of agency that the trauma has threatened. We write our trauma; our trauma does not write us. (p. 2)

The individual's experience is not realized until she engages in necessary and unavoidable conflict with experience, additional inquiry into the event and the surrounding details. These processes allow alternate responses to the event and personal control over the experiences. Like so many violent, abusive critical life events, a natural disaster takes away an individual's control over his life. Recasting that experience in words helps to heal the stresses and trauma by helping the individual learn through a rendering of the events.

Susan Burkett in the "The Butterfly Effect" narrates the progress an adult student makes over his drug and alcohol addictions by creating a narrative that describes his experiences:

> The process of writing allowed David to collect his memories of traumatic events, to focus on select ones, to elaborate, probe, and discover new relationships within them, to see beyond them, to find the new pattern, the new butterfly within him. Discovering the new pattern, David saw himself anew. Integrating patterns of powerlessness, trauma and change composed him, made him sane, and redeemed him. He called it by name. (Brand & Graves, 1994, p. 197)

This is not to say that these strategies are painless. The imagery recall and the emotional connections, which arise in memory and emotion, may cause individuals to cry and reexperience the event. Using imagery recall creates some difficult choices when working with adolescents, and the primary rule for asking someone to tell or write about their experiences is to also recognize and embrace their refusal to do so. With adolescents, as we see in the case of

Lydia, she and her brother refused to discuss the death of their best friend in Katrina's flooding.

Other literacy practices such as oral story telling (Dyregrov & Mitchell, 1992), writing as journaling, story telling, painting and drawing, and other creative arts, can be used to assist healing after traumatic events. These activities are useful in dealing with smaller children and adolescents who may have difficulty telling their experiences. The orientation here is that adolescents be given repeated opportunities to express their emotions, and they create the iconic images that are stored in memory.

These kinds of activities extended over time and with varying degrees of additional information gathering activities allow adolescents to process what happened to them and to gain control over the events. This is especially important because adolescents who are experiencing traumatic stress can lose trust in adults and withdraw into a world of hopelessness. Regaining perspective on what happened to them encourages a hopeful future as well as reestablishes trust with responsible adults. For some students, the teachers in the school have long-term contact with adolescents and can initially offer the supportive classroom environment needed to provide safety, security, and routine.

Teaching Students Affected by a Natural Disaster

My goal is not to place additional responsibilities on teachers as counselors or therapists, but to bring attention to the fact that these kinds of critical life events do inhibit learning in our students, and do affect the way they process the information and knowledge we expect them to learn in the classroom. I find myself saying something like this over and over and over again in my methods classes. Is *Romeo and Juliet* the only play that will teach students about English Renaissance drama? Is that what you are teaching? If not, then why do they have to read that play and learn about it? What is it that they are learning?

I usually am faced with a wide range of twisted expressions from a blank stare, to bewilderment, to some kind of recognition. It takes a while for the student teachers to get the "what" they are teaching when they teach any English language art, including literary samples. We cannot use the same tactics or materials or literary samples as that of traditional classroom practice. While some teachers resist the mandate to change their teaching, teachers after 9/11 found that "students' stories needed to be told so that they could comprehend the situation" (Calliouet in *English Journal*, p. 28).

Several research articles appeared after Katrina that coalesced information and pedagogical practices that would facilitate healing and learning after a natural disaster. When we think about the recovery from a natural disaster as creating stress from the trauma of that experience, we recognize that this requires academic adjustments in teaching students. Because the traumatic experience affects the brain's ability to process the emotional and iconic memory of the experience, the individual has a lack of focus; inability to concentrate for long periods of time, along with poor sleep and recurring images of the experience. These deprivations may cause adolescents to withdraw, or become more volatile, easier to move into physical violence, angry outbursts, and impatient scenes. They lose focus on a future and lose trust in adults.

According to research after the Indonesian Tsunami and published after Katrina (UNICEF, 2004), teachers need to address their students' psychological needs for support, safety, and routine. In the early days of returning to school, the research suggests teachers engage students in class discussions about what happened. These initial activities can be oral stories or written stories. After a teacher has explored what happened to the students, the lessons need to be presented in small units with multiple practice sessions over the same information (Alvarez, 2010, submitted for publication).

While teachers can resume a disciplinary based course of study, the activities still need to include activities of celebration or emotional release as the students begin the process of recovery. In the natural disaster, the process of recovery is a visible process, which in New Orleans was reflected in the state of mind of the students. This mirroring of recovery can be drawn into the classroom activities; in fact, it is crucial to do so.

The initial activities that allow for the release of the stress from the traumatic event need to be followed over time by inquiry into the natural disaster. This kind of investigation adds definition to each individual's experience, and provides an avenue through which to direct mental energy and place the adolescents within a proactive arena. They can work for the greater good of their community and take their experience and awareness into a philanthropic activity. This kind of involvement was especially relevant after the Indonesian tsunami, when so many children lost their parents that the older children and teachers began to find ways for the younger ones to be helpful and contribute to the recovery of their community, if not to their own lives.

Compensatory Strategies and the Natural Disaster

In the literacy practices and acts surrounding a natural disaster, adolescents still make compensations, just as they do in cases of other traumatic crises from violence and abuse. In this section, the reader will see more dramatic uses of specific literacy acts that speak more to the determination of adolescents to make compensations when they need to survive. They make these compensations based upon the exigent needs that are related to the survival conditions and any preexisting abuse and violent experiences. These include making up words and phrases that reflect their Katrina experience, refusing to complete written tasks, and finding alternate media to express their sorrows and distresses.

Other compensations emphasize orality over written literacy, yet the strategies are part of the literate compensations adolescents are making to maintain or regain a sense of normal. To the natural disaster victims, reestablishing a normal pattern or rhythm meant having control. Unlike the adolescent stories where abuse and violence had not affected all the members in the adolescent's life, the natural disaster eliminates personal control for everyone in some way. In that, achieving a new normal is imperative to regaining control.

In the three adolescent case studies for this section, the adolescents have distinct literacy practices, similar to those of the adolescents in Part I. Each of their compensatory strategies is intertwined with the disaster responses and stresses. However, in this section, I focus more heavily upon the teachers and their classroom pedagogy because their stories encompass the many layers a disaster has upon the teacher, the adolescents, and the community around them.

In each case, I focus more closely upon the writing assignments, lessons, and tasks assigned in English language arts classrooms. In Part I, I focused on the adolescents and their compensatory strategies in and out of school. In Part II, while I still discuss the compensatory strategies of the adolescents related to their stresses from Hurricane Katrina, the teacher data revealed that they too developed compensations, which emerged in their teaching strategies. Two of the teachers, Ms. Martin and Ms. Jane, experienced severe distress from the hurricane ignited by the loss of all their personal possessions and property. In their classroom pedagogy and philosophies about teaching adolescents, they could not dismiss their own traumatic stresses and its effects upon their teaching.

The teachers' compensatory strategies made them sensitive to addressing their own hardships after Katrina. To avoid or divert these uncomfortable references, Ms. Jane only tangentially references Katrina, and then when she does, she uses literature with thematic content that she knows will ignite references, feelings, and possibly discussion about Katrina. When Ms. Jane's emotional stresses improve, she finds that her classroom instruction and student behaviors also improve.

For Ms. Martin, her teaching philosophy and instructional pattern connects real life discussion with literary themes. Instead of avoiding these difficulties from Katrina, she engages students in direct discussion, writing tasks, and teaching materials and films that create a common understanding about how this hurricane affected everyone in her classroom, including Ms. Martin. She had firsthand experience with Katrina's savage forces, and openly commiserates with the students and brings literary activities and tasks to complement the commonly shared knowledge about Katrina in her classroom.

The one female adolescent, Lydia, developed compensatory strategies after she experienced the traumatic stresses that plagued adolescents in classrooms throughout New Orleans. In the second case study, Tyrone, the story is not one of abuse, violence, or traumatic stresses. Tyrone and his family escaped the flooding and hurricane disaster, and as a result, he didn't experience the same hardships or losses that the other stories illustrate. In spite of this, Tyrone developed his own compensatory strategies in juxtaposition to the strategies developed by his peers and his teachers.

RESEARCH LOCATION II—NEW ORLEANS

A Vignette

Everyone knows about Mardi Gras, Bourbon Street, the French Quarter, the winding Mississippi, jambalaya, and jazz. Some may even remember that we purchased Louisiana from Napoleon, who needed the money to finance his war in Europe. New Orleans is a magical place that has brewed a fine mixture from the ethnic cultures over historical time into a drink that satisfies the most difficult of palates. It is a city that does not apologize for its history but embraces the sedimentary layers of race, geography, and culture that have formed cultural fertile ground: Spanish, French, African, Cajun, Acadian, German, Italian, and Native American. Wedged between the crescent movement of the Mississippi River and Lake Pontchartrain, the below-sea-level city survives amid the forces of nature that would put it under the brackish water of the lake, sea, and river. The marshes surrounding the city and water table realities account for the unusual cemeteries lined with white-painted mausoleums. Marie La Veau, the famous voodoo priestess, lies in one such cemetery, and her gravesite is a major tourist destination.

Café du Monde survived Katrina's bashing, and it opened as soon as the all-clear was given in the city. As one of the oldest businesses in the French Quarter, the café still serves a chicory coffee latte and beignets, a New Orleans tradition. Across Decatur Street and down a few blocks from the Café is the Central Market, home to the muffalleta sandwich. It is a mouthwatering combination of olive salad, salami, pepperoni, and cheeses served on round Italian bread, freshly baked. Driving north on Esplanade Avenue, one can then find Liuzza's on the Track. This small community bar and restaurant serves the best bar-b-q-shrimp Po'boy sandwich. Mmm . . . Smells of Cajun and Creole cooking waft from the street. From the exclusive French restaurants in the Quarter like Commander's Palace to the small restaurant serving fried catfish swimming in butter and greens to the oyster Po'boy sandwiches, New Orleans serves a delightful feast for anyone willing to experiment with these tasty combinations.

This city known for its bawdy French Quarter, sultry jazz, Cajun and Creole cuisine, and its celebratory spirit also carries a history of racial and social injustices that reflect the many ideological battles about race and culture in the United States. Its schools have the academic reputation of being among the worst in the United States, reflected in the dilapidated structures McDonogh money built.

St. Charles Street divides the rich and poor sides of town. The few streetcars still running outline the long held economic and racial divisions of the city. Tulane University and Loyola University lie amongst the stately southern mansions built along the banks of the curving Mississippi, some of the highest ground in the New Orleans area. On the opposite side of town sit Southern University, Dillard University, and the University of New Orleans, formerly known as LSU at New Orleans.

On the downtown side, we have the Bywater, the Faubourg Marigny, the Seventh Ward—and after Katrina, we all know about the familiar but devastated Ninth Ward and St. Bernard Parish. Behind the buildings that line the streets lie poverty, economic racism, academic mismanagement, besides a long list of "good ol' boy" traditions that robbed resources and finances from those who deserved and needed them most. Easy to see driving along Board Street, Esplanade, Elysian Fields, St. Bernard, and others reminiscent of a Tennessee Williams play.

In late March and only in New Orleans, men compete in the "Stella Calling" contest in the Tennessee Williams festival.

Every aspect of living in such a place, the food, the drinks, the music, art, housing, has a long historical tradition that a little floodwater could not wash away. From the moment I stepped off the plane at Louis Armstrong International Airport, out onto the interstate lined with lampposts with fleur-de-lis on top, I was in love with this place. My Spanish heritage found a comfortable welcome and identification in the historical complexity of this city. The food, the music, the festivals, celebrations, and the long history we have shared as a people in becoming a United States has a place in New Orleans. "Laissez les bon temps rouler." Forever.

RESEARCH METHODOLOGY IN
NEW ORLEANS—PART II

Long before New Orleans was purchased by the United States, the Spanish and French, who gradually pushed away the Native American populations, had originally settled it. Acadians from Canada escaped down the Mississippi and built a culture we know as Cajun. Another culture was building between the African female slaves and the European men who settled New Orleans.

These "marriages" produced another culture unique to New Orleans, called Creole. While there is much dispute about what ethnic groups make up a Creole, part of it began in the questionable nineteenth century tradition of the "plaçage," a practice of arranging the liaison of beautiful African American women to European men of means. In effect, this created legitimate bigamy practices by allowing men of means to have two separate families in two separate areas of the city.

New Orleans was also the only place where African men of color could be free and own property, but there was always a geographical divide when it came to where free men of color owned property. One of the places is called the Tremé, a corner section of which still exists on the northern end of the French Quarter.[1]

The French Quarter was a specific territory bounded today by Broad Street to the north, Esplanade to the West, Canal to the east, and south by the Mississippi River. Along Canal Street, a wide expanse of land divides the city buildings from the French Quarter. This "neutral ground" was the meeting place between the French dwellers in the Quarter and the Northern business owners who settled into New Orleans after the purchase.

As for the schools, New Orleans had one of the first completely integrated school districts during the 1860s. One of Lincoln's generals, who was appointed to oversee the schools in New Orleans and to bring order to the unruly southern places, brought Caucasian, Creole, Cajun, and African students and teachers together in schools. For ten years, these integrated schools and school personnel taught side by side in relative harmony. Later, when German immigrants found their way onto the School Board, the separate but equal schooling divided race by geography and economics. African Americans had their own medical schools, teacher training schools, as well as their own elementary and secondary schools well into the twentieth century. These ethnic divisions are still present today among private and public schools.

Since the Catholic Church maintained a long presence in New Orleans, Dominican Sisters, Brother De La Salle, Jesuits at Loyola University and Jesuit High School, along with other religious orders, Catholic schools provided separate schools for African American students and Euro-American students. These racial divides remain in some schools even today, although Xavier University and Xavier High School are open to students of all races.

The public schools run by the Orleans Parish School Board have the reputation of mismanagement of its 127 public schools, and of ineffective policies to address the number of its schools in academic emergency. The elementary and high school buildings were once state-of-the-art facilities built with John McDonogh Trust funds. McDonogh's legacy was to provide financial support for schools that would house the poorest children so that they too could have an education.

The mismanagement and misuse of needed supplies and lack of accountability became lost in the "Big Easy's" lackadaisical attitude, good 'ol boy network, the geographical and economic divisions based upon race, and lost in the impenetrable layers of permissions, forms and other accounting means (Morris, 2008). These pre-existing conditions of poor performing schools, decreased investment in infrastructure repairs, and perhaps the racially bound system within New Orleans exposed these long standing conditions and traditions.

Research Questions

When I began this research project, I was an outsider to the New Orleans community. When an opportunity arose to work with the New Orleans Writing Project after Katrina hit, I decided to study the effects of a hurricane disaster upon adolescents and teachers. As I did in the Prairie High School situation, I wanted to investigate the relationship between adolescent writing culture inside and outside school, but it also meant adjusting for the hardships from Katrina. I had learned in research background readings that writing about the trauma event was helpful in reducing the effects of trauma-induced stresses and critical for healthy mental adjustments.

Since writing has been used to assist recovery from a trauma (Annan et al., 2004; Dyregrov & Mitchell, 1992; Pennebaker, 2000), I wanted to see what adjustments and necessary changes teachers made to the English Language Arts pedagogy and what writing or story telling tasks they included in response to the effects they recognized in the learning of adolescents also affected by the hurricane and subsequent events. In some ways, the violent destruction from the hurricane induced survival conditions, in addition to any life crises that individuals were already facing. In the poorest communities and schools, what would this level of destruction and academic disruption promulgate in classrooms with teachers and adolescents? As a result of these issues, there are two major research questions guiding this study:

How did the natural disaster affect classroom-teaching practices in English language arts?
What role did writing play in addressing changes in adolescent learning and behavior?

In order to answer these questions, I used the same procedures for selecting adolescents and teachers as I had with the Prairie community, with one important addition: this was a trauma zone, and many schools, teachers, and students were scattered, and former patterns for contacting principals and teachers were no longer viable. Instead, I had to rely upon introductions and references in order to find teachers and principals willing to let me study their schools and work with their teachers and students.

The ethnographic method, which I used at Prairie High School, became a mixed method research format for the New Orleans project. To understand the stresses and trauma areas teachers and adolescents were experiencing, I relied upon an existing quantitative survey on stress (Warheit et al., 1996) developed by researchers investigating stress effects after Hurricane Andrew (Appendix F). This instrument was originally developed to test for stress in adolescents, but the questions were relevant to discovering what stress meant for the teachers and created subsequent interview questions.

I used the survey data and research questions to develop the research data codes and categories for the ethnographic study of school culture, disasters, and writing (Bishop, 1999; Denzin & Lincoln, 1994; Heath & Street, 2007; Kirsch & Sullivan, 1992; Rodriguez, Quarantelli, & Dynes, 2007). In studying the classroom culture of disaster literacy, I took participant observer notes, conducted interviews using Spradley's ethnographic interview process (1979), collected material artifacts from teacher and student informants. I processed each day's visit with memos and cooked notes.

In order to develop contacts and background data, I spent the month of June 2006 in New Orleans, volunteering for various service organizations within the French Quarter and bordering New Orleans communities most devastated by Hurricane Katrina and the subsequent flooding. My entrée into the school community depended upon my being able to locate teacher research subjects through an intricate, internal referral process. By August, I had located ten teachers in five different schools willing to participate in the project. I conducted the initial interviews and collected hurricane narratives in August 2006. From August 2006 through August 2008, I visited every two months, usually staying for two weeks to a month at each visit: October, January for one month, March–April, and May.

Table 6.1.   Research Questions and Methods of Collection and Analysis

Research question	Research methods: Qualitative and Quantitative	Data analysis method
RQ1 How did the natural disaster affect classroom teaching practices in English Language Arts?	PO notes, interviews, teacher oral and written narratives; Hurricane narratives Traumatic stress survey	After transcripts were made of interviews, all notes, interviews coded for themes and taxonomic categories of disaster, teaching, and changes. 1. Simple percentages were calculated and yielded areas which most affected the teachers; 2. University of Delaware Statistical Data Center analyzed the data for correlations
RQ2 What role did writing play in addressing perceived changes in adolescent learning and behavior?	Teacher lesson plans, interviews, classroom tapes of instruction	I used Atlas ti5 for coding interviews, participant observer notes, material artifacts completed by students, and focus group analysis cross-coded with all quantitative data. Grounded theory used to establish thesis from codes and memos of all materials. All these were correlated to a time line sequence for co-occurring social events, personal conditions, classroom activities and writing or telling events and then coded for that event. I followed this procedure looking for co-occurrences of events, personal conditions and writing results, changes in behavior.

Data Analysis

The results from the surveys showed that the adult teachers experienced some stresses after the hurricane. The quantitative data suggested two categories, which helped establish the qualitative data: "hard" teaching, and personal feelings and worry about family and employment. These two categories helped me to create the codes using Atlas ti5 for all interviews, researcher memos, and notes. From the two statistical points, I framed the data analyses using the research questions; for example, if teaching was hard, what made it hard in the ELA teaching practice personally and professionally? Second, how did the adolescent behavior change in respect to the teaching and writing tasks?

I coded the material artifacts, interviews, and notes from the two categories and then assigned sub-level categories related to writing, emotional responses, teaching changes, adolescent behaviors, and hurricane experiences. For both the teachers and adolescents, personal feelings and worry about friends and family led to codes that discussed the worries the teachers had, but also reflected topics of classroom discussion and writing. Mostly these codes addressed loss, grief about family and friends, and anger at the forced changes Katrina brought to family, friends, and the safety of the familiar.

Then, I compared the codes to the material artifacts I had collected from the teachers including video clips, lesson plans, student writing tasks as reported by teachers, my participant notes, and memos. After each visit, I compared the old codes with new information in the same areas, looking for co-occurrences of events or sequences preceding any teaching tasks or writing task the teachers gave. From the completed data, I established a time line sequence to compare changes and developments across categories in the two-year period.

Research Participants

The criteria for teacher participation in the project were the following:

1. Participate in multiple interviews over two years.
2. Fill out survey on stress.
3. Allow the researcher to have access to lesson plans and other teaching materials related to writing and language arts instruction.
4. Tape classroom lessons on writing about Katrina.
5. Allow adolescents in classroom to participate in research project, if they accept invitation to participate.

After the consent forms were signed, the teachers took the hurricane survey followed by an extended interview about their experiences with Katrina, teaching career, student population, and their teaching philosophy. Each visit involved a two to three week stay, and a visit to each teacher at least twice for the entire school day. At each visit, I attended the teacher's classes, took observer notes, collected artifacts such as lesson plans, writings, or other information, and conducted an informal interview. During year one, 2006–2007, I collected data about the teacher's English language arts classroom and the writing strategies they used immediately after Katrina through the first full school year.

Each teacher was asked to keep a journal of Katrina comments or classroom references to Katrina, assignments that involved anything concerning

Table 6.2. List of Schools and Teachers Participating in the Research

School name	*Teacher name*	*Grade level of ELA*	*Discipline*	*Ethnicity, geographic identity; area of certification*	*Type of School post-Katrina*
NOHS #1	Ms. Jane	10	ELA	Euro-Amer.; NO native; ELA 7–12	Charter-NOPS
NOHS #2	Did not participate	9			NOPS before Katrina, then charter
NOHS #4	Ms. Martin	12	ELA	Afri. Amer.; native to NO.; ELA 7–12	NOPS

* All teacher names and school names are pseudonyms.

Katrina, to film a writing lesson, and keep any lesson plans that directly referred to or used Katrina as a learning activity. Each teacher selected one class of students for the research project, and then I secured the necessary parental consent and adolescent assent.

The following chart shows the biographical information for all the teachers who participated in the project over the two years.

Of the ten teachers who committed to this research project, I present the data of three teachers and the three adolescents in their classes. In one case, I have the adolescent data from one year in English language arts for New Orleans High School (NOHS) # 2; Ms. Ayms was the teacher in the second year.

The adolescent participants were selected according to the following criteria:

1. Attend school each day and have no habit of missing large numbers of classes.
2. Let me have access to all versions of writing in and out of school.
3. Be a student in the English classroom of one of my teacher informants.
4. Allow me to follow them through the school day and to after-school events.
5. Allow me to meet and talk with their parents.

I had to locate students through the English teachers because I was not allowed through the Human Subjects agreement at the University of Delaware to talk to the students without the parents' permission. This added another layer of difficulty. So the English teacher informants recommended students and then provided the students with the agreement forms. This process took part of the summer and early fall of 2007. I found three adolescents willing to participate in this project with three different teachers in three different high schools.

At this time, parents were still living in other cities, and their children were attending high school in New Orleans. Of the three adolescents, two of the families had moved since Katrina had destroyed their homes. The other family's home was not damaged, and the family returned to the city after the flooding was over and recovery started. Securing the assents of the adolescents and the consent forms of the parents took patience and persistence without trying to be a nuisance and adding to their stress.

In regards to time, this study took place over two years, but my time with each adolescent informant was limited to four visits of two weeks each. I visited each adolescent twice during the visits. During October of 2007, I was not able to visit because of an eye infection and lack of funding. I made up the time by staying longer in January 2008. The length of visits and frequency were often limited by funding allocations.

Study Limitations

The research process in New Orleans lacked the security and familiarity of the Prairie High School location. I cannot underscore enough the chaos that reigned in the first year of the study. Initially, the major problems affecting the research were locating shelter for each visit, sometimes finding materials, transportation, gasoline, and food. The scarcity of necessities was mirrored in my search to find teachers who would participate in the research project. Phone numbers and addresses that were valid before Katrina now were useless or constantly changing. Teachers, fired by the New Orleans Public Schools in September 2005, had moved and taken other more secure positions. Others had homes destroyed, moved, and were seeking employment among the schools that opened. Some of the schools were located in dangerous neighborhoods, so I was limited in my ability to follow students after school and to out of school activities, which were minimal anyway.

The schools involved in this research represent independent charter schools, charter schools under New Orleans Public Schools (NOPS), and Recovery School District (RSD) schools. The schools participating in the research are all located within what was Orleans Parish Public Schools before August 2005. In some cases, teachers lost all their teaching materials and records through the flooding or other hurricane destruction both at school and in their homes. The recollection of teaching practices recorded in the interviews served as the data about former classroom practices.

As in the case of Prairie High School, I do not offer any discussion about role of race or culture in the adolescents' writing and literacy. I had agreed to this condition for the adolescents at Prairie High School, and have maintained this throughout all the discussions of the adolescent informants in New Orleans.

In my notes about location, the schools and the particular details of ethnographic work, however, I was an outsider to the community racially and culturally. At Prairie High School, I was known to the community and found access easier into outside activities with the adolescents; in New Orleans, I had to prove myself as a trustworthy researcher who was not going to convey the particulars of the school, teachers, and students in an unfavorable light.

One principal was concerned about the research project until he understood what I was doing. He did not want the research to be directed by a critical examination of what was wrong with his school, his teachers, and the students. To represent my informants both truthfully and ethically, I was constantly aware of how I could be vigilant and respectful of racial and cultural issues that affected my informants. This required a metacognitive examination of questions, data, and meeting students after school. While I was the "least adult" with the students, I was still very much an outsider in the New Orleans world, an excellent position to be in as an ethnographer, but very difficult in the additional hazards of the trauma zone and among the historical racial tensions in the city.

In New Orleans, research involved confronting the historical issues of race and culture that were bound to any investigation. At times, I was uncomfortable in recognizing these historical boundaries inside the New Orleans schools, neighborhood communities, and the present day realities: schools with security guards, metal detectors, violence and guns, and academic failure. I had to recognize the racial tensions and existing behavioral traditions and expectations would put me in physical danger in some locations. Yet, I never felt threatened, disrespected, or unwelcome in any venue, school, or with the adolescents and teachers. They were all open and friendly, and I have unending respect for what they suffered and endured.

Given the circumstances, I was not invited to accompany the adolescents' home or to conduct further interviews. In New Orleans, I was careful about pushing into the informants' community and making the research an unwelcome intrusion into their lives. With the increase in violence within the city and in the schools, I often only accompanied the adolescent throughout the school day. Hence, the school environment became the primary research site.

Yet, despite these limitations, I was able to answer the research questions about how the disaster affected teaching and learning and the role writing played. Instead of violence from abuse and neglect, in this section, violence is the result of nature. But what I uncovered was that the violence from Katrina exposed pre-existing circumstances related to racial boundaries, economics, and academic inequalities. So investigating literacy habits and compensations that promoted writing was more layered than the previous study. Also, the culture of New Orleans played a role in how these adolescents approached their literacy compensations, and what in the school culture and curriculum inhibited and allowed resiliency and hope.

Over the two-year period, the pedagogy of teachers and behavior of adolescents changed. Yet in the layers of violence, abuse, and neglect, there is still a wonder to be found in the ways adolescents adapt and adopt survival skills in spite of horrific circumstances after a natural disaster.

NOTES

1. This information was provided by Professor Tommye Myrick, Executive Director of the New Orleans African American Museum of Art, Culture and History (located off Governor Nichols Road in the Tremé) in January of 2006.

Chapter 7

Lydia—"In Then, I New My Best Friend Was Dead"

LYDIA'S VIGNETTE

Lydia was about five feet eight inches tall and took long strides as she glided from class to class each day. Her brisk walk was often interrupted by the appearance of a friend, who reached out for a hug, a short verbal exchange, and then another hug. I saw this happen often enough, not just with Lydia, but also with the other adolescents in the research study. I came to realize it was not just a greeting but also a conveyance of comfort, understanding, and support. I never asked her about it, since I sensed it would be an intrusion, but the joyful greeting carried a hint of sadness, in the kind of knowing contact that is often exchanged at funerals.

Lydia lived in a close and large family circle. Surrounded by aunts and uncles, six brothers, and one sister, her family in school was also her family out of school. Her interests were often attached to the connection with some family member, who was able to provide her with a job or a reference that led to her involvement in some activity. Because part of her cultural heritage was Creole and Native American, Lydia also played a role each year as one of the Mardi Gras Indians. This mysterious group of performers holds its membership tightly among those born into the culture, and holds even more tightly the whereabouts and manner of their appearance and performances.

Lydia wanted to join the Louisiana State University (LSU) women's basketball team when she graduated from high school. She followed their games and knew the names of players and the coach. Although she didn't know any of the team members or coaches personally, she knew enough that she wanted to be a member of the team. While attending the university, she wanted to study to be a nurse. Lydia's mom was a health care provider, a licensed practical nurse.

Lydia wanted to follow in her mom's career. But just in case, she had taken up modeling with the local Barbizon Modeling Agency in New Orleans.

Yet through all these various career options and goals, Lydia was an enigma. This young woman had dreams and ambitions, the goals that would help her survive the stresses of critical life events. As I watched her play basketball one afternoon after school, her former coach joined me in the bleachers and started talking about to me about her. He told me that she missed practice quite often, a real inconsistency between what she said she wanted and what she was willing to do to make it happen. Lydia wanted to play basketball, but he did not hold high hopes for her success at getting a scholarship to attend LSU.

After getting her driver's license, Lydia drove her brother Brian to NOHS #1. Lydia's mom drove a small, lipstick-red truck, which I would have loved to have owned. When I met Lydia's mom, she was working as a nurse while she was going to school to be a pharmacist's assistant, in addition to raising her children. Lydia's mother was a tall, elegant woman who greeted me with a large, warm smile. With her impeccable makeup and her hair arranged in a high swirling coiffure, Lydia's mother was a strong woman who had provided for her family through very difficult times and kept her dignity and resilience. She provided a strong support and wise counsel for Lydia.

Lydia had no access to a computer other than those available in her high school computer class. Her cell phone was limited in its minutes and messaging capability.

Lydia appeared to be self-assured, goal driven, and intent. I know that she wanted me to think well of her, so she told me about her hopes and dreams. Yet, life experiences had changed this young woman over the last two years, and something had driven the change. Her grades and academic successes fluctuated. Her classes for two years had been this succession of minimal rigor and minimal academic expectations. Her teachers were sincere and dedicated, but sometimes the course content lacked rigorous and demanding academic tasks and instruction. If the teachers had had them, they were drowned in the years of academic muck, faulty administrative support, and countless pressures of meeting standardized requirements among students who brought an array of personal problems to the classrooms.

It's hard to keep hopes and dreams in such a world, but Lydia had them.

"IN THEN, I NEW MY BEST FRIEND WAS DEAD."

Overview

Lydia was born and raised in the Ninth Ward of New Orleans. Lydia's actions and story of her life after Hurricane Katrina were filled with visions of a successful basketball career at Louisiana State University, but the continuing reality of home and living crept into the vision with harsh realism. The defining memory of the hurricane was not the storm or the partial destruction of her home; it was the drowning death of her best friend. She talked about her future, but there was a sadness that surrounded any reference to Katrina, friends, and the comforts of home as it used to be pre-Katrina.

Lydia's brothers, who were also close to her friend, do not write or talk about the loss of her friend. In the months I followed Lydia, I never asked about her friend or made any reference to him because I knew she didn't want to talk about him. While there were other issues involved surrounding a large family and earning a living, Lydia's story circumnavigated this one main issue. The tragedy and loss of her friend was a personal grief she could not share with family. While the events surrounding Katrina had an effect upon her, nothing prepared her for living without her friend.

While I was not aware of all the critical life events in Lydia's life, the hurricane brought Lydia in touch with stress and trauma of a natural disaster. The loss of her home and some belongings cannot compare to the unexpressed grief that she carried for this friend. Throughout my time with her, she only gave periodic glimpses into that grief; most of the time it was hidden in a tradition of family silence and the denial of pain in the busyness of living.

Lydia's compensatory strategies were subjected to the culture of silence, but she found subtle ways to indicate her grief and desire to tell. The culture of silence at home and Ms. Jane's own pedagogical design and writing tasks inhibited Lydia's telling. In the school chaos that reigned in the early months of the fall of 2006–2007 school year, Lydia and the rest of her school community were re-assembling their lives. Learning and literacy became displaced in the search for a normal life again. Under these circumstances, making literacy compensations in writing tasks happened through layers of expressive statements, performances, and writings. In Lydia's story, we find alternate compensatory strategies in unusual contexts and media, strategies for expressing her stress and trauma.

Although Lydia's story shows us the stresses an adolescent can have after a natural disaster, she shares this stress with her English teacher, Ms. Jane. They share parallel experiences with loss and traumatic stress. As a result, I present both of their stories and experiences through their identities as teacher and student in the English language arts classroom.

Ms. Jane's Socio-Cultural-Historical Background

I met Ms. Jane in the summer of 2006, while I was volunteering in New Orleans. Ms. Jane had returned to New Orleans immediately after the hurricane to find that her home was leveled by the floodwaters and the storm. Along with the physical structure, Ms. Jane lost the entire contents of her home.

Ms. Jane had earned her degree at Louisiana State University in English Education in the early 1970s. She had graduated from a New Orleans high school and returned to teach in New Orleans after she graduated from college. Most of her teaching career had been spent at NOHS #1. The pedagogical content knowledge and disciplinary content knowledge were literature centered. Writing, film, and other media filtered into her classroom instruction, and these served to deepen the class interpretation of literary devices and themes. Her extemporaneous use of media has bearing upon her personal and academic response to the natural disaster and teaching her English language arts classes.

Ms. Jane had evacuated to Memphis, where her brother lived. Along with many other teachers and school administrators, Ms. Jane had expected to come back to work after three days. When she returned despite the danger and the conditions, Ms. Jane found a place to stay at a former student's apartment for a short time. Since the New Orleans Public School District fired all of its teachers and staff officially on September 29, 2006, Ms. Jane had to find alternate employment and housing. When she was teaching, she had held a part time job at a local funeral home.

Now, the storm brought a heavy business to the funeral home and provided Ms. Jane with much needed income. Luckily, she secured a FEMA trailer; however, FEMA parked the trailer near a graveyard. Too much death and destruction surrounded Ms. Jane.

Each night when Ms. Jane returned home, she drove down an unlighted road to an unlighted trailer. Since electricity and phone service were sparse in the early recovery period, Ms. Jane lived here alone and without any electronic or media connection to other people. She was terrified, lonely, and cried constantly. In this dark and isolated environment, Ms. Jane was worried about her high school students, and what had become of their lives.

Ms. Jane missed the students in her Rotary Club organization within the high school called Interact Club. This organization performed community service at local nursing homes and day care centers. They played games with the residents, offered musical entertainment and physical labor, if needed. Hanging on the walls in Ms. Jane's classroom were dozens of awards the group and Ms. Jane received for the devoted service to the community. After working at the funeral home in the late fall of 2005 and early spring of 2006, she was determined to reopen NOHS #1, and she turned to the Rotary Club International to help her do it.

In the summer of 2006, Ms. Jane sat outside of her school and started enrolling students in the high school, and created a list of names. The high school had been closed during the 2005–2006 school year. With determination and dedication, Ms. Jane showed the administration that indeed the students would return to the school, if the school would open for the fall term 2006.

The outside school building survived without major damage. The sturdy brick held together, but this imposing school structure hid the crumbling and neglected interior. With an appeal to the Rotary International, Ms. Jane found volunteers to come in over the summer to repair, paint, and clean the entryway area of the school building and many classrooms.

A well-known actress contributed $150,000.00 to help replace the curtains, repair light fixtures, and refinish the old hardwood floors in the dilapidated auditorium. Additional contributions helped replace the decades old seating, the 1950s hard wooden and metal chairs. In fall of 2007, one year later, this old torn and ragged auditorium was renovated with bold new velvet curtains for the proscenium stage and windows, clean floors, and lighting that actually worked.

Ms. Jane returned to her classroom and teaching English language arts in the fall of 2006. While she once intended to retire, after the hurricane, she decided to return to teaching. In her classroom, I met Lydia for the first time in the spring of 2007.

Lydia's Socio-Cultural-Historical Background

Lydia had six brothers and an older sister. The large blended family included stepbrothers and sisters. Lydia's mom and dad were never married, but both had accepted responsibility for the large family they had brought into the world. At the time I met Lydia, she was living with her mother and two brothers in a home in the Ninth Ward. Even though the property received structural damage from the hurricane and flooding, the home was not completely destroyed. Over the next six months, the family rebuilt the home. This family home and the notorious publicity surrounding the Ninth Ward made their stand in this community a standard of pride.

When Lydia's family decided to evacuate, they left ahead of the storm. Packed in the car, Lydia, her brother, and their mom tried to convince Lydia's friend to leave the area with them. Lydia's friend, Edward, along with his family, had decided to stay and wait out the hurricane. Of course, at this point, the hurricane damage was the most anyone was thinking about. The fact that the levees might breech was a possibility, but hope and trust in the engineering skills of the Army Corp of Engineers kept the levee problem behind the more immediate hurricane worries. When the levees breeched on Monday, there was little time for those who remained in their Ninth Ward homes to escape. Edward and his family were trapped in the floodwaters and drowned together in their car as they attempted to escape.

When residents were allowed to return to the city, Lydia, her mother and one brother returned to New Orleans to find an apartment in Algiers, across the Mississippi River from New Orleans proper. Lydia and her brother attended NOHS #1, even though another high school would have been closer to their home in the Ninth Ward. Lydia's father took her brothers and set up living in a trailer. Eight months after Katrina, in June of 2006, Lydia and her mom were able to return to their Ninth Ward home, even though some parts of it remained unfinished or unrepaired.

The problems of home stability didn't end with the completion of the Ninth Ward home. In March of 2007, the kitchen in Lydia's home caught fire. In an effort to put out the fire and escape, Lydia's mother was badly burned. This critical life event once again brought loss to Lydia's life, the fear that she would lose her mother after losing her best friend. The association and potential for catastrophe forced Lydia to focus once again on the emotions and images of loss. For Lydia, learning in the chaotic and sad environment at home, in her neighborhood, and at the school, was not a priority. She placed a hopeful face on it, but the daily realities of loss, and the stress of losing her home and friend, made the effort to control emotions and feelings an exigent need.

In a natural disaster and its stresses, the recovery process is mired with pits that delay the forward progress. The frustrations and hardships of everyday living aggravate the already desperate control one needs to have. Any new event or condition exacerbates the pre-existing conditions and magnifies the emotional response. For a young girl to lose the one person who is her mentor and her protector would be devastating. The burns Lydia's mother received put her in the hospital, but she eventually recovered from the burns and was able to return home.

The Themes for Writing and Disasters

Since Ms. Jane had Lydia as a student in her English language arts class, the traumas they both experienced, while different, became the focal point in their recovery process through literacy. It is important to note that neither Ms. Jane nor Lydia received any kind of counseling assistance with their traumatic stress over the losses they faced through the disaster. What we see is the way in which they arrive at a process of recovery with the literacy practices as markers of progress, or at least a conscious personal awareness of bringing their emotional stresses into an open place for reflection and discussion, even movement toward healing.

Ms. Jane's teaching and Lydia's uses of writing about the disaster vary in frequency and genre. In the early months of the first full school year after the hurricane, sharing hurricane experiences was a daily occurrence. Sometimes, a word, phrase, or reference to Katrina slipped into a class discussion on a piece of literature. If Ms. Jane engaged the students in a writing task, it became a prelude to more oral revelations about their trauma and stress related to the disaster and subsequent events.

For both Lydia and Ms. Jane, the relationship of writing about the hurricane trauma recovery took over two years to unfold. Over this time period, they shared a common pattern of activity and response to dealing with the stresses from the disaster. In order to show this, I present Ms. Jane's instructional habits and her writing assignments. I intend to highlight the consistency with which she directed each class as she confronted her own stresses and trauma from the hurricane. Through the classroom activities, I introduce Lydia and how I discovered her responses to the grief Katrina caused in her life as they emerge both within and out of the classroom.

The four themes for the writing literacy and compensatory strategies are the following: "Impermanence of Disaster"; "Avoiding Katrina"; "Breakthrough Moments"; and "Reframing the Past."

School is Home—The Impermanence of Disaster

The first theme that manifested itself in the research after Katrina's devastation was the frequency with which people physically relocated during the phases of disaster recovery. This forced condition of displacement from the natural disaster does not end with a return home, but continued through everyday tasks and continuing life crisis events.

Achieving a "new normal" routine and living condition plagued the teachers and adolescents by the daily realities of what they wanted to happen versus what could happen within the limited resources available. In the daily struggle for a normal routine, one other difficulty arose: the internal stresses from the natural disaster did not recede with the "new normal" living. These stresses had to have their own cathartic process and recuperative genesis alongside the physical restorations of place.

The natural disaster's imposed impermanence began with initial the diaspora from the city. Those who lost their physical place of home and their material belongings had to re-establish life in a new location. This involved various relocations over time, until the person re-established a home location. The difficulty was that this upheaval paralleled the internal upheavals that had not been resolved, and with each new movement to relocate, the individual created a stopgap coping of having a safe place to calm the internal upheavals.

The impermanence of the disaster drove people to find a secure place before they could begin to recapture a normalcy and safety needed to live after their losses. Ms. Jane was driven by this need to find security not only for herself but for her students from NOHS #1. With the loss of place came the loss of purpose and control. When she lost everything and had no personal family, she returned to that which made her feel useful and productive as a way to cope and regain a purpose for living.

> If I don't feel productive and I'm not happy then I will retire and do something else. Because I have not always been happy at NOHS #1, but I've always felt productive. Okay, for right now, I am at a place. I need to be here this year for two reasons. One, three reasons, one I had to re-open the school. Because I could not, I fought very hard to re-open the school. And at times totally alone I was doing that. Um, it had to reopen as a school, because kids had to have a place to have a safe education. And I have always felt safe here. And it's always felt like home. I didn't have a home to go home to, because my home is gone. My church is gone, my car was gone. I had to put my mom in an extended care facility. So, I'm all alone. I'm a native New Orleanian. But I don't have a single relative, not even a distant one here in town. Everyone is gone, except me, I'm the only one here. No one else came back. (Personal Communication, 10/25/2006)

For Ms. Jane, these upheavals started when she lost her home and belongings to Katrina. During the time of the research project, Ms. Jane found a single shotgun home to rent near NOHS #1. Inside the home, Ms. Jane had furnished it with donated items—a couch, a bed and some tables, a dresser for her clothes. Ms. Jane felt lost and alone, and the impermanence she felt as she moved from location to location brought her closer to a confrontation with her new reality in life. In times of turmoil, these personal unrelated issues erupted in the stresses and traumatic feelings, which further exacerbated any issues regarding Katrina.

Along the bedroom walls and in her bathroom hallway, Ms. Jane kept other personal items in plastic tubs. Even her clothes were relatively new, since the floodwaters had taken them as well. She kept personal treasures in special boxes and had not unpacked the boxes since the storm. Ms. Jane rarely visited her home since the storm, and employed a young person to mow the grass on her devastated property. She said that she just couldn't stand to see the damage or do anything about rebuilding. So she stayed away.

Yet, Ms. Jane had one anchor in all this confusion. She had her belief in God and his divine purpose for her.

> That's what's so weird. It's really weird. But in Memphis I applied for teaching jobs, I got one I went one day. I resigned at the end of the day. Because there was nothing wrong with it, there was nothing with the job. But, I swear I felt

God was sitting in one of the desks in the room, and he kept telling me all day that this is not where you are supposed to be. This is not where you are supposed to be, you have to go to New Orleans. And I've got to go and re-open NOHS #1. I've got to get NOHS #1 back. Because the kids in New Orleans need that school and if you stay here and teach this year, it won't re-open. And it was like he was speaking in words mean, and I, it was almost like to the point I was having to say, "Would you stop so I can think about what I am supposed to be doing right here?" And so I resigned, I went to the principal that afternoon, and I told her, that you might think I'm crazy, but this isn't where God wants me to be. I have to go where He wants me. So I came home. (Personal Communication, 10/25/2006)

Coming home in late October 2005 meant that Ms. Jane had to find a different teaching job because NOHS #1 was not opening for the 2005–2006 academic year. Three public high schools were open in the early days after Katrina: O. Perry Walker, Karr, and McDonogh 35. Ms. Jane took a position finally at O. Perry Walker H.S. for the remainder of the academic year.

I cried constantly at Perry Walker. I was constantly in tears for varieties of reasons. One of which was being afraid, another would be because it was such a sad group of people. I mean, they were just sad. They were pitiful. And then sometimes I was crying for nothing. (Personal interview, 10/25/2006)

Instead of letting this sadness envelop her in inactivity, Ms. Jane took a letter from the school board, which said that they might not open NOHS #1 because the board was not sure there would be enough students to return. Ms. Jane set up a card table and chair and sat there until she had a long list of names for the fall 2006.

So, every day from nine to one, for like two months, I sat in front of this building. As I sat in front of the school, and every day people would stopped, because they saw me sitting there. And they'd come and say, "Ms. Jane, you taught me in school. I need a place for my child to go now. How do I apply?" Lots of daddies, which was very exciting to me, lots of fathers and the father would tell me, "I'm working. I'm staying, you know, in a FEMA trailers with three other people from work, but I want my family back and my family can't come back because I don't have a place for my children to go to school. Can you help me?" (Personal Communication, 10/25/2006)

Ms. Jane revealed candidly how she responded not only to her situation but to the hardships she witnessed in others. She had lost all her personal possessions and could commiserate with other New Orleanians who experienced similar loss. Ms. Jane possessed an indomitable spirit to help herself recover by helping recover the one place of safety for all—the school. We cannot underestimate the power of the school building physically to represent a stable and safe environment within a community that had experienced such personal and physical devastation. Whatever the source of her energy and determination, she found resolve, purpose, and life in the rhetorical action of opening her school for "her" children.

As for Lydia, she and her parents evacuated before the storm, and then found living quarters near New Orleans for about eight months after they returned. Then Lydia and her family returned to their neighborhood home. The process of rebuilding and reclaiming in the 9th Ward after all the publicity was a matter of pride and reclamation of heritage. Lydia had an extended family in many areas of New Orleans. Unlike Ms. Jane, Lydia was surrounded by family and loving friends. However, tragedy struck again during the first year after the storm. The kitchen in Lydia's home caught on fire, and her mother was badly burned on her arms. Again, the fear of loss, fear for safety and protection, brought Lydia and her brother to an awareness of what they could lose again.

Even though Lydia did not lose her home or all of her possessions in the storm, she had lost her best friend. Her mother's close call with the fire created another critical event in her life, bringing awareness to the fragility of life. Lydia's mom recovered, but not before she had resumed a "new normal" life in yet another reminder of the destruction Katrina had caused. So much had happened that would be the direct result of events following and responding to Katrina's destruction and the flooding.

The opening of school brought Lydia in contact with the friends she had been separated from as a result of the storm. Given her large extended family, safe and secure in their homes, Lydia mourned her friend. As an adolescent, this was the first time Lydia had experienced the death of a loved one, a peer. She had known Edward, since she was a child. He was a frequent visitor to Lydia's home, and Lydia's brother claimed him as a friend as well. His drowning death heaped loss and grief onto recovery and healing. To go meant to leave Edward as part of a happier past.

Lydia came back to school with a heavy heart, like so many other adolescents. In her case, school became a distraction. In Lydia's vignette, I described the greetings, hugs, and embraces that brought comfort. In silence and accepted physical expressions, Lydia found comfort. She had to look forward and move on with her life. Lydia's family surrounded her with safety and security. Even though she lived in different locations following Katrina, her family prepared a home for her, a safe environment for her to live. The impermanence she lived was her personal grief with death.

Avoiding Katrina

But, we don't do Katrina at all. And it's just a rule, that's a rule he made, that's a rule I respected, you know, and you have to, you have to respect because you're not going to make any progress with somebody who isn't ready. (Ms. Jane, Personal Communication, 6/5/2007)

In the previous section, I discussed how Ms. Jane and Lydia dealt with the impermanence in their lives. Even though they both narrated their hurricane experiences, Ms. Jane and Lydia avoided Katrina discussions where Katrina became a central focus of analysis. Instead, they became involved in numerous jobs and organizational services. This behavior was reflected in Ms. Jane's classroom pedagogy.

Ms. Jane had worked part time for the funeral home before the Katrina storm. After Katrina, this became her immediate source of employment. Working long hours at the funeral home and for her church choir, Ms. Jane found solace in the work, yet the nature of the work and her living arrangement brought her loneliness and constant reminders of the impermanence of life. With this background, Ms. Jane almost singlehandedly forced the school to reopen. Her drive to reopen the school was for her benefit as much as it was for the students she cared so much about.

When NOHS #1 re-opened, Ms. Jane converted her job at the funeral home to weekend employment and found an additional part-time job working as the musical director for a small church in Mississippi. On Sunday mornings, Ms. Jane would drive two hours to provide religious music for the congregation and direct the choir.

When I visited Ms. Jane for two weeks in January 2008, she worked at school from 7:15 a.m. through almost 7:00 p.m. Several days after school, she met with the Interact Club when they performed some community service. On those evenings, she was even later in arriving home. She then got something to eat, typed on her computer, and watched game shows. Between midnight and 1 a.m., Ms. Jane fell asleep, exhausted, only to wake up at 5:30 in the morning to answer e-mail and get ready for teaching. She left very little time in her schedule for anything but work; she went from job to job to job.

Working helped Ms. Jane avoid thinking about Katrina and instead gave her a proactive resource through which to continue ignoring Katrina and all that she had lost. She knew that some of her students had lost even more than she had: they all experienced terrible losses. That silent understanding of loss allowed the students and Ms. Jane to have a referential bond that the disaster helped create between student and teacher.

Lydia's way of avoiding Katrina was very similar to Ms. Jane's method. Lydia participated in basketball; she worked weekends at McDonald's where her aunt was the manager; she took modeling lessons from the Barbizon modeling school, and was dating a young man whom she had recently met. Every time I met with Lydia, she talked about getting into LSU so that she could play on the basketball team there. Yet, her academic performance was not outstanding. Lydia wrote little and studied little, except what she could get done in classes.

Lydia's future goals after she completed high school were built around attending LSU. However, she was quick to state that if not basketball, then she would go to nursing school; and if not that, she would do photographic modeling. Lydia had alternatives and choices about her future career, but according to her teachers, her academic and athletic performance in high school presented challenges in achieving these goals.

In fact, in Ms. Jane's English class, Lydia did marginal work. Her basketball coach told me that she would never make the LSU team because she missed so many crucial practice sessions, and she wasn't dedicated enough. He said she didn't work hard enough to be able to make it. When I followed Lydia, she attended her classes and participated in the classroom work, but my conversations with her teachers and the examples of her work revealed that Lydia would have to struggle some to achieve the future she had planned for herself.

During the 2006–2007 school year, Ms. Jane reported that Lydia slept through many of the English classes in the spring. When I asked Lydia about this, she told me that she was working at McDonald's to help out her aunt. Since Ms. Jane's English class was at 7:45 a.m., this was a very early start for someone working until 12 or 1 in the morning. Lydia slept through months of classes. Ms. Jane allowed it.

Lydia's behavior in the classroom and in my meetings with her revealed to me an adolescent in deep distress. Like Diana, Lydia attended school to connect with her social group, but outside of school she coped as best as she could with the economic and emotional realities of her life. Lydia was well intentioned in wanting to do well in school, but hers is an example of the power that distress, stress, and trauma take upon adolescents who already have lived through other life crises. I analyzed Lydia's academic difficulties as signals about the effects of emotional stress upon her ability to attend to learning.

Avoiding Katrina in Ms. Jane's English Language Arts Classroom

I had a horrible experience; I don't do journals anymore because of this. I used to have kids do journals, and they would turn them into me, like once a month they'd turn in their journal notebook. And, if you didn't want me to read a journal, you could do this, you could just fold it over, and put please do not read, and I wouldn't read that one. And I would read all of the journals, except the please do not reads. Sometimes it would be like a couple of days before I would read them. On one Sunday night I was reading a journal notebook that had been turned in to me Friday, and there was a suicide note in it. And the girl had attempted suicide. She had done it. And she didn't succeed. Thank God, but I guilt tripped myself all over the place, because if I had read it when she first gave it, gave me the notebook, I could have prevented it. (Personal interview, 10/25/2006)

Often, personal experiences preempt individuals from engaging in otherwise useful learning activities. After Katrina, Ms. Jane avoided engaging in any classroom activity or strategy that had brought distress to her or would bring distress to her students. The passionate disclaimer Ms. Jane gave for not using or reading journal writing in her classroom eliminated one writing activity that we have seen to be so helpful for other adolescents. Without support or instruction, Ms. Jane's fear and personal experiences deprive the students of a meaningful and helpful writing resource. In this case, Lydia and her classmates took notes in class from a carefully constructed non-Katrina referring or inferring instructional process.

In the two years I observed in Ms. Jane's classroom, her classroom activities followed the same pattern each day:

Daily oral language edit on the board with five sentences.
Transition to literature concept for that class period
Literary example in print or non-print texts (film)
QAE between teacher and students about the reading
Assignment in notebook or some note taking activity
Closure, which involved a task for tomorrow's class

Often, Ms. Jane would invent the day's activities immediately before the class. She never provided me with a lesson plan or other kind of written preparation for her classes. After thirty-three years, Ms. Jane knew her material and relied upon the daily general plan to fill in the day at the beginning of each class. Her knowledge of the students, her experience and expertise allowed her to "read" the classroom and make teachable lessons within the moments.

Ms. Jane's classroom activities after school opened in fall 2006 avoided any direct reference to Katrina. Instead, she used literature readings that explored loss, hardships, betrayal, anger, and frustration to navigate a discussion, offering students an opportunity to reference Katrina. Through this indirect process, Ms. Jane and the students were safe from Katrina topics, yet the indirect references allowed them to discuss Katrina while NOT discussing Katrina. In one interview, Ms. Jane revealed her philosophy about Katrina in writing tasks and literature she assigned:

> Because some kids were telling me, still, my kids, I did not make them write about Katrina all year. I never once made them write about Katrina because I had kids like Brian, Lydia's brother, who told me straight up 'I am not going to talk about this. I am not going to write about it. You are going to have to give me a zero if you make me because I'm not doing it. I don't want to talk about it.' And I decided from the beginning that I was not going to make anybody do it. I would give them experiences. I would give them situations where they could if they wanted to. And occasionally they would say something more, more verbally than writing.
>
> They were much more willing to talk about it than they were to write about it, but even Brian won't even talk about it at all. I mean I still have gotten nothing. He had this opportunity and I got nothing from him. He did not do it. And he has told me straight up, that his relationship with me is much better because of the fact that I have not been [forceful with the writing]. And as far as I'm concerned I never would because when he's ready he will. And hopefully somebody will be there. Hopefully the right somebody will be there. When it's time you know. That's all I can hope for, and I have to pray for him if that happens, because he's just not ready, he's just not ready. Now, he will talk to me about the fire, he will talk to me about his mom's burns, about the kitchen burning down, all that, that he can talk about.
>
> But, we don't do Katrina, at all. And it's just a rule, that's a rule he made, that's a rule I respected, you know, and you have to, you have to respect. Because you're not going to make any progress with somebody who isn't ready. And he's going to be ready one day. He's going to be ready one day and maybe he's just going to be a junior, okay so he's still got two more years at NOHS #1, maybe he'll feel that the door is open, and if he's ready to talk to me, he can come to me because I did respect it. (Personal Communication, 10/26/2006)

Ms. Jane's philosophy and praxis for the students who had lost as much as she had was to invite discussions about their suffering, but not to force the discussion or the written exercises. In this atmosphere of respect and trust, so crucial to establishing and rebuilding the trust between adults and adolescents after a natural disaster trauma, Ms. Jane was able to navigate a compensatory curriculum. In Ms. Jane's case, what determined the curricular choices was her established experience with language arts content teaching practices to the exclusion of activities that would cause any kind of additional stress and trauma for the students.

Her pedagogical compensations included a structural pattern of instruction that controlled the classroom lessons and activities into a safe zone that didn't intrude upon her own stresses and traumatic problems or her students. She left enough room in the literature selections to allow students who wanted to talk about their Katrina stresses, problems, and experiences to talk. She provided writing activities and discussions, which tapped the problems the students were facing with Katrina.

On the other hand, the overall instructional pattern was predictable, consistent, and paced. Important similarities existed between Ms. Jane's English language arts instructional patterns and Ms. Plummer's senior writing project. Both possessed consistency, connection, choice, and conflict; however, in the comparison between Ms. Plummer's and Ms. Jane's teaching designs, both teachers structured their lessons with the four components, even though they applied them differently.

Ms. Jane found peripheral ways to address the stresses from Katrina by offering limited access and discussion through literary references, and allowed students to make statements and connections themselves through the literary readings and writings. Her way of compensating in the classroom pedagogy is to invite oral discussion and references based upon a literary theme. She compensated for the more direct witnessing of the stressful experience by providing alternatives, which she could then incorporate into any literary lesson.

Ms. Jane's English language arts curriculum was constructed on a literature study and analysis, with writing assignments interspersed with writing analysis tasks related to the literature or in imitation of the literature study. In her reluctance to openly discuss Katrina and have students write texts, she interjected writing tasks when she saw the need, but she never pressed students to write or speak about their experiences with Katrina. The subtle and tangential writing opportunities respected Ms. Jane's belief that the students would respond when they were emotionally prepared to openly discuss the issues. In the discussions to follow, I sequenced Ms. Jane's use of writing and literature as it opened opportunities to directly discuss Katrina.

Writing Tasks in Ms. Jane's Classroom

The first writing tasks Ms. Jane gave when school opened in fall 2006 was a group assignment to write a Cinderella story. The students had to write the story from another character's or object's point of view, not Cinderella's. The story had to have a first-person narrator.

What happened to this assignment revealed the way in which these "avoiding Katrina" writings were still about Katrina and the lived experiences that the students brought to the task. Ms. Jane didn't have to ask about Katrina because the students were using the immediate lived experiences and casting them within the story. The writing task allowed the students to make choices about their writing, not as much as Ms. Plummer's Senior Project allowed, but nonetheless, there was choice and consistency in the pedagogical choices Ms. Jane made.

Many students who returned to New Orleans for the fall of 2006 were not able to attend the same neighborhood school that they had attended before Katrina. Many of the students who now attended NOHS #1 had been students in other New Orleans public schools in academic emergency. As a result of the neighborhood displacement and reorganization, students in Ms. Jane's class were not part of the NOHS # 1 culture. In her description of this writing assignment, Ms. Jane's considered writing tasks activated the hurricane realities the students brought to the task along with the cultural and racial tensions that permeated the difficult adjustments to change.

> About twenty of the groups did the ugly stepsister, and it was ghetto. It went straight and I mean ghetto, really obnoxious ghetto actually, um, you know, you must remember because we hardly have a ghetto here. I think they were writing like that because they were living that experience. [Some of the students] always lived in the projects, and projects didn't come back. And they wrote in really heavy ghetto. And I think, they actually, that it's a signal to me, that they are missing their former life. Now, I had some children who were in the groups that they wrote [about] the ghettos stepsister who were horrified because that's not a part of their lives at all, and they got very upset because they didn't want their names to be on that . . . (Personal Communication, 10/25/2006)

In this writing, the "ghetto" language refers to the use of Ebonics within the culture of another geographical area of New Orleans and the language students used that was particular to their neighborhood school and housing community. At NOHS #1, the new students and the former students conflicted over their identities and values being represented through alternate language patterns. Instead of seeing this as a deficit to their story, Ms. Jane interpreted it as a contextualized message about the storm, and the very different effect it had upon her mixture of students from different schools and neighborhoods. NOHS #1 is not far from the neighborhoods that would have used the heavier ghetto Ebonics.

The schools and neighborhoods are geographically within a five-mile radius, yet the use of language was as clear a geographical marker as any street or neighborhood location. This also meant that the degree of displacement would also be located in the geographical zones that mark racial and cultural lines in New Orleans. In the use of language through this story, we have multiple layers of stresses that boiled through the story construct as well as the language used to reveal it.

In a second writing, Ms. Jane asked her students to write to students in Florida who had experienced the same displacement after Hurricane Andrew.

My first encounter with Lydia in Ms. Jane's classroom was reading the letter Lydia wrote about her experience with Katrina.[1] Through this letter, Ms. Jane learned about the loss of Lydia's best friend.

> . . . I am writing this letter because my English teacher read your letter to me. In since you told me something about you, I am going to tell you something about me. In the letter you said it's boring where you live. Well, for me, New Orleans are fun, but I am still mad for the devastation we had dilling with Katrain. Since Katrain come my life never been the same in will never be. Let me tell you why. A day before Katrain come my family asked one of my best friends to come with us during the time we was getting ready to go, but he refuse to so we left it as that. So we left for the hurricane. We went 3 different places, but we end up in Houston Taxes. When we got to Houston we watched the news and seen New Orleans underwater in then I new my best friend was dead. That was a hard pill to swallow. I know that I did not explain a lot about me, but I just wanted you to see what we went through down here in New Orleans losing everything and can't talk to our love ones anymore. (Letter, 3/27/2007)

This letter is an example of one writing task Ms. Jane often gave in the 2006–2007 academic year that referred to Katrina. As per her own teaching philosophy, she invited students to exchange letters with high school students in Florida, many of whom had lived through Hurricane Andrew. This initiative then provided an opportunity for students to engage or refuse to discuss what happened after Katrina. These writing tasks were authentic writing tasks, but Ms. Jane did not follow with revision, editing, or any other advice for adjusting the form. This lapse of detail may have accommodated students who did not want to write about their experiences, but as we have seen in other adolescent narratives, the depth of revision is a component for building language skill and healing.

In the other samples from this writing assignment, many students took the opportunity to discuss their own issues with Katrina. Their stories reflected experiences similar to Lydia's story: the escape plan, the arrival in a destination city, finding news about the flooding and destruction, and for some, moving again, once it was apparent that they couldn't return home immediately. Many of the students expressed anger at what happened to their homes, their possessions and their losses. In the following exchange with Ms. Jane, she recalled how the word "Katrina" provoked responses:

> D: What did you notice during the year? Where did Katrina come up?
>
> J: She, I'll call her she—Katrina—came up unscripted. I wouldn't really bring her up, but say, "That's like Katrina. That's like what happened to us after the storm." You know, and they would make reference to it. And they would make very relevant references.
>
> D: Can you recall any of these specifically?

J: In "A Rose for Emily" by Faulkner, when I was talking about holding on to the past that Faulkner, one of Faulkner's themes is holding on to the Old South and holding on to the past, totally the extreme that she ended up killing her lover, to hold him there so he wouldn't leave her because she was holding onto the past so strongly. And one of the kids in the class said, "That's like us with Katrina, because we don't want to let go, we want things the way they used to be." And then they started talking about that in the class about how NOHS #1 is not the same as it was. And how the city is not the same as it was, how, you know, we have to adjust ourselves, and be willing to accept things, accept change and we don't want to. (Personal Communication, June 2007)

In three separate references to teaching children and adolescents after a natural disaster or other crisis event (Damiani, 2006; Kliman et al., 2005; Tisserand 2007), all the authors advise teachers to offer opportunities for students to express their feelings in writing, drawing, discussion, or musical opportunities. No student should ever be forced to discuss or write about their experiences, but instead, as Ms. Jane realized that students do need opportunities to tell.

The invasive part of traumatic stresses is that they do not automatically fade away after the event has ceased, or the home has been repaired and rebuilt or after a certain number of years. Those who do not have some kind of direct intervention may carry traumatic stress for years. With this fact at the forefront of instructional pedagogy in times of crisis, teachers need to be prepared to adapt pedagogy and content materials. It will not be business as usual for many of these students, and students affected by violence, abuse, and natural disasters whose families do not have a stable living environment or economic security. They already have traumatic pre-existing conditions that complicate any further life crisis events and reactions to them.

Ms. Jane's indirect approach to providing literacy interventions for her students' stresses based upon her insider understanding of the cultural, historical, and experiential events not only about Katrina but about New Orleans was critical for both Ms. Jane and the students. She respected their refusal to openly discuss their experiences with Katrina; however, we see that through the indirect literary setup of parallel thematic discussions, students discussed the stresses and experiences without having to reveal memories too personally held. The literary discussion acted as a tool through which the students made critical analyses of the literature and relied upon their immediate hurricane experiences to connect and make meaning.

Breakthrough Moments

Writings that the adolescents and teachers completed about their natural disaster experiences varied in genre, material, and delivery in various ways.

In the three years I spent in New Orleans after the storm, I found that people found very creative ways to address their losses and experience through writing. Some expressed anger; some were funny and satirical; some were composed with sadness and power. The immediate responses were survival signs like the postings by FEMA and rescue teams on the homes: the infamous X marking with abbreviations and numbers. Another was the names, address, and phone number of a home's owner, indicating where they had relocated, often a spray-painted message on the remaining wall of a house.

On city walls, street signs, wherever a message could be painted or attached, words helped spread news and information. These were signs of life and recovery. These same kinds of messages occurred in other displays. One day after school, while I was waiting to meet Lydia's mother, Brian, her brother, happened to meet us. He wore a T-shirt with a picture of Edward silkscreened across the back, and the date that he died. I have seen these types of memorials on trucks and cars: the name, with an emotional appellation and the date the individual died. I asked Lydia if that was the picture of her friend, and the only response was a solemn, "Yes." Her brother turned away from us, and then she walked away from me. In that moment, silence said enough. It wasn't time to talk about Katrina or Edward.

I consider these types of expressions symbolic written texts work as visual rhetoric. Everyone in New Orleans who sees the shirt and dates will understand. There is no need to ask because the story is common enough to anyone who survived the storm. There was an innate need to tell the truth about what happened, especially about the traumatic feelings and stresses. The compensatory strategy being employed here echoes the adolescents' use of pictures to narrate events, provide context and meaning.

In this unexpected writing on Brian's shirt, the memorial words spoke what Brian and Lydia couldn't discuss out loud. The need to express emotions was greater than the code of silence surrounding Edward's death. These compensations, while not part of a classroom writing pedagogy, revealed that adolescents find alternate ways to communicate, and writing pedagogy can assist them in finding effective means of expression by providing options in terms of materials, genres, and symbolic use of language that communicates and expresses.

Breakthrough moments happened sporadically. In the code of silence that surrounded the classroom instruction and Lydia's life around Katrina, I had to investigate other means and ways of compensations and written discourse. The breakthrough moments were unexpected statements, questions, or actions that provided a personal revelation about Katrina. These situations occurred without any warning or signal, and often erupted in unrelated contexts, but these seemingly unrelated contexts exposed the layers of stresses beneath the surface and connected the present to the past.

One such moment occurred when Ms. Jane asked me to read several short stories she had written. I told her I would, and she sat on a chair while I read them. It became apparent that she wanted me to read them while she was there. While the stories were not about Katrina, they were filled with symbols and metaphors relevant to Ms. Jane's life. We talked briefly about the stories, and then Ms. Jane asked, "Do you think I need help?"

In the two years I had been coming to New Orleans and observing in Ms. Jane's classroom, she had been quite open about her stresses and trauma related to Katrina, but she kept it out of her classroom instruction. Knowing that I was an English teacher too, she used these short stories to initiate a discussion that really had nothing to do with her short stories. I was surprised when I reflected back on this event how Ms. Jane had employed writing as a tool to approach me about current research on trauma and stress and what I had observed. I said, "Yes, I think you could benefit from talking to a professional about all that you have suffered through Katrina and mourn your losses." After that, she nodded and walked out of the room, taking her copies of her short stories with her.

Lydia's breakthrough moment occurred when we were walking from her ACT prep class down a hall to her next class, computers. The hallway to the computer class just happened to pass the Nurse's office. Lydia stopped by to talk to a young woman sitting in the office who was obviously very ill. The nurse started talking to Lydia about how she was doing. Without transition or introduction, she mentioned how she lost her best friend in Katrina and she had no one to talk to. The nurse told her to come back and see her, for she knew someone else who had also lost a dear friend and they could share their stories. Lydia turned and left the room, and without comment to me, she started chatting about her next class. During the day, she made no further reference to the statement she made to the nurse or about Katrina.

Each of these incidents illustrates how deep our need is to tell about the stresses and trauma in our lives. We also see that adolescents and adults find ways to compensate for the environmental restrictions, which prohibit them from expressing their feelings. While these breakthrough moments are not literacy events or compensatory strategies as have been discussed in this book, they detail the importance of telling, narrating, and expressing these critical life events, and how important it is to express them through language, directly or symbolically.

Some Way Out

In April of 2008, when I returned to New Orleans for the final visit, I found Ms. Jane much changed in attitude and spirit. She was quick to tell me she had had a very changing experience around Easter of 2008.

In March, near Easter, Ms. Jane was searching for some sacred music to use for one of the Easter week services. As she searched for the music, Ms. Jane realized that all her sacred music was lost to the flooding from Katrina. Ms. Jane said at that moment, she crumpled to the floor and started sobbing. A high school student, James, was with her at the time. After he heard Ms. Jane's story, he asked Ms. Jane who the composer was and whether the composer was still alive. Yes.

James went to the Internet, found the composer, discovered his phone number, and called him. In James' telling of Ms. Jane's story to the composer, the composer offered to replace her music the following year, 2009, and work with her to help the choir perform his music. Ms. Jane was overcome not only by his generosity to her, but by her student's quick thinking and proactive assistance on her behalf. Ms. Jane officially let go of the past, and found new hope and resiliency in a student's generous assistance.

During this research process in the disaster area, I witnessed complicated, significant reactions and situations, but their meaning belonged in the hands of a professional psychologist. Yet, these breakthrough moments were important literacy moments because of referential use of reading and writing in conjunction with personal trauma and stresses. These moments and others like them brought an awareness of personal growth and development in terms of how the natural disaster changed their lives.

During the 2007–2008 school year, Ms. Jane saw academic improvement overall.

> My kids are doing, I mean, they're much more involved in the work and more enthusiastic about it and seem more interesting in learning than they did last year. Last year they didn't seem to learn a thing. They are desperate to be kids. They are begging all year to do activities; they want things to do. (Personal Communication, 4/9/2008)

The academic progress occurred gradually over the two years, parallel to the recovery in process for Lydia and Ms. Jane. In the early days of 2006, when school reopened, school life was about reestablishing that normal rhythm. It was about surviving. For the teachers and students, the natural disaster experience had changed their lives and their realities. Now, they had to recapture a desire and future vision for this new world.

Some Way Out—Ms. Jane's English Language Arts Classroom, Year Two

In the second year I spent in Ms. Jane's classroom, the school administration required every teacher to write the following items on the classroom chalkboard each day: Do Nows, Warm Up, Objectives, Content Focus, Guided Practice, Independent Practice, and Wrap-Up. Ms. Jane's explanation was,

"I've seen it on the junk that they give me in those professional development [sessions], and they want us to put that stuff on the board." In addition
to these demands, the teachers were required to give weekly assignments or
tests that evaluated students on some aspect of the curriculum every week.
Ms. Jane's "do now" had been her daily edit practice. In the following discussion, Ms. Jane explains her literature-based program of study, with the daily
edit and vocabulary words added for emphasis, and defends her instructional
habits that in her mind meet the district's required teaching format.

> My vocabulary happens once a week. I give them twenty words. I have four
> components: I have editing, the vocabulary, my literature, and the way I teach
> literature is to start with Dr. Seuss because I know that I am going to start with
> Poe. I start with an author; I give a lecture about that author's life and how they
> fit historically into American Literature and into American history. I lecture
> about the author's life, they take notes and I have an open notebook quiz at
> some point during the year on the author. We read something by the author,
> we have a lecture about the author, we read something [else] about the author,
> and we watch something by the author also because I know they do really well
> with television and video. So. I try to make every author a combination of
> reading, knowing, where they fit historically, who they were, how their work
> relates to their lives. We always try and say you know about his life? Why did
> he write this? What do you think his purpose was? (Personal Communication,
> April 2008)

Ms. Jane meandered non-sequentially through American Literature: Salem
Witch Trials, *The Scarlet Letter*, Emily Dickinson followed by the Harlem
Renaissance poets, then to the authors from the south and New Orleans:
Faulkner and local favorite Tennessee Williams. When I questioned Ms. Jane
about writing, she said that they write. "And they write after Hawthorne.
They write. They always have to write an essay, and if they agree or dis-
agree with that and come up with their own argument, as persuasive essay. I
do things along the way. They write poetry after the Harlem Renaissance."
A partial example follows from a poem a student created after the Harlem
Renaissance poetry study:

> We real cool. We stayed in school.
>   We didn't need a pass, 'cuz we stayed in class,
>   Didn't cause a fight, we did it right
>   We stayed in school. Now we make the rules.

Along with poetry, Ms. Jane gave a resume writing assignment. This assignment asked the students to write a resume for the author they were studying.
In Ms. Jane's classroom, the writing tasks seemed to be an extemporaneous

idea projected within the existing literature study, and related tangentially. In respect to writing and trauma interventions in English classrooms, Ms. Jane's pedagogy attached writing to literature. If the students made connections to Katrina within the writing tasks, then she accepted these as part of the literary analysis.

> D: What has changed?
>
> J: Last year that [Katrina] was kind of like all we talked about. It was just not them. It was me, too. All of us, we kind of didn't have room in our lives to talk about anything else almost because you [were] still living in the FEMA trailer and trying to find a contractor or looking for a place to live. You know it's hard [to learn] when you still feel you're homeless and when you've lost everything you owned.
>
> D: Are you making progress?
>
> J: I'm making progress and good stuff is happening in my classes. And I have kids who are learning all . . . way more so than last year. I told you we've been surviving. Now it's time to thrive. We aren't surviving; we have survived. It's time to thrive, and if we just keep surviving, we don't go anywhere . . . (Final interview, April 2008)

As this interview revealed, Ms. Jane's English language arts curriculum reflected her own biases and experiences with writing, which is narrow and often extemporaneous. She clearly has a literature-based program, which doesn't provide enough opportunities for students to express their stresses from the natural disaster. However, Ms. Jane was responsive to the students' reluctance to talk about Katrina, primarily because of Lydia's brother, Brian. That one statement led Ms. Jane to restrict writing topics, and since literary analysis has traditionally been the accepted content discipline to the English language arts classroom, she remained comfortable within this content. Yet, in her own words, she avoided the direct writing tasks because she lived the students' own reluctance.

In one area, Ms. Jane's limited writing demands followed a major component of healing after a natural disaster: psychological literature advocates no additional pressure be placed upon students or adolescents to discuss or reveal anything about the trauma they have experienced. They should have many opportunities in the classroom setting, but no student should be forced to participate. Ms. Jane's approach took this caveat to the extreme in terms of letting one student's reluctance to control the writing opportunities. In spite of these sensitivities, the students who might benefit from a more open and direct approach to the stresses were left to find their own emotional releases in the peripheral reflections and classroom recitations about Katrina.

When the teachers themselves are also affected by the critical event, it is necessary to address the psychological effects upon the adults so that they can gain some relief and healing before and during the times they work with children. Both psychological and financial means of support need to be offered to teachers, and Ms. Jane's story and teaching show us the influence disaster stress has upon a teacher and the resulting teaching pedagogy.

Lydia's Breakthrough Moment

One curious thing I noticed about Lydia one day was the tattoo she had on the front of her forearm: it was her mother's name. This tattoo was very important to Lydia. After the loss of her friend, Edward, and the fire in the family home that destroyed part of the rebuilt home, this second critical life event drove Lydia to face a difficult reality: the pain from the loss of Edward to the possible loss of her mother. This second event caused a change in Lydia's behavior, which she realized:

> Well, when Katrina came, I was kinda grouchy. Like I told you, I lost my friend in Katrina. I had to, like, live through it 'cause it's life. So, that was a big change also. Calling them or, you know, my mom cooked certain things on certain days just because she knows that's what that person wanted to eat. His favorite was turkey necks, so every time mamma cooking, it'd be like, "Well, son, I cooked turkey necks." So now, we cook turkey necks and now everybody just look around and wonder. (Personal Communication, 4/10/2008)

When I asked her about the changes she observed in herself after the flood, and the rebuilding of their home, she told me she began modeling with a local agency. Lydia seemed to be searching for some positive image or help with her self-image to give her a maturity and sophistication that other avenues had prevented. These critical life events drove Lydia to take some personal action. Instead of using literacy, she made a pro-active and physical compensation that gave her a different demeanor and control to accompany the changes she realized.

> Well, I was the type person that, I didn't want anybody to tell me nothing. But once Katrina came, my mom set me down and was talking to me like, "When you grouchy, you not gonna get far in life with that attitude" So sweet talk . . . It really works like, cause now, like, I have people looking at me for differently. (Personal Communication, 4/10/2008)

According to Ms. Jane, the fire in early March of 2008 had caused a change in Lydia's behavior. Ms. Jane recalled that Lydia worried every day that her mother would not make it or that she would be left without her. The tattoo on Lydia's arm, her mother's first name, now made sense. Children fear the loss of a parent, and given what Lydia had lost, this crisis event added another layer to her emotional response concerning loss of someone she loved.

Both Ms. Jane and Lydia had navigated around their Katrina experiences, and I equate these personal maneuvers with the compensatory strategies. With the limitations on writing tasks in school and out of school, they found more pro-active avenues through which to construct expressive and responsive strategies to their stresses. Ms. Jane and Lydia create for themselves activities and busyness that they strategically adjust to exigent life situation, waiting for a new normal to settle in.

I struggled with the lack of writing Ms. Jane required in her classroom, but I came to understand that compensations regarding natural disasters carry a wide range of reactions and coping strategies dependent upon the level of stress and trauma. Both Lydia and Ms. Jane avoided writing tasks as evidenced in Ms. Jane's classroom philosophy and Lydia's sparse writing examples. Yet, the written compensations were substituted with reflective oral patterns of communication and symbolic uses of language. While this may not be the best of methods in which to address adolescent behaviors related to stress and trauma, it does reiterate the need for sensitivity in requiring certain content material, written tasks, and story telling opportunities.

I saw Ms. Jane employ an oral narrative activity in one class. In what appeared to be an inspired moment, Ms. Jane broke from her accustomed learning sequence and said to the students, "If you have a story, tell a story." Ms. Jane began narrating some historical event from New Orleans' past. Since the students appeared not to know much about the history of New Orleans and what existed prior to their birth dates, Ms. Jane regaled them with stories about people from the community and her life. She had used this narrative style as a transitional strategy to introduce a literary idea, especially when the literary example was from a New Orleanian author (Faulkner, Williams, Chopin, and Whitman), but I had not seen her do this as a lesson in oral narration. The students followed this one lesson inviting the students to tell their stories in class.

In the subtle telling of her own stories, Ms. Jane demonstrated a new teaching compensation in this activity. Because she does not often give them writing tasks that allow them to tell stories, she does this through her extemporaneous assignments. In January 2007, Ms. Jane had finished a modern American play, and then gave the students time to develop their own plays and perform them in the classes. This was relatively early in the recovery phase of Katrina, but students embraced this activity. These activities were haphazardly included in the established pedagogy and depended upon how Ms. Jane read the needs of her students.

I would like to suggest that if Ms. Jane had offered more activities like the play writing or letter writing activity we saw Lydia complete earlier, these opportunities would provide a much needed expressive outlet than her established pattern of instruction. I think from the responses both from those who engaged with the activity and those who did not, the majority of students didn't reject the issues of Katrina. In fact, the students needed to tell their stories in order to process what had happened to them. Ms. Jane controlled this compensatory strategy because she couldn't process her own trauma or stresses.

I came to see Lydia more through Ms. Jane's eyes and through the eyes of her other teachers. In school, the teachers viewed her as academically lackadaisical and unprepared for her classes. She would take notes while I was observing, but then teachers would tell me that her attendance was sporadic, and she often didn't have work completed.

In the beginning of her junior year, Lydia turned sixteen and began driving. Ms. Jane equated an adolescent getting a driver's license with decreased interest in anything academic. At the same time Lydia learned to drive, she took a job at McDonald's, she had a steady boyfriend, and social activities were on the increase. While one could say that these situations were a rite of passage among many adolescents, Lydia's story for this research showed the normal rites of passage were complicated by the abnormal conditions surrounding the disaster. While the world around strove to bring normalcy back to the school and life, the adolescents and teachers created an alternate classroom space, a surrogate picture of what can be to temporarily replace what is.

WHAT WE LEARN FROM LYDIA AND MS. JANE

From the data presented by Ms. Jane and Lydia, we have two complementary situations that show us how the traumatic stress of a natural disaster influenced learning and writing practices. For Ms. Jane, her own disaster experiences limited what she was able to embrace in adjusting her classroom instruction. She avoided the very writing and telling experiences that students needed but also what she needed.

Ms. Jane's ELA pedagogy reflected thirty-plus years of knowledge about adolescents, and what she determined was the best way to reach them. While Ms. Jane avoided the direct telling and writing assignments about Katrina, she recognized that the recovery process and the narrative stories could be restrained until individual students needed story telling about their Katrina experiences. Until that time, she would initiate small indirect writing tasks and oral activities that released the stress value on the Katrina emotions but never engaging students in overt stress interventions.

Instead of compensatory strategies for adolescents, Ms. Jane's story provides the first illustration of compensatory strategies used by a teacher. Ms. Jane's traumatic stresses manifested themselves in her classroom instructional design. Ms. Jane does not have a writing program into which she could inject writing. Ms. Jane assigned writing, but I never saw her teach writing.

Ms. Jane's compensatory strategies limited the writing tasks that were referential to Katrina. Her story telling strategies were related to literature themes and personal anecdote, which revealed homegrown knowledge about New Orleans. While the administration imposed classroom pedagogical structure upon the teachers, since the school was in academic emergency, Ms. Jane didn't make many changes, since she saw her pattern of instruction as meeting the new requirements.

While Ms. Jane blocked too many Katrina activities and references, she never stopped any student from making Katrina references or connections in the classroom. She respected the students' rights to address their emotional stresses and experiences when they could willingly tell and reflect. She is a dedicated and devoted English language arts teacher whose own stress and traumatic experiences served to make her more sensitive and compassionate toward the changes and needs of her students.

Ms. Jane's situations echoes what Ms. Martin (chapter 8) strongly advocates: teachers need to receive professional support, financial support, and administrative support in order to be psychologically and academically ready to meet the adolescent stresses a natural disaster brings to the classroom. This includes information about curricular adjustment, pedagogical and instructional alternatives. Without these visible supports, the teachers are left to handle both their own stressful situation and the changes in adolescent behavior.

Lydia told us how traumatic events affect the process of recovery and coping. In her family situation, the family avoided discussing Edward's death, and Lydia seemed afraid to break the silence. Instead of using writing or telling to express herself, she responded by creating pro-active compensatory strategies. The compensatory strategies in Lydia's case include memorializing on shirts, the tattoo, and through the preparation of familiar food. While these are very different compensations than adolescents made in the previous stories, I maintain that they are nonetheless compensatory strategies. When the other adolescents did not have resources in the classroom to address their stresses, they created them.

In Lydia's case, she is restrained in the classroom and in her personal grief. In saying this, I am not making a negative critique of Lydia's parents or of her teachers. Without even journaling activities, Lydia has no visible support or instruction for using writing for expression. Lydia told me she did not write at home or keep a journal. The lack of writing expectations and experiences means that Lydia does not have a default writing system to adapt, adjust, or even just use to express herself. In that, she compensates within the symbolic use of limited language expression.

Lydia's compensatory strategies emerged through her symbolic use of language, which had to carry meaning and personal expression. Lydia was fighting through so many losses that we should not be surprised at her lack of academic engagement and productivity. The pile of stresses and losses Lydia faced were indicative of an adolescent unable to think with such emotional heaviness in her life. Yet, like Danielle and Diana, Lydia was able to see growth herself through her struggles with loss. In similar circumstances, Diana sought employment at the diner; Lydia worked at McDonald's.

It is interesting to note that this push for employment may signal that the academic purposes are not relevant enough to sustain adolescents' interests. I am suggesting that after disasters, more classroom activities need to promote pro-active engagement that put adolescents to work on community and school sponsored programs to help with the reconstruction. Give them something to do to help others, and by doing so, help themselves. They gain self-awareness and self-knowledge through these various strategies—they can learn through the activity about surviving traumatic loss.

In the few writing samples Lydia produced for Ms. Jane, she discussed her stresses and feelings in cold and simple detail. The misspellings and informal language patterns were constant in her other writings. I never saw Ms. Jane demand revisions or editing. The grammatical and spelling mistakes were supposed to be alleviated through the daily oral language and vocabulary tests that were part of the classroom instruction.

We learn that stresses from natural disasters are nonetheless stresses that cause dramatic changes in adolescents' abilities to learn, write, and engage in literacy. We also learn that teachers can be active facilitators in the recovery process, especially if they are supported with information about how to address these adolescent behaviors related to traumatic stress.

NOTES

1. Lydia's writings are presented as she wrote them, including her spelling, grammar, and punctuation.

Chapter 8

Tyrone—"Doing Me Is What I Do Best"

TYRONE'S VIGNETTE

Tyrone is the last of eight children in his family to graduate from high school. The position as the last child gave Tyrone some special privileges: a number of places to visit across the United States. Perhaps, most important in respect to the events of August 29, 2005—a number of places to escape the flooding waters and destructive fury of Katrina.

In his last year of high school, Tyrone enjoyed a large circle of friends, whom he courted during every break between classes. He would find a friend, exchange some common hand greeting, and then quickly say, "Hey, man, whad ya know?" I watched him greet his female friends more closely, a hug, a whisper in the ear, a sleight of hand that conveyed some mutually understood message. When he accepted a role as a research informant, he introduced me to his friends, saying, "She's writing a book about me." Then he smiled and hugged that friend quickly and then grabbed the next friend, and the process repeated itself.

Tyrone, according to his teachers, caught a dreadful case of senioritis when he began high school. Even the principal shook his head while watching the smiling and "cool" moves of Tyrone and his friends. In classes, teachers often shook their heads as Tyrone tried to smooth his way around assignments and disciplinary remarks that often chided him for his tardiness and incomplete assignments. Despite what this might say, Tyrone was on the honor roll.

The charm and smooth talk didn't work on everyone, especially his female teachers. They knew too well that he would make a play for getting out of work sooner or later. His English teacher was particularly bombarded with these appeals. "Ms. Martin, if you write my final research paper, I will pay you a hundred dollars. Serious. Come on, no one has to know. I'm good for it, and it will be good for you, too." Ah, but Ms. Martin found no sincerity in such statements, and quickly told Tyrone where to sit, what not to say, and how to remember what she said.

After school, Tyrone drove away in his brand new car, a birthday/graduation gift from his parents. One day while sitting in his computer class, Tyrone was furiously sending text messages over his new iPhone. After answering the latest phone messages, he was intent on locating a man's Gucci belt on eBay, while the computer teacher went around the room to help other students with a survey.

After graduation, Tyrone's employment plans were unclear. He toyed with joining the Air Force, going to college, or setting up a business. All of this was to be decided after several summer vacation trips to visit brothers and sisters in other states, after a huge graduation party, Memorial Day party and some rest after a strenuous senior year and senior trip to Florida and Disney World.

"DOING ME IS WHAT I DO BEST"

Overview

Tyrone escaped Katrina by living with his older brother outside of Atlanta. He spent an entire year attending another school in which he made many new friends. Tyrone is one of the exceptions to the stories we hear about Katrina; he had a good experience attending another school, had a comfortable, stable home away from New Orleans, and the family home, though flooded, was repaired so that the family could return in the fall of 2007. Tyrone lost no immediate or extended family members and was supported and protected by his large family and parents.

Tyrone's story is one of privilege among so much desperation. Tyrone's friends and classmates experienced more of Katrina's fury than Tyrone did. He seemed unaffected by what happened to his hometown city, even his friends. When I asked him questions about Katrina and his experiences or what he knew of his friends' experiences, his answers were evasive. At times, it appeared that he could not really understand what I asked him, and my attempts to simplify the question only made his answers more elusive.

Nonetheless, I include Tyrone's story even though his personal story does not include the stress or violence. Not every adolescent has the horrific histories that are the presented in this book; however, in Tyrone's social and academic life, his friends and his teachers were affected by the storm. By studying Tyrone, I had access to his friends and teachers, many of whom suffered traumatic stresses of loss and displacement. Through his friends and teachers, we have more details and evidence about teacher and adolescent compensatory strategies after a natural disaster.

Tyrone avoided writing except on the cell phone or on the computer. Much of the "written work" he was given in classes was comprised of worksheets, note taking, math problems, or physics problems. Like Lydia, Tyrone only wrote in school for assignments he was assigned. He did not write outside of school, keep a journal, or use writing literacies other than what was required.

Instead of self-sponsored writing, Tyrone responded to visual images in crafting and using literacy. Like Chase and Diana, Tyrone worked from the visual images to create texts and read texts, an interesting way to survive the academic tasks he had to complete in school. So, in the search to understand writing to survive for one student who didn't experience the trauma and tragedy, I studied him among the teachers and friends whose stories were devastating. What does writing to survive mean for an adolescent who escaped the ravages of Katrina, but is surrounded by it?

Ms. Martin was a teacher still fighting through the agonies of Katrina, along with many of the students in her senior English class, while Tyrone remained seemingly untouched and unencumbered by the horrific stories of loss and tragedy of his friends and his teacher. So, this story, unlike the others in this book, focuses on the tragedies surrounding one adolescent and one teacher who instituted in her English language arts classroom interventions to mitigate the trauma and stresses students were facing from Katrina and the ongoing recovery process. Her awareness of her own traumatic stresses gave her a compassion and understanding awareness of how this affected the students in her classroom. This socio-cultural-historical scene brings the tragedy from a natural disaster clearly in focus.

Even so, we learn that not all the children from New Orleans experienced the loss and pain that the news images conveyed. It also should disrupt our conceptions of race, culture, and economic privilege in New Orleans. In spite of this, even one so privileged has to survive—that admittedly is what Tyrone did best.

Tyrone's Socio-Cultural Background

Tyrone's family was large and was made even larger by the number of aunts, uncles, second cousins, and extended family members. His father had retired from the U.S. Postal Service, and the family lived in a comfortable middle class suburban home in New Orleans. I do not know whether Tyrone's mother had a professional occupation, but she and his father had raised eight children. Tyrone was the last one still at home. Among the older siblings, one brother had joined the Air Force and Tyrone considered following in his footsteps. The others lived across the southern tier of states, and they had a variety of professional occupations.

Tyrone had been born in New Orleans. As the baby in the family, he had a much wider worldview, given the various geographical locations of family and his travels. He seemed comfortable with going other places and living in unfamiliar situations. He spent the year after Katrina attending a public high school outside of Atlanta. At the school in Georgia, he told me he became a bit of a celebrity, as the only student attending the school because of the hurricane devastation in New Orleans.

Tyrone's dress often included an expensive addition to the required school uniform restrictions. It might be a wristwatch, a Gucci belt, or a pair of popular sneakers, all in the required school colors, but nonetheless, an expensive article of clothing. Of course, there was the new car, which he had received for his grades during his senior year. Tyrone worked at the local Wynn-Dixie, and this employment provided him some extra income and after school activity. Tyrone had joined no sport teams or school clubs and organizations.

There is one final detail about Tyrone. One day we were talking, and I noticed that Tyrone had long fingernails, the small finger on each hand. The nail was at least two inches long. During an interview, I asked about the long nails, because each of the boys seemed to protect or favor the finger with the nail on it. Tyrone and his friend revealed that if a person has long nails, it meant that he had money and didn't have to work hard. Instead of being a sign of wealth and status that might provoke criticism or resentment, Tyrone openly paraded this status symbol. In this attitude, he was not alone.

Ms. Martin's Socio-Cultural Historical Background

Like Ms. Jane and Lydia, Tyrone's English language arts teacher, Ms. Martin, had faced all the horrors captured in the news, newspapers, and subsequent discussions and information about Katrina. Her story encapsulated the worst stories broadcast about Katrina. She lost her home in Katrina's wake, had to be rescued from the roof of her mother's home, spent three days on the bridge waiting for rescue, slept on the floor in the convention center, and then was air-lifted to Corpus Christi, Texas. There, she, her mother, and two sons lived with a family for a month.

The host family bought them clothes, gave them money, and offered whatever hospitality they could. Ms. Martin's Katrina effects continued throughout the two years I observed her classes. Her car was stolen and used in a drug fight. In another incident, two young thugs killed her next-door neighbor, and now she feared for the safety of her two boys. During the same time frame, she developed debilitating health problems, including shoulder pain and insomnia.

Ms. Martin was born and raised in New Orleans. She attended NOHS #4 as a high school student and graduated from Xavier University in New Orleans with a teaching certification in the early 1980s. Almost immediately after she graduated, she returned to NOHS #4, and had been teaching there for thirteen years when I met her.

Before Katrina, Ms. Martin had lived in a home in the Ninth Ward with her two sons. After Katrina, she moved into the Marigny, a geographical area adjacent to the French Quarter. Other events that happened after she returned to NOHS #4 in January of 2006 are revealed in future discussions of her instructional strategies.

During the two years I conducted research in Ms. Martin's classroom, she developed various health related problems: debilitating shoulder pain, sleep apnea, and increasing tiredness and exhaustion. Ms. Martin admittedly said that she did not take home any school related work. She taught her classes, and then returned home to address the growing number of Katrina related issues and her children's needs. Along with these issues, Ms. Martin, a tall, attractive woman with short cropped hair, had recently become engaged. This relationship and her fiancé's growing emotional troubles from his Katrina experiences, took any residual energy she might have had. When their relationship ended in the spring of 2008, she said she felt better and had regained some of her energy.

Ms. Martin was a teacher who kept her students' confidences and provided them with other grooming and hygiene products when she realized the students were in desperate trouble. She welcomed students into her home when they had nowhere else to sleep or shower. Like Ms. Jane, Ms. Martin was a dedicated teacher, who, despite her own traumatic experiences, intervened and helped the suffering adolescents she taught.

Tyrone's Visual World of Literacy

Tyrone used various visual media to assist him with writing assignments, building knowledge, and gaining facts; in effect, learning and making knowledge. Reading meant interpreting pictures, gathering information from the spoken narrative and visual codification in the films or other visual presentations of information. As the principal of NOHS # 4 said one day, "Computers and technology. They [adolescent students] adapt it to their purposes, and it is very different from what we as teachers want them to do" (Personal Communication, 1/14/2008).

Tyrone's use of visual media and computers directed his major compensatory strategy. While the principal meant that the students are searching and texting when they should be using the technology to assist their learning, they are learning to adapt their skills with media to meet their needs. The following story is a vivid example of how rapid communication through computer technology provoked a violent incident.

One Friday night, the NOHS #4 was having an open dance after the basketball game. Just as the dance began, gunshots rang outside the gym doors. This was later discovered to be a retaliatory strike for a comment someone had made on a MySpace page. The dance was immediately cancelled, and the police began their search for the shooters.

This was one dramatic instance of how violence infiltrated the New Orleans schools after they had opened and tried to reestablish normal extracurricular opportunities. What is more alarming is the use of MySpace as the social forum for the gang rivalry and vendetta challenges among high school–age students. The large opportunity for literate acts to precipitate violence only echoes the principal's astute comments about students and lessons out of the context. Here is another example of the compensatory strategies at work in similar ways to those being used by Chase.

During the academic day, Tyrone had one computer class. His computer teacher had so many obligations in addition to teaching computers that the classroom instruction was often interrupted by someone's need for a computer repair, a computer test administered, or an administrative computer emergency. Tyrone took advantage of these diversions to conduct searches, answer emails, look up clothing items, and then when required or monitored, he completed an assignment. Tyrone's computer teacher believed in his ability to utilize his computer savvy for some future employment and professional application.

Tyrone nudged his fellow students for answers and information, leaned upon friendships and courtships to provide him required classroom preparations. His process was to find the quickest way to get the work completed, whether he borrowed, improvised, or created a few moments before or while it was being collected in class. When he was given a computer assignment, he would look up the answers on the network systems, paste them in, and then go back to searching for that Gucci belt on eBay. At least five times an hour during the school day, Tyrone was checking his iPhone and texting. If he was not working on the computer, he was using an alternate electronic tool.

MS. MARTIN'S ENGLISH 12 CLASSROOM

We have a set curriculum that we're given by the state of Louisiana that I absolutely do not follow. I believe that learning should be interesting for children in that it should be something that they can apply to their lives. If you cannot connect English, Math whatever with real life experience, children will not learn. What I tell kids the first day of school is that this is a class on life. It's not just—they know that it's English on their schedules, but I tell them this is a life class. And I say yes you are going to learn this survey of British Literature or survey of American Literature or whatever, but you are going to learn more about life. (Personal Communication, August 2006)

In this statement, she outlined a curriculum that purposefully employed connection between learning English content and life. This philosophy guided her pedagogy and writing assignments long after she faced the stresses from Katrina.

In the New Orleans of the eighteenth, nineteenth, and early twentieth centuries, separate secondary schools and universities existed for African American students to gain secondary school diplomas and college degrees. An African American child could go to college and become a doctor, minister, teacher, but he would attend the African American schools. Some of these legacies still hold within the demographics of schools within the New Orleans Public Schools.

Ms. Martin's high school, NOHS #4, was a McDonogh school that was given to the African American community after a petition by a group of influential black citizens to the New Orleans Public School Board. John McDonogh, a nineteenth-century philanthropist, left an endowment to build schools in poor communities so that all the children in a community would have a place to learn. The African American group wanted a high school for their children, and they were eventually given a McDonogh school. Today, NOHS #4 is a college preparatory public high school within the New Orleans public schools with a solid reputation for producing quality graduates, and one of the few high schools run by the New Orleans School Board that is not in academic emergency.

Any student who attended NOHS # 4 knew this reputation and was proud to graduate from the school. With a long history as a known and respected teacher, Ms. Martin had students clamoring to be in her English classroom during the senior year. More important to our discussion, her pedagogical pattern of instruction drew upon the fact that Ms. Martin shared her life experiences with the students alongside every literary discussion.

Ms. Martin's story about Katrina recalled the most tragic sequence of events that were captured by the news: she and her family were rescued from the roof of a flooded home, taken to the bridge over I-10 and stayed there for three days, spent additional nights in the horrendous conditions within the convention center, and then air-lifted to Corpus Christi, Texas, where a family housed Ms. Martin and her two sons for three months. Ms. Martin lost everything in her New Orleans home, including the structure. Her only remaining possessions were those left in her classroom at NOHS #4.

Ms. Martin's English language arts curriculum was centered on the study of British Literature in the twelfth-grade year. She took students through a chronological study of the British canon, beginning with *Beowulf*. Her classroom instruction followed this pattern:

1. She assigned a reading and questions from the textbook.
2. While the students were completing this, she took attendance, answered questions from absences, solved school-related issues surrounding her role as advisor for the girls' dance squad, her role as assistant director of the play, and her role as English Department Chair.
3. Then after twenty minutes, she began class with an oral summary and question and answer about the readings.
4. After the class had proved to her that they had comprehended the reading's message, she began to expand the discussion to the thematic content of the piece as it addressed real life.
5. She ended class with a quick summary of the next day's lesson and homework preparation.

Ms. Martin altered this pattern occasionally by having students write in their journals and orally share all or part of their writing, if they wanted; then she invited students to place the journal writing in the garbage. She used the journal writing to bridge to the literature study for that day, extrapolating and reflecting the reading's thematic content with real life content in a classroom discussion.

Writing tasks in the classroom were separated by purpose: academic and personal. The writing assignments were limited to the literary analysis essay, academic summary of materials, and analytical pieces, such as the summative research paper. Similar to Ms. Jane's writing requirements, writing was assigned with guidelines, but students did not receive direct instruction in how to write, accompanied by practice writings and revision techniques.

The personal writings focused on personal responses to any critical life event occurring with the students and were initially related to Hurricane Katrina. Ms. Martin had students each year who begged to be placed in her classes; she was not an "easy" teacher, and I asked myself throughout the study what drew students to her and her classes. As she described herself, "I am loud. I'm tough on these kids. I'm real about life, and they still beg to be in my classes" (Personal Communication, August 2006).

Ms. Martin demonstrated her philosophy in a classroom exchange with Tyrone. Tyrone had returned from the senior trip, and he wanted to know if Ms. Martin had missed him. When she responded, Tyrone cowered, as if he had expected her to confirm that she had missed him, and returned to his seat in the room while Ms. Martin addressed the confusion over the final portfolio requirements. (See appendix G.) He was concerned that he hadn't finished all the work for the final portfolio since school ended May 9, and he expected to graduate. During class, Tyrone spent his time quietly whispering to students near him or, when he sat behind a young woman, he played with her hair throughout the class. It seemed as if Ms. Martin ignored his inattentiveness and focused her energies on students more interested in completing the project.

Tyrone and Friends

Tyrone surrounded himself with friends at every possible interlude. Before school, students gathered in the first floor outdoor courtyard. Then, as each student took a seat in class, Tyrone located himself near a student with whom he could talk during the class, unless, of course, he had an assigned seat. In physics and math, Tyrone sat near students who helped him with the information. He wasn't often prepared.

Yet despite this dependence, Tyrone shared a friendship with many of the male and female students he introduced me to over the school year. He found every opportunity in the day to find his friends: between classes, at lunchtime, and before and after school, when he planned the next meeting. At the lunch break, Tyrone would not eat in the school cafeteria; instead, he would meet friends in the courtyard during lunch and strictly socialize, greeting one friend and then another.

> DA: What's important for me to know about you?
> Tyrone: I told ya. Nice guy. Cool. Like to have fun. Gentleman. Courtesy for others. You know, I look after people. (Personal Communication, April 2008)

Tyrone's image was important to him, and through the school day, he worked that image as I have described. However, whirling around Tyrone was another world of experiences.

Tyrone introduced me to a young woman who had been selected by Spike Lee and Soledad O'Brien to tell her Hurricane Katrina experience. Eleven high school students had been given video cameras to record their stories about Katrina two years after the storm. The result was a production called *Children of the Storm*, available on CNN at the following URL: http://www.cnn.com/2007/US/08/28/Soledad.childrenofstorm/index.html. These children of the storm told about lost hopes, shattered dreams, and dismal living conditions. Tyrone had been living near Atlanta since October of 2005, and hadn't returned to NOHS # 4 until the fall of 2007. By introducing the girl to me, Tyrone showed me his popularity and attempted to provide me with information about Katrina he didn't have.

The students affected by Katrina existed all around Tyrone—some of them in very desperate need for help. During English class one day, Ms. Martin directed the students to a reading from Chaucer, and then the students were to answer the chapter questions. She gave them this task because she had to leave the room to take care of some student matter. Tyrone read in starts and fits, asked other students what the piece was saying, and then the whole class gradually veered from the content reading into personal discussions. When Ms. Martin returned, class continued as I have described. However, there was one student who remained slumped over in his desk; his head wobbled on his supporting hand, and then he would abruptly awake. Ms. Martin said nothing to this student.

After the class, she told me that the student was a heroin addict; so were his parents. Rather than send him to the principal, where he would certainly be disciplined, she kept him in her classroom. She had counseled the student, but it had little immediate effect on his situation. At the beginning of class, Ms. Martin had given the student some mouthwash, soap, and some cologne or aftershave. She told him to go to the bathroom and come back to class not smelling like drugs, and try to be alert. This was the young man who kept nodding off.

In her final interview, Ms. Martin raged against the school system and the lack of psychological support it offered to students. The drugged young man was just one instance of the hidden conditions of students living in poverty and in dysfunctional family environments before Katrina. After Katrina, the situation only became worse. Tyrone observed the events in class but said nothing about the young man or his drug use.

This story and many others like them stalked the halls in NOHS #4. Teachers did what they could, like Ms. Martin, but the overwhelming need for help was beyond what any one person could provide. In schools where the students already had diminished resources and financial and emotional difficulties, a natural disaster situation exacerbates these conditions. As we see, this young man cannot focus or attend to learning. Unless there is a more dramatic and committed intervention, this young man's ability to succeed and escape is diminished.

In a focus group interview with Tyrone's peers, I learned that the students were tired of Katrina. From their stories, it was clear that they had found resiliency and were able to move past their experiences. Each of the students related to me a lesson or some real thematic understanding about their experiences. They were tired of writing about Katrina, tired of hearing about it, but were certainly willing to offer their observations about what had changed in their lives and in school because of Katrina. The one echo from all the students was that "New Orleans will never be the same. It's different now."

As I probed with questions, the students recalled the inconveniences of living with relatives, who at times demanded money from the guest relatives. This surprised the other students who were listening: that family would require payment for the living accommodations, regardless of the reason. The students had various stories about their experiences: some hated being in another town and school; some found that when their home was rebuilt and they returned, they were normal and safe again.

When I asked about the difference in the quality of education they had received in their Katrina schools versus NOHS # 4, their experiences brought them a new respect for the education they received. When they compared the teaching styles and rigor demanded of them at NOHS # 4 versus their alternate Katrina school, the students found appreciation and realization about what was important to learning and being associated with a quality education. Many of the students blamed Katrina for their drop in grade point because they couldn't learn in environments they didn't like.

One student who escaped to Mississippi found the number of pregnant girls in the school to be "so sick." These alternate schools forced them to compare the values of NOHS # 4 with those of other schools. From that experience, they arrived at a new respect for their academic preparation.

> But then at the same time, you have to realize that NOHS # 4 is one of the highest schools, like one of my friends, now she goes to [another high school in New Orleans]. We had to write terms papers in order to graduate and she was like, "Term papers? We ain't doin' no terms papers!" And I am like, "You dumb, 'cause you gonna need to know how to write those term papers when you get to college. And see, other college. Now, you don't have to go. But that's what the curriculum is. (Personal Communication, 1/18/2008)

One of the most fascinating aspects of this conversation was the students' belief that if the people who were poor and lived in the Ninth Ward and housing projects would just get up and work instead of expecting someone else to help them, they would be better off. There was little compassion for the thousands of people who lost their homes, who lived in poverty through no fault of their own. While the students reported on their newfound appreciation for the school, they failed to understand the systemic and institutional forces that contribute to poverty and injustice, even though some of the students whom they were talking about sat next to them in classrooms.

Finally, when I asked about what Tyrone learned from his Katrina experience, he said:

> T: This year has, yeah, a lot better. Um, mainly because, like, everybody's putting that past 'em. So, everybody's trying to like move on, and it's better.
>   DA: Do you think you can move on? Have you moved on?
>   T: I don't really think about it. Like, to be honest with you, like, I try to, you know, look past that to the future. 'Cause, I mean, I *am* the future. (Personal Communication, January 2008)

Tyrone and friends were a complex group of self-reliant adolescents who hadn't experienced the financial and material destruction to home and family that many students in the school had. This sequence of stories illustrated the variety of experiences students brought to Ms. Martin's classroom. Tyrone's responses indicated that he didn't think about Katrina; now that his friends moved on, he could, too.

Surviving was dealing with the inconveniences and unexpected changes that the storm had brought to the larger New Orleans community. They had survived the storm with their families. They had to survive the writing of those required term papers which gave them so much status among the other high schools. Yet, students who suffered from the ravages of violence, poverty, abuse, and other issues were hidden by their silence in the classroom. Louder voices, more recovery assistance, and resiliency spoke so loudly that those still in need were lost, except for the compassion and awareness of a teacher.

WRITING ABOUT KATRINA

Not all the students in Ms. Martin's English 12 class had Tyrone's support system. While Tyrone sat in her classes, behind the scenes, Ms. Martin listened to stories of students who lived in the upstairs rooms of a partially gutted house while their parents worked in another city. These adolescents lived alone all week until the parents arrived on the weekends to buy groceries and to check up on their children. Sometimes, it was even longer between visits. Another related fact was that the numbers of students who used drugs and alcohol increased, and students engaged in more risky sexual behaviors. These behaviors are indications of unresolved traumatic stresses in adolescents.

Ms. Martin found that she had students in her classes who had not experienced the same horror with Katrina. In the fall of 2007, she showed her class Spike Lee's film *When the Levees Broke*. For those students who lived through the experience, the film brought back difficult and emotional memories. Some students sat fascinated by the pictures because they had escaped and not returned to see the devastation until the city had cleaned up the cars, refrigerators, mud packed areas, bulldozed entire neighborhoods, and buried the dead.

In the fall of 2006, I provided Ms. Martin with the three sets of thirty *Time* magazine issues that had been dedicated to Katrina, which had been graciously donated by *Time* to the school. The students in her class did a response paper and an investigation into the truth of the magazine articles by interviewing people who had lived through the experience. Some of the students resented these tasks since they had lived through them. Ms. Martin was attempting to provide the class of students an informed context about the Katrina destruction and flooding so that all of the students would have a common reference. She needed the common frame of reference for her English class to understand what was a reality for New Orleans, and for her to survive teaching it.

In the 2006–2007 school year, Ms. Martin often gave her students journal assignments. I have described her writing assignments as academic and personal. Journaling was a personal activity she invited the students to do when she felt that they needed to express some emotions, as well as a regular learning activity on literary themes and personal connection. In the first year of school after Katrina, she asked students to write about their ideas, feelings, or something that was troubling them that day. She followed the writing activity with an opportunity for students to share or read from the journal entry. Then, she invited students to throw the papers away so that no one would read them.

These writing activities provided Ms. Martin a time to engage in her teaching philosophy about life. Katrina had dramatically changed her life, and she wanted to share her experiences with her students in order to extract from the discussions some common purpose and meaning after the indiscriminate destruction Katrina had caused and brought upon people's lives. The writing provided a point of departure through which to also view the thematic messages of literature, which was the dominant language arts being covered in the curriculum.

Many of the literary themes could be generally extrapolated to complement an emotional reaction or lesson provided by Katrina. This type of activity is critical for some students' intellectual survival after a natural disaster. In the journal activity as Ms. Martin designed it, she gave the students an opportunity to recount and release the problems they were facing in that moment. If the students wanted to, they could then tell what they wrote about and the class members had an opportunity to commiserate on their shared experiences. This emotional release opportunity is critical to rebuilding trust and releasing the emotional blocks that dominate critical life events and traumatic stresses. In the writing opportunity, Ms. Martin had found a way to provide students with the release and assure them of privacy.

While teachers are not trained counselors or psychologists, they have to confront the real psychobiological manifestations (van der Kolk et al., 1996, pp. 228–229) of trauma in the classroom. If teachers expect students to continue to learn, they must address the real consequences of the traumatic stresses, even if these stresses are not severe. Like Ms. Plummer, Ms. Martin had an instructional process that provided the kind of emotional and intellectual support needed by students who were surviving a traumatic life event. The journaling activity prior to the literary instruction released an emotional barrier to engaging in more analytical tasks.

While I never saw Ms. Martin write a lesson plan or make an entry into a journal, she told her story with each lesson, and moreover, she offered to share personal details about her life, what she thought they meant, and how she used these lessons to strengthen her own resolve to recover. Ms. Martin's teaching philosophy was based in a connection between literature and real life.

Yet, the writing tasks were so distinct in form that the connection from personal to academic was not encouraged, nor any more authorial control established through revision and editing conferences or instruction. Her challenge to the students was to meets the demands of the course and use literature to confront the challenges and conflicts in life. Her connection to the literature often challenged commonly held opinions and points of view, which Ms. Martin had no problem in addressing or raising.

In part, I believe that these elements are what made Ms. Martin's class so desirable to students, even though they would have to write unwelcome academic themes and essays. While her pattern of instruction was based in her intuitive teacher knowledge, the students responded to her methods in two specific compensations: the journal writing and the connection of literature to life discussions made the English student culturally and personally relevant.

Visual Literacy and Tyrone

How [do] I learn? I learn from watching things. Like . . . I can. . . . like you were just, like, just told me to just [sit] there and just read something. I'd probably take forever just to catch on. But if I can actually watch you do something. That's why I like math a lot. Because when I ax the teacher to write out a problem on the board, I can be right there with her. (Personal Communication, 4/11/2008)

To Tyrone, writing was arduous, not fun, and certainly not compatible with his visual preferences in learning. So studying his writing habits and composing processes meant that I had to understand these strategies as different literacies, similar to Chase and Diana.

The computer became his preferred writing tool and what sources and information he could access. Tyrone didn't see that writing and typing on the computer and accessing information was writing and literacy. Remember Randy and his fishing log? Through the computer, he collected ideas by locating reviews, YouTube passages and clips, criticism, and other sources of information. Then, he used the visual information he had collected to produce a written document, yet Tyrone wouldn't consider his typing and searching as literate acts. Nonetheless, his computer skills allowed him to meet the academic requirements and complete assignments. While we might consider Tyrone's academic work ethic questionable, he does introduce another compensatory strategy that is dependent upon visual comprehension as a pathway to learning.

James Gee's work *What Video Games Have to Teach Us about Learning and Literacy*, illustrated the seductive nature of visual images and progress challenges that are met with immediate rewards. Tyrone created a picture from the visual information presented to him by translating selected images into a visual pastiche that reflected what he wanted to say. With each success and access, Tyrone had achieved another level of success and understanding, just like the reward system in the video game.

When Tyrone had the visual image accompanied by the oral narrative, he learned. I wondered how the oral and visual instructional pattern in the classroom was replicated through the electronic media, the video games and web sites. Chase declared his process with self-awareness and deliberate intent to capture language patterns. Tyrone used media, but he didn't possess the same deliberate awareness or compensations. Nonetheless, he created written compositions using these media resources.

The context for his written composition was the required senior research paper on a novel. Tyrone selected *War of the Worlds*. As the following discussion illustrates, I am not sure Tyrone really knew what he was doing.

> D: What did you do the research paper on?
> T: The *Water Worlds*
> D: Is that the one with Kevin Costner?
> T: Yeah, but they had a move with, um, Tom Cruise in it.
> D: Then, I am getting confused.
> T: I didn't do it on the book, I do the [report] on the movie.
> D: Oh, you did it on the movie.
> T: I did it on the book. (Personal Communication, April 2008)

If this sequence of questions was not confusing enough, I came to realize only after reading his research paper that he had confused Costner's *Waterworld* with the Tom Cruise version of *War of the Worlds*. The title of his paper was "The Affect of a Martian Attach in the *World of the Worlds*." I provide page 1 of her paper (Figure 8.1) with Ms. Martin's comments.

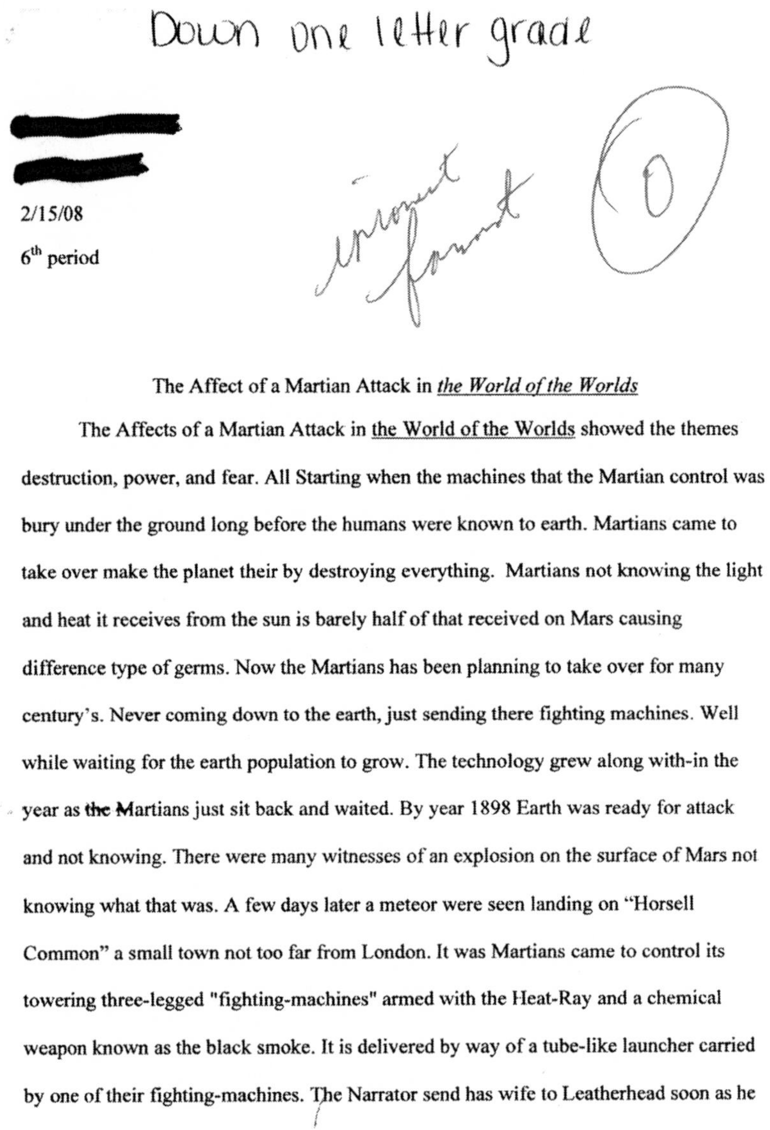

Down one letter grade

2/15/08

6th period

The Affect of a Martian Attack in *the World of the Worlds*

The Affects of a Martian Attack in the World of the Worlds showed the themes destruction, power, and fear. All Starting when the machines that the Martian control was bury under the ground long before the humans were known to earth. Martians came to take over make the planet their by destroying everything. Martians not knowing the light and heat it receives from the sun is barely half of that received on Mars causing difference type of germs. Now the Martians has been planning to take over for many century's. Never coming down to the earth, just sending there fighting machines. Well while waiting for the earth population to grow. The technology grew along with-in the year as the Martians just sit back and waited. By year 1898 Earth was ready for attack and not knowing. There were many witnesses of an explosion on the surface of Mars not knowing what that was. A few days later a meteor were seen landing on "Horsell Common" a small town not too far from London. It was Martians came to control its towering three-legged "fighting-machines" armed with the Heat-Ray and a chemical weapon known as the black smoke. It is delivered by way of a tube-like launcher carried by one of their fighting-machines. The Narrator send has wife to Leatherhead soon as he

Figure 8.1.

In preparing a draft of his paper, Tyrone's sources included the radio version of *The War of the Worlds*, two DVDs of the movies (the 1953 and 2005 versions), a dictionary for themes (he used destruction, power, and fear), an audio book of H.G. Wells' *The Time Machine*, and one Internet source for *The War of the Worlds*. The Internet source and Tyrone's paper show a similarity of phrasing, revealing a reliance upon the Internet source to direct the paper. I offer below a brief quotation from the Internet source, followed by Tyrone's version for his research paper, as he wrote it:

> After the attack, the narrator takes his wife to Leatherhead to stay with relatives until the Martians are killed; upon returning home, he sees first hand what the Martians have been assembling: towering three-legged "fighting-machines" armed with the Heat-Ray and a chemical weapon: "the black smoke." (www.online-literature.com/wellshg/warworlds)
>
> It was Martians came to control its towering three-legged "fighting machine" armed with the Heat-Ray and a chemical weapon known as the black smoke. It is delivered by way of a tube-like launcher carried by one of their fighting machines. The Narrator send has wife to Leatherhead soon as he found out about the attack. (Tyrone's research paper, 2/15/2008)

Tyrone's written text showed he co-opted the Internet source for the major word phrases, which he took from the video story, *War of the Worlds*. He continued the general story under the three thematic headings of destruction, fear, and power using the same phrasing co-optation.

By comparing the above two passages, we see the direct use of the Internet source, while Tyrone attempted to create his own sentences. Some might call this plagiarism rather than any actual use of visual literacy. As Howard (Eisner & Vicinus, 2008; Howard, 1995) has suggested, Tyrone's method of writing may be plagiarism, but it may also be a patchwork design. He borrowed from the visual media to help him piece together a written sequence. While I would suggest that this mirrored Chase's manner of creating texts, Tyrone's process indicated that he too was piecing together a written narrative using these computer generated images and source.

His use of narrator as a character rather than the awareness of the first person narrator showed his summary was based not on having read the book, but upon the internet and DVD versions of the story. Second, even though the title was presented correctly in all of the resources, Tyrone incorrectly gave the title in our interview and in the paper by calling it World of the Worlds. Not only was this an inattention to detail and inattention to the research in his writing, but his dependence upon the Internet and DVD sources for the paper do not reveal his understanding of the story beyond the story line.

The first line of the paper indicated the themes he intended to discuss, which I have already alluded to. In the paper, after the summary paragraph, he included three long paragraphs each beginning with one theme. Then, he related the story that showed this theme, generally. He presented no discussion or analysis but just recounted the story's main events. At the very end of the paper, he shifted to the second person narrator point of view and summarized the meaning in the following manner:

> Some mainly the outcome to this story the "*World of the Worlds*" is that you don't always have to be big to come out on top because the smallest thing under your nose could kill you.

The subject and verbs lacked agreement, as if Tyrone were combining his own thoughts with the text he was co-opting, and their intersection produced this awkward phrasing. His reliance upon the Internet and DVD for the contents of the paper presented evidence of the visual compensations Tyrone made in order to produce this written text. Ms. Martin directed Tyrone to revise his paper because it did not meet her formatting requirements. Admittedly, this was a poor-quality writing sample, but it reflected the type of written work Tyrone produced: quickly done, unedited, and superficial.

Even though Tyrone assured me he had read the book, he visually read the book from the DVDs and the Internet sources. For students like Tyrone, who are visual learners, technology access provides multiple and varied access to the visual renderings of literary information. I do not dismiss the poor quality of his writing, but he showed his growing reliance upon technology for research evidence, that was once relegated to library books and refereed sources. With access to more information and sources, there is a greater need for discernment and critique when students rely upon these visual images to create meaning and make meaning. With technology, the visual material with oral narrative provide a powerful tool for expanding literacy, but without restrictions and accountability, students may use these sources in place of real literacy and learning. In the discussion surrounding compensatory strategies, Tyrone has created one that he used to circumvent learning and writing. Again, here is evidence that students do not always use what we teach them as we intend, but clearly for their own purposes.

Tyrone's reliance upon visual images continued to cause difficulties for him in his English class. Whether we can attribute this to his causal study habits or his unique compensatory strategies of visual imaging, Tyrone explained about his process and reading and learning in English this way:

> T: But like, if you just tell me to just read this and do this work, and I'm telling you know, like, don't catch on to that. Like, when we had computers, I caught

on so quick, like I was like passing everybody in that, and I caught on so quick, you know and everything. Algebra I. That was right before the storm. And now you know what I like to do. I like to see stuff.

D: Is English hard then?

T: Yeah, So I do a lot of imagining. You know, like I try to imagine things. Whenever I'm reading, I try to imagine like it's right there in front of me.

He further explained this when he attempted to recall William Blake's poem, "Tyger, Tyger, Burning Bright."

T: I tried, I remember 'cause, in the poem, he was like, he was axing the tiger who created you, that's what I am talking about. Yeah, so you know, I tried to picture that. You know, that I was like, in the jungle, watching it. Try to picture like you know it was a movie instead of just reading it.

D: Is that how you read?

T: I cannot read and not visual it. You ask me about it and I'll tell you what I saw in my imagination. (Personal Communication, April 2008)

Tyrone clearly outlined the learning process as a visual learner, but his English class depended upon traditional forms of reading in class, discussion, and then writing assignments. Tyrone never admitted frustration or dislike of the subject, but clearly favored classes and subjects that demonstrated a process; for example, his math course. His compensatory strategies led him to use the power of images. The difference between the compensatory strategy and his visual learning process occurred in his deliberate use of images to produce texts. The images provided the words and ideas Tyrone co-opted and reshaped into an understanding and a product. When he cannot operate in the visual, then he can't read, and I would suggest, write.

When it comes to writing, Tyrone has shown us the intersection of his visual literacy and his written literacy. He wrote through the visual images by using them as a pathway to understanding. When I looked up the website on H.G. Wells which Tyrone cited, the cite had an organizational pattern, color, images including a picture of H.G. Wells, and limited text to read. Yet, this site gave him the abbreviated verbal outline for his paper, which he transferred to a written format. In the following interview with Tyrone, he shows a lack of purpose and audience, and demonstrates his reliance upon oral forms of communication.

T: I don't, you know, like, I don't have nothing to write. I don't have nobody to write to. Whenever I have to tell 'em to, I just tell 'em.

D: During the story, what did you do? After the storm, when you were in Atlanta?

T: I just called people, and like, I might write somebody on My Space, you know, but like write you a letter or something like that, nah.

D: Well, tell me. What do you do? I mean, you read and write in school. Do you do reading and writing outside of school?

T: Yeah, MySpace all day long. I'm the king. I have thirty-four thousand views. (Personal Communication, April 2008)

Tyrone viewed texting on his phone, and the images and words he created on his MySpace and Facebook pages, as writing. However, these were linked to the electronic tools and visual images and sounds. Students like Tyrone viewed writing as a school related task, even though the skills they learned through the school-sponsored writing were used in other contexts and with other tools. Again, in his process, we see the recurring theme of adaptation, co-optation, and distortion of academic instruction and disciplinary content.

Ms. Martin's division between academic writing and personally sponsored writings only served to reinforce Tyrone's use and concept of writing. In the personally sponsored world, there were no assessments or teacher-directed responses to corral the student's writing style or task. The exigent need was personal and, therefore, preference in genre and communication style was relative to the individual student and the purpose. To that end, this compensation, in complement to his visual learning style, managed the visual images so that he achieved the written product.

Tyrone did not just offer us a very intimate portrait of composing through visual practice. His process further illustrated how his particular learning style applied to instructional practice in the classroom. As mentioned earlier, Tyrone favored mathematical studies and courses that use numbers: he learned from teachers with a combined visual and oral classroom lesson:

> I learn from watching things. Like, I can, you were just like, just told me to just sit there and just read something? I'd probably just take forever to catch on. But if I can actually watch you do something, That's why I like math a lot. Because when I ax the teacher to write out a problem on the board, I can be right there with her. (Personal Communication, April 2008)

Here we see the visual dependence upon a physical action and the coordinating verbal explanation. Visual learning for Tyrone was not just constructing meaning through the visual images, but he also heard the content being constructed while he "saw" what to do and how to do it. Without the oral instruction accompanied by the visual, he cannot reach understanding.

Tyrone provided two other important components to his learning process: Teachers had to do the "visual stuff" and to keep it interesting.

> You gotta compare, you now, we read something that happened like a thousand years ago. She would compare it to now-a-days stuff. So, you know, to be honest with you, I don't care what happened ten years, then thousand years ago. But like, when she compare it to like 2008, it make a lot more sense to me. You know what I am saying? (Personal Communication, 4/11/2008)

Locked inside of Tyrone's learning process was the required link to relevancy. This theme resurfaced in educational literature in culturally relevant pedagogy, differentiated instruction, and other pedagogical processes (Ladson Billings, 1994; Tomlinson, 2000). Students like Tyrone need to have the visual instruction paired with the oral discussion and the personally relevant connection established.

His visual process showed us to what lengths students go to ignore the content knowledge in lessons that they cannot process for understanding, and the compensations that they make to arrive at knowledge we often did not intend. Tyrone's process showed us again the need for personal connections adolescents need in order to process the disciplinary content. This is especially difficult in English when Tyrone resisted the reading materials unaccompanied by any visual description other than contemporary events connected to the content.

TYRONE'S RESPONSE TO KATRINA

Tyrone's story about Katrina was not a story about traumatic hardship, but Tyrone had memories and stresses from experience nevertheless. When I asked him what changed about him from the sophomore student he was before the storm until now as a senior in high school. Tyrone said that he learned the value of a dollar. He was seeking another job when I asked him what he was doing in school and out of school. In school, he was just trying to graduate, and out of school he wanted another job. While he was in Atlanta, his parents stopped providing him with an allowance and clothes, so he had to find a job.

> I was always, always get like the finer thing in life. Even when I move out there, I was able to get some of those things. Like, I used to go to school and didn't have to worry about nothing, and nothing like that. Then, I came back, it was . . . all the teen attractions and stuff like that, hangout stuff, all that stuff was gone. (Personal Communication, April 2008)

Tyrone and his friends often talked about how much they grew from their experiences with Katrina. For some, the hardships came in the form of changes in the physical geography, learning different cultural behaviors in their diaspora, which brought them into conflict with their own values and living habits. Katrina disrupted more than just the housing: it offered these adolescents a unique opportunity to learn about life, living and the future.

> I grew a lot much older, a lot much more wiser, and I'm much more mature. I realized that it's all about me, and I have to look out for the other stuff—the future. (Personal Communication, April 2008)

I was unsuccessful in securing more writing samples and assignments, which Tyrone had supposedly completed for his classes. Neither Ms. Martin nor Tyrone provided a copy of his additional writings or the final literary portfolio (Appendix G). Tyrone graduated in May 2008 from NOHS #4.

WHAT WE LEARN FROM TYRONE

Tyrone presented a unique challenge among the other desperate and difficult circumstances surrounding the other adolescents in this book. However, through Tyrone's story, we learned other stories from individuals responding to the traumatic stresses; including Ms. Martin and descriptions of other students in her English and sitting next to Tyrone. At times, it is hard to see through his egocentric choices and learning processes. As he told me," It's all about doing me. It's what I do best." In some sense, this was Tyrone's survival mechanism. He was self-aware and through his visual compensations was self-educating.

We have all had students like Tyrone in our classrooms: privileged, charming, and academically casual about learning. These students can incite frustration to see such potential being wasted. In spite of his attitude, Tyrone shows us that adolescents with different learning styles operationalize the literacy preferences and habits they have developed to compensate in producing school based documents, and most probably with greater ease, personally relevant documents and texts outside of school.

One thing we do learn from Tyrone is that an adolescent doesn't have to have a history of violence or abuse or traumatic stresses to create learning strategy compensations. Even though he was surrounded by the other harsh stories, he survived relatively unscathed and still needed to develop learning strategies to compensate for his own learning style. Through this analysis, we see more evidence about teaching visual and auditory learners.

Tyrone has introduced the idea that connection and choice are not only relevant to the production of writing, but also to the pedagogical design of a lesson. He shows us the reciprocity of visual and oral instructional patterns for visual learners, but as teachers, this means that the lessons and then the practice of the disciplinary concept must extend the use of oral and visual. The visual here represents a picture, a text, a chalkboard demonstration, and any other print or non-print text that is being used to teach. Expressed as a mathematical equation, it is a representational sequence of activities for the visual and oral learner:

+ personal choice/connection to learning concept
+ visual and oral examples and/or visual examples with clear oral explanations
+ teacher-scaffolded/guided practices, visual and oral
+ individual practice leading to independence
+ more guided practice; an explanation with new visual samples
+ oral synthesis and reflection on learned concept
+ relevance for the students between canonical materials and life
= learning

While the equation is not dissimilar to what many teachers use as their instructional sequence, it places emphasis on repetition and guided practice, choice, and personal relevancy.

Another detail we learn from Tyrone and his peers is the growing importance of computer assisted learning and meaning making, especially when they complement a student's visual learning style. The easy access of these technological tools invites students to use them without critical analysis as to their appropriateness and reliability and to plagiarize. These undesirable uses along with other causal co-optations of easily accessible sources draw attention to the growing need for further teacher vigilance on assessments for writing tasks that rely upon computer based information sources. A very different picture emerged by comparing Chase's use of electronic sources with Tyrone's method, but they were using them in distinctly personal ways that make them compensatory strategies.

The role of computer generated information and the language use it provides to students presents teachers with an entirely different writing process. Ms. Martin used the writing process in her classroom, but Tyrone clearly compensated at the various junctures to invent what he had to have written for class, but by not using the traditional writing of texts from the head; instead, with a few strategic choices made, Tyrone realigns the writing process into a visually based composing process that allows him to produce a written text.

Finally, we learn that teachers experienced traumatic stresses, and that these conditions had significance in their teaching strategies. Both with Ms. Martin and

Ms. Jane, teacher intuitive knowledge of both their students, disciplinary content, and their teaching philosophies affected what instructional strategies they adapted to meet the behavioral changes in the adolescents in the their classrooms.

From the collective voices of the adolescents, the traumatic stresses and the repeated discussions about the traumatic events need to be replaced by an assumption of a new "normal" pattern to life. To this end, we see again the use and importance of journaling in the teacher's interventional teaching strategies. While there is not evidence about the development of writing strategies in classrooms over the recovery phase, we hear the adolescents and teachers indicate that story telling and journaling are connected to reestablishing learning. One more thing to write about and survive.

Chapter 9

Writing Across Trauma, Tragedy, and Adolescence

The history of teaching writing to adolescents is a complicated but relatively short one, depending upon how far back we reach to gather the principles. Indeed, education theorists since G. Stanley Hall in the late nineteenth century have continued to investigate the biological, intellectual, and social characteristics that identify adolescence as a separate stage in human development. Over the last forty years, the teaching of writing or composition has found a disciplinary identity, especially after the Dartmouth Conference in 1966. Expressivist theories of writing have been part of rhetorical history and composition studies history. Given the conventions of expressivist writing, the evidence presented in this book advocates for a new writing pedagogy that is based in the Expressivist traditions, a neo-Expressivist writing pedagogy for adolescents.

COGNITIVE, SOCIAL, AND EXPRESSIVIST WRITING PEDAGOGIES

An effective writing pedagogy for students considers the emotional/affective brain processes related to knowledge making and traumatic responses. Its attention to the affective/emotional connections needed by these kinds of students means that all the students in the classroom have a truth to investigate and tell, regardless of the conditions, since the affective-cognitive process has primacy in adolescent development.

I would be remiss if I did not address those teachers, theorists, and researchers who are proponents of cognitive process theories and socio-cultural theories of writing. The cognitive process proponents invoke writing through the rhetorical exigency and then a recursive sequence of cognitive operations. While the cognitive process theory (Flower and Hayes, 1981) describes the operational and rhetorical aspects of cognition as the primary process of knowledge making, it ignores the affective conditions that are connected to thinking through language and ideas. Indeed, the primary statement in all the theories is to describe writing and brain operations that would promote better writing. For two decades Cognitive process theory was an influential theory, being quickly implemented into textbooks and by teachers as the pattern for teaching writing. The omission of the emotional component to cognition for adolescents, and especially for those adolescents subjected to violences, is not addressing pedagogy for the way adolescents learn, and truly adjusting to their needs and abilities.

Similarly, social-cultural theories of teaching writing draw awareness to the role a person's social environment has upon early language development and cultural patterns of literacy. With the theories of Vygotsky, Bakhtin, and Lacan, researchers focused on identifying the process of literacy and language use that were operating through the social and cultural communities. Examples of these include Heath's ethnography (1983), which identified the cultural differences in language use between two geographically close communities. Another example of the social-cultural theories of literacy was represented in the work by Scribner and Cole (1981), which brought awareness and evidence to cultural and social contexts in an individual's literate acts.

While I consider the socio-cultural-historical theories of mind attentive to language acquisition processes and the importance of culture in determining some language patterns and uses, they do not give enough attention to the affective dimensions of information processing in adolescents so vital to their literacy development. I see the socio-cultural theories and constructivist theories as important teaching considerations with respect to cultural and social identities; however, these theories place language as subject to external forces, and not within the biological dimensions of literacy development.

In the implementation of socio-cultural theories, writers became part of a community, and learned to write through conferencing and sharing of writing (Daniels & Zemelman, 1988). Others paid more attention to the culture and ethnicity of adolescents who needed a culturally relevant program similar to what Heath suggested in her book (Ladson-Billings, 1994). While the socio-cultural theories demanded that teachers of writing consider the cultural dynamics in the language students brought to school, there was difficulty in describing a pedagogy that would accommodate cultural, dynamic systems for written literacy. At some point, literacy acquisition included reading and writing with the understanding that literacy was not broad enough to encompass the developing skills needed for computers, media, and other electronic communications. Writing texts seemed to reframe the writing touchstones of choice, audience, and purpose under the writing literacy umbrella (Gallagher, 2006). Professor James Britton was a primary thinker and proponent of a study on adolescent writing processes. This seminal publication brought to the composition arena a theory of learning and thinking related to language development. Britton's influence and research impacted U.S. thinking and research on writing and teaching of writing to adolescents. Both *Language and Learning* and *The Development of Writing Abilities (11–18)*, written with Tony Burgess, Nancy Martin, and Alan McLeod, theorized and investigated how language development and writing are connected. Along with James Moffett, Britton's work provides the touchstone for linking adolescent writing development and Expressive discourse.

Other writing pedagogies have relied upon expressivist writing practices but have not named it as such: Harste, Short, and Burke (1988) for children, Atwell for the middle grades, and Moffett for the secondary grades. From the late 1990s to the early twenty-first century, the direction of composition pedagogy has marked middle school and high school writers who need more age and culturally appropriate strategies and practices. Contemporary writing texts branched to include multiple genres (Bomer, 1995; Romano, 2000), or outlined the specific practices of successful individual teachers (Tsujimoto, 2001) to considering the role of media and computers in the teaching of composition (Wysocki et al., 2004).

Expressivist writing and writing pedagogy have existed alongside of the social-cultural, constructivist, and cognitive theories. In some cases, with its historical tradition of being associated with writing therapy (Bracher, 1999; Desalvio, 1999; Harris, 2003), the Expressivist tradition created a different approach to the teaching of writing (Elbow, 1990; Harris 1997; Thompson, 2000). In school writing, the formal essay, the Bain modes of discourse, or Kennevy's discourse for standardized testing and the writing process dominated writing instruction. Nevertheless, Expressivist adherents and researchers have continued to foster the value of Expressivist theories of writing (Brand & Graves, 1994; Harris, 2003; MacCurdy & Anderson, 2000) and found its theoretical verity in the writing of individuals who have had traumatic experiences.

Years ago, I had the privilege of taking a course from James Moffett. I have used his textbook not only in my high school classroom but also as an Expressivist/Developmental writing pedagogy sample for my pre-service teachers. When Moffett tried to implement his writing program in one community, it was met with resistance and controversy (*Storm on the Mountain*). While the ideas contained within the *Teaching the Universe of Discourse* and his subsequent textbooks for *K-13, A Student-Centered Language Arts and Reading*

Curriculum were developmental and expressively focused, some found them to be so revolutionary that they presented a curriculum that was antithetical to the community's expectations.[1] However, his curricular plan for writing discourses included a full spectrum of genres, readings driven by the narrator point of view, and an extended process from investigating writing ideas by recording, reporting, abstracting, and theorizing.

Gabrielle Rico in *Writing the Natural Way* also provides an affective, brain based method for discovering the stories we have to tell. Her inventing procedures help each writer discover how ideas are connected and then sequenced. The actual invention process of writing down and organizing ideas allows each writer to see his/her mental links between ideas. These techniques are under-utilized by teachers in writing instruction.

Another writing teacher and author, Ken Macrorie, in *Searching Writing* and *Telling Writing*, exemplifies the Expressivist tradition by using the narrative traditions of telling stories as the foundation for developing expository texts and research texts. His work embraces the need for students to tell stories, and then use that story format to develop their ideas in another genre like exposition and research. In his work, he privileges the narrative genre, instructs in narrative conventions that serve as the foundation for building idea awareness which can be translated into a multiplicity of genres and attentive to the shifts of purpose, audience, and style such moves would require of writers.

Perhaps the most influential writer, teacher, and theorist in developing the Expressivist tradition is Peter Elbow. His long list of essays, books, and articles refine and define an active Expressivist tradition. He codifies such procedures as free-writing as an invention procedure for the discovery and connection of ideas. His works have been referenced and cited throughout this book.

My intention is not to list every published book that explicates a writing program from the early 1980s forward, but to show the major works that have influenced contemporary writing pedagogy. As the reader can see, the Expressivist tradition has developed alongside other writing pedagogy and writing theory since 1966, Dartmouth Conference and advent of composition studies. However, while all these texts/events are useful and relevant depending upon the teachers' intentions and beliefs about teaching writing, they are purposefully dependent upon some individual aspect of writing, and not necessarily intended for inclusion in a secondary language arts program.

Each writing programs is based upon a theory, belief, ideology about the teaching of writing intended to present the latest outlook or distinct approach and application; however, some principles tend to emerge from these texts that I believe are the main principles about teaching writing that every ELA writing teacher needs to embrace. The Neo-Expressivist Pedagogy states what those principles are and attaches research data and historical data to the significance of the approach.

We have seen the life crises that adolescents have faced, and how they have used the compensatory strategies and literacy strategies to orchestrate learning and finding solutions to the daily problems they encounter. This search process is constructive and is driven by an exigent need. Chase's case study most directly illustrates this process, even though Diana's process for escape and coping is directed by a need to establish independence and show learning. Through the self-defined goals of need and desire and teacher-driven academic goals these adolescents were operating within a zone of development, and from their testimony, forming concepts about life and its operations.

THE TRAUMA CONNECTION IN THE EXPRESSIVIST TRADITION

What becomes an implicit message from the adolescents' case studies is that writing is something one does for school; writing for life is something one does outside of school to live and learn about what's really important. When we consider the degree to which violent acts have become so commonplace, asking adolescents to write literary essays and explore disconnected topics for writing will not address the complicated learning contexts that adolescents bring to the classroom or increase literacy. In the growing violence that adolescents face in schools, at home and on the streets, writing is a conduit to learning in all phases of education.

Before this discussion moves into the specific theme for this book, I want to revisit an idea that makes this discussion on literacy and trauma relevant for all adolescents in every classroom. I am not suggesting that there be one writing program for adolescents who have experienced trauma and another for students who have not experienced the dramatic life crises presented in this book; I am suggesting that the writing pedagogy and attention to compensatory strategies that guide creating lessons for the traumatized group will be effective for all students.

What we need is a writing pedagogy that can encompass the modern literacy demands and yet also reflect the realities of adolescents' lived experiences. This reality may intrude upon the pedagogical practices that educators have relied upon. As we have seen in the case studies, tasks such as literary analysis require language skills that may be as creative and sophisticated as any piece of literature. Without a different pedagogical approach to writing,

these creative expressions are locked into conformity and forms of normal-
ized writing genres like the essay and Bain's modes of discourse. Adolescents
can use the language of their world to transform themselves; we have to get
out of their way.

Merely offering journal writing activities and choice of topic are super-
fluous to generating meaning unless they are mixed with design, personal
relevancy, and directed or framed with rhetorical purpose. Then, students
will experience language and writing as a tool necessary for their survival
and evidence of their growth and development. As teachers, we can no longer assume that the students in our classrooms share a common experience,
cultural touchstones, and other learning references. Quite the contrary, traditional essayist writing pedagogy wants to normalize writing expression into
an economic function assessed by a single exam. Accountability is one thing;
teaching all learners is another.

Paolo Freire has thoughtful critique for us in this regard. His critical pedagogy and theories also apply to adolescents. At the mercy of adults, adolescents who are victims of violence and abuse know too well about oppression
and oppressors. Some who are excluded from mainline acceptance, brutalized
for their differences and eccentricities grab onto the power of violence to
attempt vindication and brutalize the oppressors who have oppressed them for
so long. I am not being melodramatic here, but after ten years of research with
adolescents and consequences of violence, language power is the powerful
vehicle of transformation for those subjected to traumatic stresses. Teachers
have to show adolescents how to use it, and as college educators, we have to
prepare future teachers to do so.

The case studies show us that adolescents do use literacy to meet their
immediate needs for survival to name the world they live. While we want
them to apply the language skills and use them independently, we need
to support writing activities and pedagogy that allows them to do so.
Sandwiched between childhood and adulthood, this developmental time is
strategic with changes critical of identity and personal integrity. What better
system to adopt than to use an adolescent's natural inclinations to draw him
further into considered discussion and controversy using language: to name
himself, and the world around him. The process of conscientization is very
much like the process of development for adolescents in that this is a period
of rapid transformations and the development of a personal power that can
literally transform a life.

In disconnected writing classrooms, the adolescent has one less place to
exercise any control. Surrounded by adults, adolescents use writing to control
what they can in that adult world either by responding to adults directly or
by engaging in writing that acts as a surrogate for the control adults seem to

have. In effective writing programs that attempt to engage adolescents with the immediate circumstances of their lives and use those experiences and information in conjunction with objective research materials, the adolescents engage willingly in writing tasks. O'Connor's work (1996) records the plays that O'Connor's students wrote about the difficult situations in which they lived. This writing gave form and power to what otherwise would have been considered a harsh condition that prevented learning instead of a condition that became a fertile ground for learning.

If we learn anything from the research case studies, O'Connor's work and Erin Gruwell's *Freedom Writers*, we learn the power of written experience and the mental and emotional transformation that it brings within and outside the classroom. It is not a panacea for social and emotional ills, but a constructive tool that uses the material of life to learn in ways that cannot be induced by academic assignments like the one on *Julius Caesar*.

Teaching the way adolescents learn is not easy. The dramatic changes in their development and individuality make any one writing program untenable. However, the principles outlined in the case studies illustrate a series of correlative components that make teaching writing successful. Those elements are consistency, conflict/challenge, connection, and choice.

Consistency is the maintenance of revision and editing over an extended period of time for one piece of writing. Consistency also establishes the maintenance of standards and clear goals for writing.

Conflict/challenge establishes the level of engagement, signaling where in the writing task the adolescent can find purpose and personal relevance. This also means that the writing tasks are intended to provoke challenge with long held opinions and beliefs or ideas through directed inquiry into a single subject. When the adolescent assimilates and associates with the established knowledge and then engages with conflict and challenge to those ideas, she reaches an engaging in knowledge making through knowledge telling.

The conflict/challenge component parallels the internal conflict for students who are living in traumatic situations or facing past traumatic conditions; conflict/challenge points to the realities of adolescents' changing developmental needs and the everyday conflicts they face as well as considering those students' whose lived experiences aren't defined as traumatic. Even so, we have seen how traumatic experiences and their emotional memory impose intellectual and physical hardships on their development, especially in a world with increasing violence. In terms of brain process, the conflict opens up emotional channels through which the inquiry can activate reflection, awareness, and cognition.

Choice is the continued call from so many writing teachers, such as Donald Graves (1983), who places choice at the beginning of engagement and purpose to any writing project. If the writing project is about learning to write, choice allows the adolescent to engage and begin attaching knowledge that adolescents already possess and binding it to emotional relevance and personal involvement.

The fourth and final element, connection, provides the guiding relevancy for all the other elements. The theorists and teacher writing researchers keep calling for connection and personal relevancy within writing classrooms. The connection has to be for the students to make and the teacher to allow individually: "If we are ever to become artful teachers, we must attend to this battle for attention. We must find some way to encourage our learners to want to use their reason" (Zull, 2002, p.76). What better connection than to associate content knowledge and personal knowledge in experience? Ms. Martin and Ms. Jane showed these qualities in their instructional patterns between the literature and life lessons.

These four elements comprise a pedagogical guideline for creating writing tasks that address the individual needs of all the adolescents in our classrooms. Let me digress for a paragraph or two, and reiterate the importance of using more details from brain theory and trauma theory. The most important reality about the brain is the relationship of cognition to feeling. They are intricately bound together in the making of knowledge.

> Knowing is a feeling. Not only is knowing a feeling *getting to knowing* is full of feeling. Those feelings are part of cognition. Our emotional centers trigger our Hypothalamus, and the writing of our bodies, to produce characteristic body feelings as we struggle with problems and solve them. (Zull, 2002, p. 73)

When we discuss making writing tasks effective for all students, we also must recognize the biological and mental patterns that establish knowledge. Adolescents are in the process of rebuilding brain connections; the amygdale drives the emotional responses as they link them to memory. Learning and literacy happen within the struggle.

In the case of personal experiences, these may be stored as "episodic memories": they are the memories we reweave as we recreate an event or an episode in our life (Zull, 2002, p. 80). When the traumatic levels of stress become so overwhelming, these brain operations of rational thought can literally shut down our ability to process information. Our brain is attending to the more important needs of survival, and the chemicals that the body sends due to the stress can impede memory and recall processes.

Therefore, if we want to engage students in learning and writing, we have to engage them at the memory and emotional levels and work with the natural brain processes. For students in stress, the brain's ability to process information has to have another entrance in order to operate. The emotions provide a key to the entrance, and then we have to move students to exploring the interior through memory and reflection activities.

I have seen writing being assigned rather than taught. Some teachers are not fully aware of the background and historical forms that determined the shape of modern literary genres such as literary essay analysis, comparison-contrast essays, persuasive essays, other modes of discourse, and expository-based assigned writing tasks. In light of the case studies, only rational activities are actually counterproductive to evidence presented. If nothing else, this evidence should direct us to question more how we are teaching writing, why we are teaching it to adolescents. What do we want them to be able to do with this literacy skill?

We have seen teachers discuss the slow process of learning that affects students who live and have experienced trauma from violence, abuse, and other factors. In order to re-establish a learning environment for these students, we need to rely upon the four elements for providing immediate writing and story-telling conditions and opportunities. These will be followed by extended opportunities to investigate a topic and then be challenged in one's thinking and ideas about that topic. Furthermore, we also realize that students make dramatic compensations when their needs are not being met, and they adapt what we are teaching. If we direct content instruction to fit into personally relevant learning contexts, the results could reveal more literate growth and amelioration to the traumatic stresses.

From the case studies of adolescents and their English language arts teachers, we gather a picture of the design of a writing pedagogy that addresses the needs for students experiencing life crises, but also a program that utilizes the creative and natural learning processes of each adolescent. In this case, the teacher is a guide and mentor throughout the process, and learning is the product both can embrace.

Mark Bracher, in the *Writing Cure: Psychoanalysis, Composition, and the Aims of Education*, clearly delineates the similarities of psychoanalytic pedagogy and the goals of Expressivist writing. The caveats from a number of compositionists, Expressivist theorists, and educators warn of the dangers of teachers using such clinically based procedures in the classroom with young students, since teachers are not specifically trained or have knowledge as to how to apply the principles of psychoanalysis and the stories they might engender from students (Johnson, in Anderson & MacCurdy, 2000). Bracher invites teachers to use the principles of psychotherapy to shape classroom-writing tasks, revision tasks, and teacher commentary on papers. He suggests that written discourse reflects the psychological state of the individual; that language use and misuse are in part manifestations of intellectual and

emotional conflicts within the individual's life. While theorists debate these
issues, we cannot ignore evidence that shows us that writing about traumatic
events can nonetheless be therapeutic and healing and aligned with natural
processes of literacy.

As Louise Desalvio describes in her book *Writing as a Way of Healing*
(1999), the names of many established writers show us how these writers
used writing as a way of surviving their lives: Alice Walker, Tim O'Brien,
and Isabelle Allende, to name a few. Desalvio shows how these writers used
their craft to write their way into a healthy mental state; that writing was
the vehicle that helped them survive and not succumb to the mind-numbing
violence they experienced. Building a writing program at the secondary level
that is respectful of all the experiences that students bring to the classroom
and mindful that teachers are not therapists is still possible.

In *The Psychology of Writing: The Affective Experience*, Professor Brand
outlines the affective cognitive process, which directs our intake of sensory
information, including those unexpected and traumatic events that happen
but don't necessarily register through cognition initially. Her research case
studies attempt to show the emotional/affective processing during writing.
She details the historical development of the affective/emotional aspect in
the psychology of writing experiences. Her work offers a genuine, research
and history based validity to the affective experience in writing. Her historical outline integrates brain processing information, literary and philosophical
texts as well as her own research case studies. The important conclusions
of her work fill a needed discussion on the affective role in composing and
cognition. As Peter Elbow states in the introduction to *The Psychology of
Writing,* her work provides the composition field with evidence and intellectual depth to the role emotions play in composing, and gives us the language
and discourse to further develop conversations and research on emotional/
affective role in writing/composing.

The uses of writing in psychotherapy and counseling venues have provided the research background that allows us to pursue more integration
of these results into composition pedagogy. This is especially relevant for
teaching adolescents whose life experiences contain years of traumatic
stresses from abuse, violence, and disasters. Since research has shown that
these events impact an adolescent's ability to process information and to
think, then different pedagogical strategies are needed to reach these individuals. After all the research reports and the evidence presented in this
book, the possibility exists for a pedagogy that bases itself in the Expressivist traditions, accepts the caveats of professional writing therapy, but
still promotes a writing pedagogy that will address the needs of traumatized
adolescents and their peers.

NEO-EXPRESSIVIST WRITING
PEDAGOGY FOR ADOLESCENTS

I want to suggest a new writing program for adolescents based upon the four principles of connection, conflict/challenge, consistency, and choice that provides specific pedagogical guidelines using Expressivist precepts in writing and writing pedagogy (Elbow, Rico, Graves) for adolescents. I call this a Neo-Expressivist writing program, heavily based in evidence from Expressivist writing researchers, authors, and educators cited throughout this book.

Understanding that the Expressivist tradition, long associated with therapy and traumatic stresses, can be used to structure a viable writing pedagogy for adolescents, I have detailed a teaching approach derived from the case studies and the historical development of the Expressivist tradition in composition. The major precepts for this Neo-Expressivist writing pedagogy for adolescents are the following: student-writer-author, choice and genre, goal setting, connection, pedagogical consistency and revising consistency, and finally conflict/challenge.

The Expressivist tradition of writing and writing pedagogy, first, places the writer as the author and director. The author selects the topics from an expressive need to tell her truths and explore them, reflect and deepen understanding through deeper inquiry. In Neo-Expressivist pedagogy for teaching writing to adolescents, the student-writer-author has to develop this identity and be encouraged to tell. This positioning gives the student writer a different purpose within the classroom. The complementary instructional strategies are designed to show students how to achieve clearer expression of their ideas.

If we believe that students have a truth to tell and that as the teacher, our responsibility will be to draw that truth out and assist the student in reflecting, challenging, and constructing written discourses, then as educators we are embracing a very different teaching agency. In this position, we become the mentors and motivators in the search for self-expression. We have to believe that through this process, the student writer will discover and develop sophisticated skills with language and personal identity through reflection and critique.

The second precept gives the students control over topic choices, but the choice involves more than just selecting the immediate idea. The topic selection may contain the key to what blocks an adolescent's literacy abilities, written expression, and compensations. Other researchers and compositionists have heralded the call for student topic choice (Graves, Bomer, Tsujimoto, Atwell), but a Neo-Expressivist writing pedagogy contains additional teaching procedures that must also accompany the choices of topics. The role of the teacher is to help the writer discover what he thinks and/or to provide a safe learning environment in which to tell.

This tenet requires a different teaching position than most secondary teachers use in the classroom. In many classrooms, adolescents are given a model to follow, a specific genre to imitate, the generic "essay" name assigned to any writing students do. Very little time is given to investigating the genre most appropriate for the students' ideas. This can lead to some degree of chaos and uncertainty in terms of what the students are directly learning. This monologic writing approach excludes crucial elements related to purpose, audience, and genre. Instead, the process assumes that the student will transfer skills to other writings (Foertsch, 1995).

As we have seen in the case studies, teachers who plan a writing pedagogical program around topic choice and literary references do provide a wide range of writing experiences. Imitating literary models provides practical options for students when they do have more control over their writing form. Again, this harks back to the question about what we expect adolescents to learn about writing when we explicitly teach writing. Writing is often assigned but not taught.

In the Expressivist tradition, every person is a writer with ideas and a message, but few adolescent writers have substantial experience writing in other genres. Without this experience, students may not be able to see their ideas in a specific writing form, or experiment with transferring an idea from one form into another. Adolescents need experience and the chance to write in a wide range of genres including narratives and non-fiction writing of all kinds. Danielle's case study illustrates the power of this position.

The Neo-Expressivist pedagogy also means that the adolescents are writing to name the life they are living through a concentrated study of a chosen topic, and to complicate and experience a type of expertise through composing various pieces that reflect their interests and help them make meaning of their day to day life: examine it, reflect upon it, and express it without consequence or retribution.

We have seen evidence and research data that shows that individuals need to tell their traumatic experiences in order to gain agency and control over the experience. By doing this intense story formation, they can release the traumatic stresses and regain a control that is necessary to building pathways for literacy development. The use of the language symbol system forces them to convert these experiences into discourse. This process alone is important to resiliency, to literacy development and to using the traumatic experience as a powerful transformative tool. The topic choice has both emotional and cognitive relevance for assisting the student in learning.

Moreover, teachers will need to provide a variety of writing experiences in various genres that model topic selection and message through specific forms. The process of choice embraces clarification of message, word choice, and genre. This broadening of the experiences with writing provides teachers and students with more opportunity for expression and allows those students for whom trauma and stress rule their lives a safe place to tell.

In the Expressivist tradition, practitioners value the inventive stage of discovery of an idea or topic for writing. These are not teacher-driven or selected, but entail providing students with an array of invention strategies that provoke ideas and topics for writing. The student writer is the author. Too often invention strategies are relegated to brainstorming or mapping instead of sustained discovery strategies over several days to weeks using a variety of discovery ideas including classical inventive strategies from the topoi (common places for inventing and finding ideas). These also include journal writing, free writing, brainstorming, or other inventive strategies that prompt the discovery of ideas. However, there is one condition to using these strategies: they must be connected to other writing activities and have a clear purpose, either developing writing skills or discovering truth and ideas.

Third, goal setting in the Neo-Expressivist pedagogy is essential. The ability to set goals and create strategies to reach those goals is essential for healthy personal and intellectual development. The clarity and directness with which the goals are made visible assists in establishing agency and control. The teacher and student writer can negotiate, for example, how many writings a portfolio will contain or a format for the final product; what will the writings need to demonstrate in terms of skills and knowledge about writing; the role of genre conventions; the students' own writing goals for the course or semester; and finally, the clearly stated writing goals for the course. In other theories like the cognitive process theory of writing, goal setting was a cognitive function in the process. In this Neo-Expressivist pedagogy, the goal setting drives ownership for the writing being considered within the course or project.

In preparing a Neo-Expressivist writing program for adolescents, teachers isolate the central theme or vision on the writing rather than literature. The literacy goals for the curriculum need to be clearly stated within the language arts disciplinary requirements. As teachers are subject to state mandates, the curriculum may need to be adjusted, but still can cover all the language arts grade level expectations.

In the writing-centered model, literature study functions as support and illustrative study for the writing genres. Teachers and students select reading material based upon their subject choice as well as read certain canonical works relevant to their academic studies. We have seen these harmoniously function in ELA classrooms with Ms. Plummer and Ms. Martin. As the literate language arts expand to include visual literacy and media literacy, the literature and writing can now engage video productions, films, and more modern media usage as viable forms of discourse. In fact, using these contemporary genres and literacies may have more expressive appeal to adolescents, and help them learn the literacies and expressive discourses they need to survive.

The fourth element is connection: connection between the student's interest, emotional needs, and the structure of activities may define the effectiveness of the program. In the various studies presented, the connection between the assigned work and its relevancy to the students' personal needs often determined the literacy learning. In the biological evidence presented, the brain disconnects certain thinking pathways as the result of the trauma. In order to reconnect the "thinking" pathways, the individual has to reconnect the pathways establishing new connections and personal relevancies. Through writing and telling stories of the traumatic experience thaws the freeze, an individual can reclaim both the emotional and cognitive processes to think, to feel, and to learn.

On the pedagogical level, the connection between the various classroom strategies and material content has to complement these mental processes. In the various descriptions of adolescent reasoning and processing, the connection begins in the classroom with the material helping the student to access her prior knowledge, thereby creating a foundation for building new associations and assimilations.

The fifth element involves consistency. Consistency is the one necessary teaching element that provides control in the Neo-Expressivist program. It allows the student and teacher to have a disciplinary program that provides individual exploration, depth of inquiry, and transformative revision process. Especially traumatic subjects or ideas need to have objective and alternate positions presented. As students delve into their topics, they are gaining information and expertise in their area but also have models and patterns for expressing similar ideas. If students will read when they are interested, then this system provides literacy support.

These tasks become important in writing literacy as a personal power to use language, and transform an adolescent's life. At the very least, these writing activities have the potential to empower adolescents. I have used the case studies to illustrate that one of the hallmarks of adolescent development is the establishment of an individual identity. Adolescence is the protracted period in the growth cycle where adolescents are finding and searching for their separate identities. This mark for identity is consistent with Expressivist writing theory, which utilizes writing to capture personal idea discovery; furthermore, writing it down and telling the story in present time offers a system for reflection and self-awareness, as we have seen in the case studies of Chase, Diana, and Danielle.

Consistency is also necessary throughout the course. Instead of one or two writing conferences on a certain piece of writing, the teacher may need to read revisions of a paper nine or ten times, as we have seen with Ms. Plummer.

These deep revisions are the pathways to great skill with grammar, paragraphing, syntax, and other literary devices we want students to develop in their writing. While teachers can rely guardedly upon peer writing groups, teachers need to expect that less skilled students will need more scaffolded conferencing and attention.

Conferencing involves more than error correction or commentary that directs the writer to meet the teacher's personal goals. Instead, the conferences allow the writer to make deeper connections, reflections, and critique of his own writing. The student-writer explores his own intent through the revision process. In this aspect, the grammar correction, phrasing, and other structural or mechanical concerns become part of the consistent depth of inquiry into one's topic and its written form. Also, the consistent and expected use of writing conferences creates a "writer" mentality through which the writer takes ownership over his text, another important aspect of Expressivist writing. Consistency means the sustained and maintained expectation of excellence, and the teacher and student work together to achieve that goal in the conferences, peer writing groups, and through classroom instructions.

The final element, and perhaps the most important aspect of the pedagogical program, is to provide challenge or conflict. Adolescence is a period of biological changes and upheavals as they reach toward adulthood. The internal and external crises that arise in every adolescent's life are relevant in the immediate moment. Their social world consists of building relationships, losing relationships, finding other relationships, and discovering how to be in their immediate world. The extra crises from violence and disaster only complicate this process, and strip the traumatized adolescents from engaging in their development with traumatic memories, experiences, and encumbrances. Moreover, every adolescent needs to write to survive, but especially those whose lives are complicated by private and public violence.

Challenge and conflict are necessary components in any writing program because they are natural processes that instruction needs to complement. Challenge in this connotation means creating a writing classroom that invites and structures challenges to the adolescents' acquired literacy skills and provides a gateway through which to use these acquired skills whiling gaining new ones, building upon their prior knowledge and experience. The challenge enters the classroom through choices in reading and writing, the demand for language use skills developed through conferencing and revision. These manipulations with language are the tools for building language power and expression, even though the student might not see their immediate worth.

Challenge/conflict create a zone of proximal development (Vygotsky, 1983; Dixon-Krauss, 1996) where the adolescent cannot supply all the information, and then strives to find answers in ways similar to what the students have shown us about their compensatory strategies. The conflicts students already bring to class from their everyday lives as well as the biological conflicts in psychological development provide plenty of discord for learning. The discord created in writing tasks and assignments has the power to open a closed pathway by circumventing established patterns of learning. In some cases, the conflict/challenge naturally exists for those students living in traumatic conditions. The external conflict or challenge in the classroom is intended to complement the internal challenges and provide direction and inquiry to probe for solutions and understanding.

Instead of providing answers, the teacher provides pathways for finding information and expressing ideas through engagement with many forms of written and oral discourses. The students determine some of these; teachers determine other discourses for a specific illustration of a writing technique. Instead of the emphatic reliance upon the generic "essay" as nomenclature for the writing adolescents do in high school, the teacher now has the obligation to show students other options for expression.

The Neo-Expressivist Pedagogy for Teaching Writing to Adolescents offers each teacher a writing instructional program that will address her school district demands for language arts writing content knowledge, accommodate the emotional process that adolescents engage in to write and think, and to begin to accommodate the traumatic conditions that plague many of today's adolescents.

For all the students who live in extreme conditions and with traumatic stresses, we need to address their literacy needs as actively as we address the students who do not live with these conditions. The violent outbursts, revengeful and frustrated individuals who lash out at perceived injustice with violence seem to dominate the news with increasing frequency. Our students witness these acts every day. These public and private violences affect adolescent learning, their survival, and their development. Changing the way we teach writing to adolescents who live with the public and private violences will mean that these children will have an instructional intervention that can serve them throughout their entire lives, and teach them the power of language to heal and to survive.

NOTES

1. See *Storm on the Mountain* by James Moffett for the full account of what happened in the community.

Appendix A

Syllabus for the Senior Project (Block Scheduling)

Term 1	Literature
Week 1 Aug. 21–23 Thinking about Topics	Introductory Exercises
Week 2 Aug. 26–30 Draft Autobiographical piece (Choose Full-Length Book)	Autobiography/Biography
Week 3 Sept. 3–6 Revise Autobiographical piece Draft descriptive piece	*Beowulf*
Week 4 Sept. 9–13 Revise Descriptive Piece Draft Poetry Analysis	*Beowulf*
Week 5 Sept. 16–20 Revise Poetry Analysis Conduct Interview with worker Magazine Article # 1	Terkel/*Canterbury Tales*
Week 6 Sept. 23–27 Draft Interview Piece Magazine Article #2	*Hamlet*

(Continued...)

Term 1	*Literature*

Week 7
Sept. 30–Oct. 4 Magazine Article # 3   *Hamlet*

Week 8
Oct. 7–11 Select and Finalize Piece
   for Publication

Week 9
Oct. 21–23 Student/Teacher Grade
   Conferences
Revision time
Exam

FULL-LENGTH BOOK FINISHED

Term 2	

Week 1	*Brave New World*
Oct. 28–Nov. 1 Draft Poetry Analysis	Magazine Article # 4

Week 2   *Brave New World*
Nov. 4–8 Revise Poetry Analysis
Magazine Article # 5

Week 3   "A Modest Proposal"
Nov. 11–15 Draft Persuasive Piece
Magazine Article # 6

Week 4   *1984*
Nov. 18–22 Magazine Article # 7

Week 5   *1984*
Nov. 25–26 Draft Conclusion

Week 6   Romantic Poetry
Dec. 2–6 Revise Conclusion   Draft original poem

Week 7   *Dead Poets Society*
Dec. 9–13 Revise original poem
Draft Introduction
Artwork

Week 8
Dec. 16–19 Revise Introduction

Week 9
Jan. 6–10 Cover, Table of Contents
Bibliography
Pagination

Week 10
Jan. 13–15 Presentations of Senior Project
Final Exam

Appendix B

Danielle's Writings

Name of writing	Genre	Date of drafts	Exigent situation	Type of revision
Life event	Autobiographical narrative	8/28/96	1st Eng. class writing on topic of divorce	None
Important Person—Dave	Description of significant person in narrative	9/4; 9/13; 10/14	Teacher-initiated	Various times
Test on *Beowulf*	Poetry in rhyming couplets	9/19	Examination	None
Literary discussion of poetry—Jason Talmadge	Literary analysis with 1st-person narrator	9/6; 10/14; 10/20	Senior project	Reduction of text; clearly summarize poem; confusion in narrative; verb tense shift
In-class prose writing describing a nature scene	Changed to poetry during 2nd draft of text 9/25	9/24; 9/25; 10/9	Class assignment	Word choice; irrelevant details
Magazine article report form	Supplied by teacher	10/9	Senior project	None
Interview to be written as a character description—Todd	Series of interview questions written into a series of paragraphs describing a person	10/23; 10/30	Senior project	Storytelling not clear to reader; tense shifts; accurate form of words

(Continued...)

Name of writing	Genre	Date of drafts	Exigent situation	Type of revision
Poetry analysis with anecdotal reflection— Identity	Summary/analysis/ anecdote/reflection of anecdote to summary	10/31; 11/7; 11/10	Senior project	Information not available
Define culture, for Sociology class	1 paragraph of definition	11/11/96	Class assignment	None
Booklet of writing for Spanish class, published under Danielle's Spanish name	Various single paragraphs that each deal with a thing in life: TV; favorite animal; work; friends	First-quarter writing assignments collected for parent-teacher conferences in November.	Parent-teacher conferences	Points given and some grammatical elements corrected in Spanish-language use
Persuasive piece	Letter to mother	Think-aloud protocol 11/19, 1/20	Senior project	Teacher remarks
In-class writing: what you are is where you were when	One long paragraph + 2 sentences	11/20/96	In-class writing	Points given only
Introduction for senior project	Series of narrative memories about what she remembers	12/5;12/12	Class assignment	None
Writing poetry	Series of sentences set up as stanzas	12/12	D. found poem, and it served as background for this writing	Pick words more carefully if it is to be part of portfolio
Syllabic poem	Each line must have 10 syllables	12/18/96	Class assignment for students to learn to count syllables in stanzas	Completed in class in peer-editing group
Poem for portfolio	Sonnet using syllables from previous exercise in class	12/12/; 12/18	Class assignment	Group editing project
Personal letter	letter	12/9	Need to settle a past situation with a far-away old boyfriend	None

Appendix C

Chase's Writings

Name of writing	Genre	Dates for drafts	Exigent situation	Type of revision
Childhood memory	Narrative	9/5; 9/11	Class assignment	Teacher's editorial corrections
Significant Person	Character description	9/25	Class assignment	Teacher's editorial corrections
Setting	Autobiography statement about important place	10/1;10/2; 10/3	In-class writing assignment from short story study	Typed from hand draft; teacher's editorial corrections
Immigrant	Biography	10/3	Class assignment	Teacher editorial corrections
Summary-FHU	Story summary	10/9	In-class assignment to check study reading	None
Story of love	Narrative	10/15	Single emotional effect	None
Social promotion	Journal turned into writing	10/3	Newspaper article about school board decision	Teacher's editorial comments
Single emotional effect	Narrative about two young girls	10/15	Write a story with a single emotional effect	Teacher's editorial corrections

(Continued...)

Name of writing	Genre	Dates for drafts	Exigent situation	Type of revision
Letter to Judge	Letter for 11/20 court date	10/22	Speeding ticket	None
Family origin	Narrative	10/26	History class	Teacher's grammar/ sentence corrections
Persuasive letter intended to be editorial	Information turned into letter intended to be persuasive	11/25–12/5	Class writing assignment	Revisions don't reflect any consistency after teacher comments
History report	Reporting facts about Cold War	12/11	Report required for grade in history class	None that I have
Summary of novel, characters, and reaction	Three separate writings that addressed the three titles	Turned in December/ January; assignment given in October	Report on novel student was reading outside of class	None
Final exam in English	Narrative about future life	1/15	Final exam	None

Appendix D

Diana's Writings

Name of writing	Genre	Dates for drafts	Exigent situation	Type of revision
Folktale/myth writing	Summary and comparison	8/31	Class assignment	None
Comparative history assignment— Athens and Sparta	Essay	9/12	Class assignment	None—one draft only and then graded by teacher (B)—comments suggest third-person narr. pt. of view instead of first
Proverbs interpretation	Journal entry for English class	Every day of class except exam days; collected four times: 9/20; 10/21; 11/22; 2/13	Class assignment to write and interpret proverb	Teacher collects periodically and then returns them to students with comments
Name paper	Narrative/ exposition	9/19; second draft 9/25; third draft 10/12; final draft after 10/12—no exact date	Class assignment	Peer editing on 9/23; Diana had not completed draft
"My Mind Is in a Daze"	Journal and poem	10/4	Fear of being hurt by new love	None

(Continued...)

Name of writing	Genre	Dates for drafts	Exigent situation	Type of revision
WSAS Exam	Essay portion of test; persuasion writing prompt	10/21	State-mandated testing of sophomores	No revisions; completed in 20 minutes
Destiny is not left up to chance.	Persuasive speech invented and prepared in writing before delivered to class	11/5; final 11/11	Class assignment	Outline of speech 11/5; teacher corrected and added details; second outline and rough draft 11/11
Novel response	Expository writing about *Jane Eyre*	12/2	Class assignment	One draft and teacher comments that edit her phrasing
Test on *Jane Eyre*	One essay question about the novel	12/4	Essay exam	None
Poetry presentation on Alice Walker poem	Oral presentation with written analysis	Not known	Class assignment	Teacher comments on rubric
College letter	Letter of application to Oklahoma St. U.	12/3; 12/11	Writing of letter for computer class	English teacher reviewed and edited it
Jose	Personal letter	12/10	He sent her money to come to Oklahoma; she is returning a letter	None
Kathy	Personal letter to friend in Michigan	12/10	Letter from her friend	None

Name of writing	Genre	Dates for drafts	Exigent situation	Type of revision
Report for health class on alcohol and drugs	Series of questions and written answers	12/6	Class assignment	None
Response report on *Lord of the Flies*	One-paragraph response to statement from the novel	1/6	Class assignment	None
Journal—kept hidden behind dresser	Don't know	Various	Times of emotional stress	None

Appendix E

Persuasive Speech Assessment

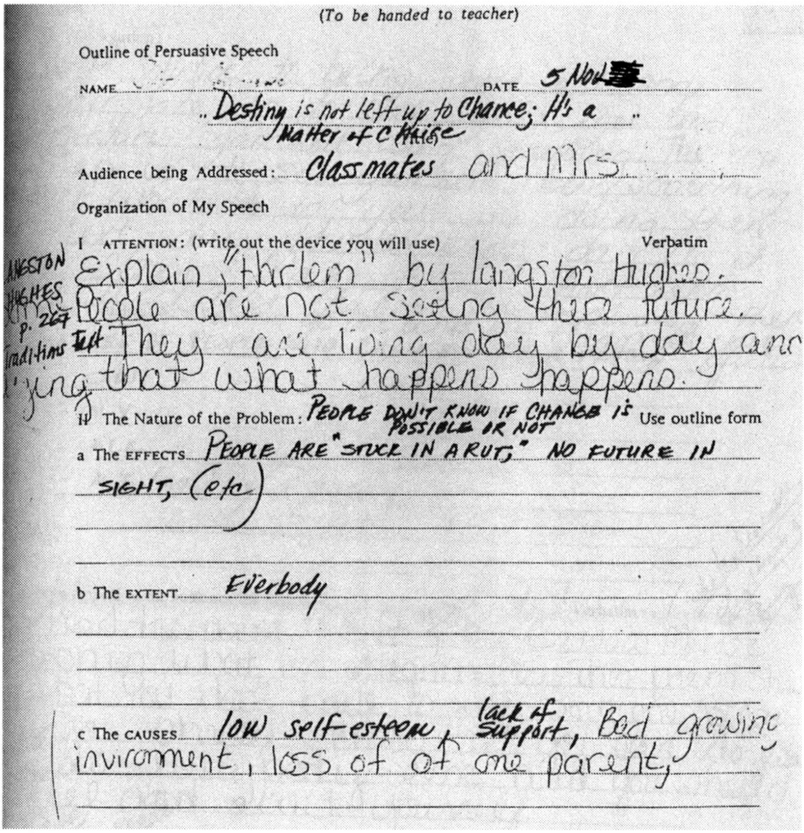

(To be handed to teacher)

Outline of Persuasive Speech

NAME .... DATE 5 Nov 翌

.. Destiny is not left up to Chance; It's a ..
Matter of Chhise

Audience being Addressed: Classmates and Mrs. ....

Organization of My Speech

I ATTENTION: (write out the device you will use)   Verbatim

LANGSTON HUGHES p. 264 traditions Expl

Explain "Harlem" by langston Hughes.
People are not seeing their future.
They are living day by day and
'ing that what happens happens.

II The Nature of the Problem: PEOPLE DON'T KNOW IF CHANGE IS
POSSIBLE OR NOT   Use outline form

a The EFFECTS PEOPLE ARE "STUCK IN A RUT," NO FUTURE IN
SIGHT, (etc)

b The EXTENT Everbody

c The CAUSES low self-esteem, lack of support, Bad growing
inviroment, loss of of one parent;

Figure E.1.

245

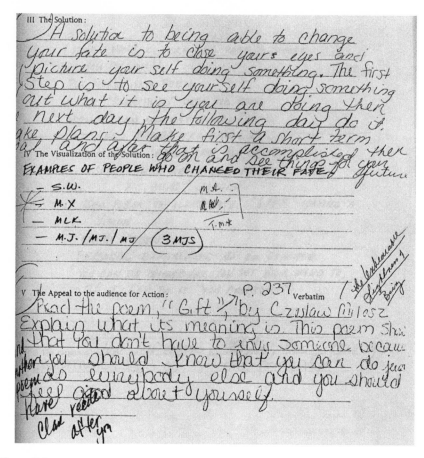

III The Solution:

A solution to being able to change your fate is to close yours eyes and picture your self doing something. The first step is to see your self doing something out what it is you are doing then next day, the following day do it. ake plans. Make first a short term and after that accomplished ther go on and see things for your future

IV The Visualization of the Solution:

EXAMPLES OF PEOPLE WHO CHANGED THEIR FATE

- S.W.
- M.X
- MLK
- M.J. / MJ. / MJ (3 MJS)

M.A.
M.W.
T.M*

V The Appeal to the audience for Action: P. 237 Verbatim

Read the poem, "Gift", by Czslaw Milosz Explain what its meaning is. This poem sho that you don't have to envy someone becau: you should know that you can do jus as everybody else and you should feel good about yourself.

Figure E.2.

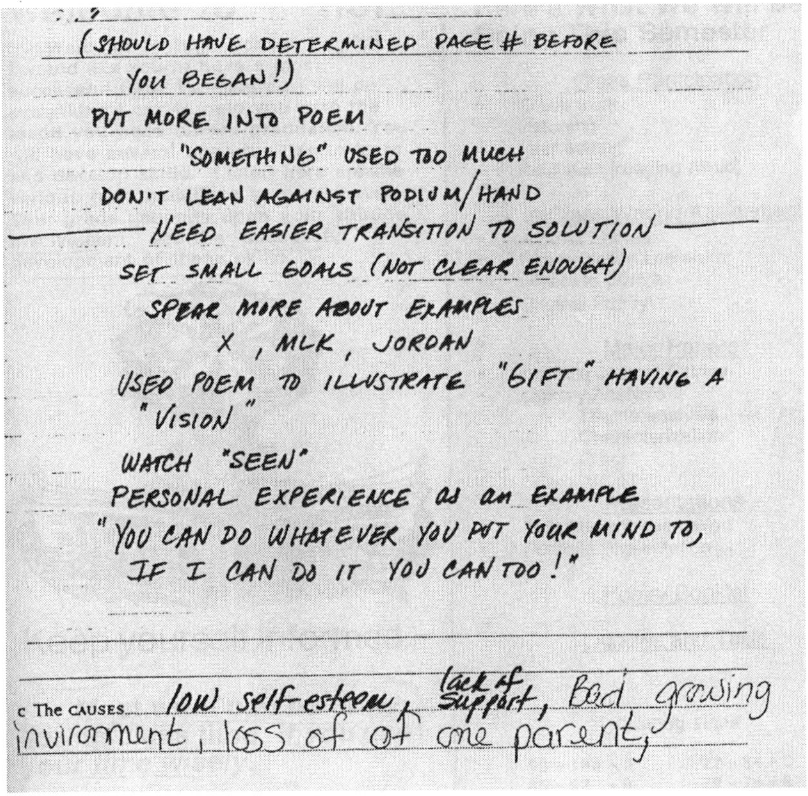

(SHOULD HAVE DETERMINED PAGE # BEFORE
    YOU BEGAN!)
PUT MORE INTO POEM
        "SOMETHING" USED TOO MUCH
DON'T LEAN AGAINST PODIUM/HAND
——————NEED EASIER TRANSITION TO SOLUTION ——————
SET SMALL GOALS (NOT CLEAR ENOUGH)
    SPEAK MORE ABOUT EXAMPLES
            X , MLK , JORDAN
USED POEM TO ILLUSTRATE "GIFT" HAVING A
    "VISION"

WATCH "SEEN"
PERSONAL EXPERIENCE as an EXAMPLE
"YOU CAN DO WHATEVER YOU PUT YOUR MIND TO,
    IF I CAN DO IT YOU CAN TOO!"

c The CAUSES *low self-esteem, lack of support, Bad growing invironment, loss of of one parent,*

Figure E.3.

Appendix F

Hurricane Information Survey
(Warheit et al., 1996)

Please answer with the following selections: Never, Sometimes, Often, or Always for each of the following conditions which directly relate to you about your experiences *immediately after* Hurricane Katrina.

	Never	*Sometimes*	*Often*	*Always*
1. I had trouble sleeping				
2. I had bad dreams or nightmares				
3. I feel upset and restless more than usual				
4. I felt the need to be alone				
5. I got into more verbal arguments than usual				
6. I got into more physical fights than usual				
7. I cried more easily				
8. I was concerned about where I would go to school or work				
9. I missed other family members				
10. I felt very sad about damage to our home or things				
11. I felt very bad about being away from my own home				

	Never	*Sometimes*	*Often*	*Always*
12. I worried a lot about what was going to happen to me and my family				
13. I felt worried and anxious about things in general				
14. I was very sad, moody, and depressed				
15. I got into more trouble at school than usual				

Appendix G

English IV Literary Portfolio Project

English IV (Honors and AP)
Literary Portfolio Project

The Literary Portfolio Project is the final extensive writing assignment for the English IV (Honors and AP) course. Completion of the portfolio is **mandatory**, not optional. Each component of the portfolio will demonstrate your ability to write both informally and formally. While the portfolio contains various pieces or parts, it will be graded as a single unit. Each part of the portfolio should be complete, thorough, and correctly formatted. The entire portfolio must be typed and turned in on or before April 15, 2008 (by 3:10 p.m.). The **MLA** style is the only accepted format for this project (unlike the research paper, the portfolio is **single-spaced**). A sample portfolio is included in this packet.

The Literary Portfolio Project includes the following components:

Author's Letter (1 page)—this piece is a letter to your reader, that introduces him to you as a writer. In the letter you may describe your style and outlook on different types of literary writing. The letter should include a brief description of each part of the portfolio and the reason(s) why it was chosen to be a part of the portfolio project.

Informal Thinking (1 page)—this piece is any entry included in your journal from this class (from any quarter). Rewrite your first thoughts on the topic discussed in that particular journal; then write your second or current thoughts on this topic. Although this is informal writing, it should be thorough, tasteful, and inoffensive.

Short Analytical Essay (1-2 pages)—this is a formal essay that analyzes the following quote by Alfred Lord Tennyson: "Tis better to have loved and lost than never to have loved at all." In a multi-paragraph essay discuss the validity or inaccuracy of such a quote. Remember, this is formal writing. Thus mechanics, usage, vocabulary, and spelling are very important.

Narrative (1 page)—in this piece relate a personal story that supports the thesis statement (main idea) of your short analytical essay. (You may want to change names, in your narrative, if privacy is an issue for classmates who may be discussed in the story).

Responses to Educational Journal Articles (1 page)—this piece will include brief summaries and your responses to two articles found in educational journals (articles will be provided in class). Your response should include, but is not limited to, answers to the following questions: What have you learned from the article? What is most interesting about the article? If you could meet the article's author, what one question would you ask him? Why?

Bibliography

Adolescent programming experiences during conflict and post conflict: Case studies. (June 2004). New York: UNICEF.

Alvarez, D.M. (2010). "I had to teach hard": Teaching and trauma after Katrina. Under review at *The High School Journal,* Fall 2010.

Alverman, D.E. (ed.) (1998). Reconceptualizing the literacies in adolescents' lives. Mahweh, N.J.: Lawrence Erlbaum Press.

Anderson, C.M., and MacCurdy, M. (eds.) (2000). Writing and healing: Toward an informed practice. Urbana, Ill.: NCTE.

Atwell, N. (1987). In the middle. Portsmouth, N.H.: Boynton/Cook Publishers.

Barenbaum, J., Vladislaw, R., and Schwab-Stone, M. (2004). The Psychosocial aspects of children exposed to war: Practice and policy initiatives. *Journal of Child Psychology and Psychiatry,* 45 (1), 41–62.

Barrett, E.J., Ausbrooks, C.Y., and Martinez-Cosio, M. (2008). The school as source of support for Katrina-evacuted youth. *Child, Youth and Environment,* 18 (1), 202–235.

Barton, D., Hamilton, M., and Ivanic, R. (2000). Situated literacies: Reading and writing in context. New York: Routledge.

Berger, G.R. (2006). Memory: Illustration-brain regions. *Psychotherapy and Neuroscience.* Retrieved March 1, 2010 from http://www.nature-nurture.org/index.php/ptsd/memory/illustration-brain-regions/.

Bishop, W. (1993). Writing is/and therapy? Raising questions about writing classroom and writing program administration. *Journal of Advanced Composition,* 13 (2), 502–516.

———. (1999). Ethnographic writing research. Portsmouth, N.H.: Boynton/Cook.

Bissex, G. (1980). Gnys at wrk: A child learns to write and read. Cambridge: Harvard University Press.

Blitz, M., and Hurlbert, C.M. (1998). Letters for the living: Teaching writing in a violent age. Urbana, Ill.: NCTE.

Bomer, R. (1995). Time for meaning. Portsmouth, N.H.: Heinemann Publishing.

Bozhovich, L.I. (1980). Stages in the formation of the personality in ontogeny. *Soviet Psychology*, 19, 61–79.

———. (1979). Stages in the formation of the personality in ontogeny [II], *Soviet Psychology*, 17, 3–24.

Bracher, M. (1999). The writing cure: Psychoanalysis, composition and the aims of education. Carbondale: Southern Illinois University Press.

Brand, A.G. (1989). The psychology of writing: The affective experience. Westport, Conn.: Greenwood Press.

Brand, A.G., and Graves, R.L. (eds.) (1994). Presence of mind: Writing and the domain beyond the cognitive. Portsmouth, N.H.:Boynton/Cook Publishers.

Brandt, D. (1990). Literacy as involvement. Carbondale: Southern Illinois University Press.

Britton, J. (1970). Language and learning. London: Allen Lane, The Penguin Press.

Britton, J., Burgess, T., Martin, N., and MacLeod, A. (1975). The development of writing abilities (11–18). London: MacMillan Publishing.

Brock, S., Lazarus, P., and Jimerson, S.R. (2006). Best practices in school crisis prevention and intervention. Bethesda, Md.; NASP.

Brooke, R.E. (1991). Writing and sense of self. Urbana, Ill.: NCTE.

Bruner, J. (1986). Actual minds, possible worlds. Cambridge: Harvard University Press.

Cohen, J., Mannarino, A.P., and Deblinger, E. (2006). Treating trauma and traumatic grief in children and adolescents. New York: Guilford Press.

Csikszentmihalyi, M., and Larson, R.(1984). Being adolescent. New York: Basic Books.

Cushman, E. (1998). The struggles and the tools: Oral and literate strategies in an inner-city community: Albany, N.Y.: SUNY Press.

Damiani, V.B. (2006). Crisis prevention and intervention in the classroom: What teachers should know. Lanham, Md.: Rowman and Littlefield Education.

Denzin, N.K., and Lincoln, Y.S. (1994). Handbook of qualitative research. Thousand Oaks, Calif.: Sage Publications.

DeSalvio, L. (1999). Writing as a way of healing. San Francisco: Harper Collins Publishing.

DeStiger, T. (2001). Reflections of a citizen teacher. Urbana, Ill.: NCTE.

Dewey, J. (1939). Experience and education. New York: MacMillan.

Dixon, J., and Stratta, L. (1986). Writing narrative and beyond. Canadian Council of Teachers of English.

Dixon-Krauss, L. (1996). Vygotsky in the classroom. White Plains, N.Y.: Longman Publishers.

Dyregrov, A. (1991). Caring for helpers in disaster situations: Psychological debriefing. *Disaster Management*, 2 (1), 25–30.

Dyregrov, A., and Mitchell, J.T. (1992). Work with traumatized children: Psychological effects and coping strategies. *Journal of Traumatic Stress,* 5, 15-17.

Dyson, A.H., and Genishi, C. (eds.) (1994). The need for story: Cultural diversity in community and classroom. Urbana, Ill.: NCTE.

Eisner, C., and Vicinus, M. (eds.) (2008). Originality, imitation, and plagiarism: Teaching writing in the digital age. Ann Arbor: University of Michigan Press.

Elbow, P. (1973). Writing without teachers. Oxford, UK: Oxford University Press.

———. (1990). What is English? New York: MLA & NCTE.

Emig, J. (1971). The Composing Process of Twelfth Graders. Research Report #13. Urbana, Ill.: NCTE.

English Journal. (2006). Looking forward: Teaching English after 9/11. 96 (2).

Erikson, E. (1968). Identity, youth, and crisis. New York: W.W. Norton & Co.

Fetterman, D.M. (1998). Ethnography: Step by step. Applied Social Research Methods. Thousand Oaks, Calif.: Sage.

Finders, M. (1997). Just girls. New York: Teachers College Press.

Fine, M. (1991). Framing Dropouts: Notes on the politics of an urban public high school. Albany, N.Y.: State University Press.

Flower, L. (1994). The construction of negotiated meaning. Carbondale: Southern Illinois University Press.

Flower, L., and Hayes, J.R. (1981). A cognitive process theory of writing. *College Composition and Communication,* 32 (4), 365–87.

Foertsch, J. (1995). Where cognitive psychology applies: How theories about memory and transfer can influence composition pedagogy. *Written Communication*, 12 (3), 260–383.

Foucault, M. (1972). The archeology of knowledge and the discourse on language. New York: Pantheon Books.

Freire, P. (1970). Pedagogy of the oppressed. New York: Continuum Publishing Co.

Gallagher, K. (2006). Teaching adolescent writers. Portland, Me.: Stenhouse Publishers.

Gardner, H. (2006). Multiple intelligences. 2nd Edition. New York: Basic Books.

Gee, J. (2003). What video games have to teach us about learning and literacy. New York: Palgrave MacMillan.

Gilmore, P., and Glatthorn, A.A. (eds) (1982). Children in and out of school: Ethnography and education. Philadelphia: University of Pennsylvania, HBJ & Center for Applied Linguistics.

Goenjian, A.K., Molina, L., Steinberg, A.M., Fairbanks, L.A., Alvarez, M.L., Goenjian, H.A., and Pynoos, R.S. (2001). Post-traumatic stress and depressive reactions among Nicaraguan adolescents after Hurricane Mitch. *American Journal of Psychiatry,* 158, (5), 788–794.

Graves, D. (1983). Writing: Teachers and children at work. Portsmouth, N.H.: Heinemann Publishing Co.

Gruwell, E. (1999). The freedom writers diary. New York: Broadway Books.

Harris, J. (1996). A teaching subject: Composition since 1966. Upper Saddle River, N.J.: Prentice Hall.

———. (2003). Signifying pain: Constructing and healing the self through writing. Albany, N.Y.: SUNY Press.

Harste, J., Short, K., and Burke, C. (1988). Creating classrooms for authors. Portsmouth, N.H.: Heinemann.

Hartman, C., and Squire, G.D. (2006). There is no such thing as a natural disaster. New York: Routledge.

Heath, S.B. (1983). Ways with words. New York: Cambridge University Press.

Heath, S.B., and Athanases, S. (1995). Ethnography in the study of teaching and learning of English. *Research in the Teaching of English*, 29 (3), 263–287.

Heath, S.B., and Street, B. (2007). Ethnography: Approaches to language and literacy research. New York: Teachers College Press & National Conference on Research in Language and Literacy.

Howard, R.M. (1995). Plagarisms, authorships and the academic death penalty. *College English*, 57 (7), 788–806.

Hull, G., and Schultz, K. (2002). School's out: Bridging out of school literacies with classroom practice. New York: Teachers College Press.

Jackson, S., and Rodriguez-Tomé, H. (1983). Adolescence and its social world. Sussex, UK: Erlbaum Press.

Jarrat, S. (1991). Feminism and composition: The case for conflict. *Contending with Words: Composition in a Postmodern Era*. New York: MLA.

Jensen, E. (1999). Teaching with the brain in mind: Practical application of brain research. Learning, Emotion, and the Brain Conference at University of Wisconsin-Madison, Feb. 25.

Johnson, T.R. (2000). Writing as healing and the rhetorical tradition. Anderson, C., & MacCurdy, M. (eds.) *Writing and Healing*. Urbana, Ill.: NCTE.

Kirsch, G.E., and Mortensen, P. (1996). Ethics and representation in qualitative studies of literacy. Urbana, Ill.: NCTE.

Kliman, G., Oklan, E., Wolfe, H., and Kliman, J. (2005). My personal story about Hurricanes Katrina and Rita. San Francisco: Children's Psychological Health Care.

Knobel, M. (1999). Everyday literacies: Students, discourses and social practice. New York: Peter Lang.

Ladson-Billings, G. (1994). The dreamkeepers: Successful teachers of African American children. San Francisco: Jossey-Bass Publishers.

Levine, K. (1986). The social context of literacy. London: Routledge & Kennan Paul.

Lewis, C., Enciso, P., and Moje, E.B. (2007). Reframing sociocultural research on literacy: Identity, agency and power. Mahwah, N.J.: Erlbaum.

Lincoln, Y.S., and Guba, E. (1985). Naturalistic inquiry. Newbury Park, Calif.: Sage Publications.

MacCurdy, M.M. (2007). The mind's eye: Image and memory in writing about trauma. Amherst: University of Massachusetts Press.

Macrorie, K. (1970). Telling writing. New York: Hayden Book Co..

———. (1984). Searching writing. Upper Montclair, N.J.: Boynton/Cook Publishers.

Mandell, N. (1988). The least adult role in studying children. *Journal of Contemporary Ethnography*, 18 (4), 433–465.

McCarthy, M. (1987). Stranger in a strange land: A college student writing across the curriculum. *Research in the Teaching of English*, 3, 233–265.

Mead, M. (1961). Coming of age in Samoa. NewYork: Harper and Collins Publishers.

Miller, D.S., and Rivera, J.D. (2007). Landscapes of disaster and place orientation in the aftermath of Hurricane Katrina. In Brunsma, D.L., Overflet, D., and Picoiu, S. *The Sociology of Katrina*. Lanham, Md.: Rowman and Littlefield Publishers.

Moffett, J. (1968). Teaching the universe of discourse. Boston: Houghton Mifflin.

Moffett, J., and Wagner, M.J. (1976). Student-centered language arts and reading, K–13: A handbook for teachers. Boston: Houghton- Mifflin.

Moje, E., and O'Brien, D. (eds.) (2001). Constructions of literacy. Mahwah, N.J.: Lawrence Erlbaum.

Moll, L. (Ed.) (1990).Vygotsky and education. New York: Cambridge University Press.

Morris, J.E. (2008). Out of New Orleans: Race, class, and researching the Katrina diaspora. *Urban Education*, 43 (4), 463–487.

National Institute of Mental Health (2003). Child and adolescent violence research. http://www.nimh.gov/publicat/violenceresfact.cfm.

New London Group (1996). A pedagogy of multiliteracies: Designing social futures. *Harvard Educational Review*, 66 (1).

Nunley, K.F. (2003). How the adolescent brain challenges the adult brain. Retrieved February 17, 2003 from http://help4teachers.com/prefrontalcortex.htm.

Nystrand, M. (1997). Opening dialogue. New York: Teachers College Press.

O'Connor, S. (1996). Will my name be shouted out? New York: Touchstone Press.

Peek, L. (2008). Children and disasters: Understanding vulnerability, developing capacities, and promoting resilience—an introduction. *Children, Youth, and Environments* 18 (1), 1–29.

Pennebaker, J.W. (1990). Opening up. New York: William Morrow and Co.

———. (ed.) (1995). Emotion, disclosure, and health. Washington, D.C.: American Psychological Association.

———. (2000). Telling stories: The health benefits of narrative. *Literature and Medicine*. 19 (1), 3–18.

Pratt, M.L. (1991). Arts of the contact zone. *Profession*, 91, 33–40.

Reich, J.A, and Wadsworth, M. (2008). Out of the floodwaters, but not yet on dry ground: Experiences of displacement and adjustment in adolescents and their parents following Hurricane Katrina. *Children, Youth, and Environment*, 18 (1), 354–370.

Reid, W.H., and Wise, M.G. (1995). DSM-IV training guide. New York: Brunner/ Mazel Publishers.

Reijneveid, S., Crone, M., and Verhulst, V.V. (2003). The effect of a severe disaster on the mental health of adolescents: A controlled study. *The Lancet*, 362, 691–696.

Rico, G.L. (1983). Writing the natural way. Los Angeles: J.P. Tarcher, Inc.

———. (2008). The power of story. Spring, Tex.: Absey and Co.

Romano, T. (1995). Writing with passion in life stories: Multiple genres. Portsmouth, N.H.: Boynton/Cook.

———. (2000). Blending genre, altering style. Portsmouth, N.H.: Boynton/Cook/ Heinemann.

Scribner, S., and Cole, M. (1981). The psychology of literacy. Cambridge: Harvard University Press.

Smagorinsky, P. (1995). How English teachers get taught. Urbana, Ill.: NCTE.

Solsken, J.W. (1995). Literacy, gender, and work in families and schools. Language and Educational Processes. New York: Ablex Publishing.

Spradley, J. (1979.) The ethnographic interview. Orlando, Fla.: Holt, Rinehart & Winston.

Stake, R.E. (1995). The art of case study research. Thousand Oaks, Calif.: Sage Publications.

Thompson, T. Jr., and Massat, C.R. (2005). Experiences of violence, post-traumatic stress, academic achievement, and behavior problems of urban African-American children. *Child and Adolescent Social Work Journal*, 22 (5–6), 367–393.

Tisserand, M. (2007). Sugarcane academy. Orlando, Fla.: Harcourt, Inc.

Tomlinson, C.A. (2000). Differentiated instruction: Responding to the needs of all learners. Alexandria, Va.: ACSD.

Tsujimoto, J. (2001). Lighting fires. Portsmouth, N.H.: Boynton/Cook/Heinemann.

van der Kolk, B., McFarlane, A.C., and Weisaeth, L. (1996). Traumatic stress: The effect of overwhelming experience on mind, body, and society. New York: Guilford Press.

Van Maanen, J. (1988). Tales of the field: On writing ethnography. Chicago: University of Chicago Press.

Voices of hope: Adolescents and the tsunami. (2005). UNICEF. Adolescent Development and Participant Unit, 3UN Plaza, New York.

Voss, M. (1996). Hidden literacies. Portsmouth, N.H.: Heinemann Publishing Co.

Vygotsky, L. (1962). Thought and language. Cambridge: MIT Press.

———. (1978). Mind in society. Cambridge: Harvard University Press.

Warheit, G., Zimmerman, R., Khoury, E., Vega, W., and Gail, A.G. (1996). Disaster-related stresses, depressive sign and symptoms, and suicidal ideation among a multi-racial/ethnic sample of adolescents: A longitudinal analysis. *Journal of Child Psychology* 37 (4), 435–444.

Weems, C.F., and Overstreet, S. (2008). Child and adolescent mental health research in the context of Hurricane Katrina. *Journal of Clinical and Adolescent Psychology*, June, 487–494.

Wolcott, H.F. (1990). Writing up qualitative research. *Qualitative Research Methods Series 20*: Newbury Park, Calif.: Sage Publications.

Wolf, M. (1992). A thrice-told tale: Feminism, postmodernism, and ethnographic responsibility. Stanford, Calif.: Stanford University Press.

Wolmer, L., Laor, N. Dedeoglu, C., Siev, J., and Yazgan, Y. (2005). Teacher-mediated intervention after disaster: A controlled three-year follow-up of children's functioning. *Journal of Child Psychology and Psychiatry*, 24:11, 1161–1168.

Wysocki, A., Johnson-Eilola, F., Selfe, C., and Sirc, G. (2004). Writing new media. Logan: Utah State University Press.

Zemelmen, S., and Daniels, H. (1988). Community of writers. Portsmouth, N.H.: Heinemann.

Zull, J.E. (2002). The art of changing the brain. Sterling, Va.: Stylus.

Index

abstract thinking, 146
adaptation: of media, 102–3; rule of, 22–23
adolescence: brain in, 7, 134, 142, 224–25; cognition in, 10, 13, 15–16, *16*, 53, 134, 145, 147, 217–18, 226; coping strategies in, 143; crisis of, 8, 9, 53, 88, 95, 104, 231–32; desires in, 95; emotion during, 10–11, 225; employment in, 192, 196, 223; female, 106; flow in, 16–17, 147; Hurricane Katrina's effect on, 148, 202–3, 204, 214; identity during, 8, 47, 53–54, 78–79, 95, 130–31, 230; individualism in, 53; language use in, 14; learning in, x–xii; needs in, 103, 104, 136, 137, 204, 221, 222; oppression in, 222; research methodology, 33–34, *34*, 37–38, 158, 161–62; rites of passage in, 190; self-awareness in, 102, 104; story telling in, 119; substance abuse in, 106; trust in, 12, 144, 151, 152; violence during, x, xii–xiv, 8–9, 12, 13, 218, 221; young adulthood phase of, 53, 56–57, 95
affective-volitional tendency, 10
African Americans, 156

ages, 30
Algiers, 170
Alverman, D. E., 17
American Psychiatric Association, 141
amygdala, *146*; cognition from, 10; emotion in, 95, 224; flow and, 147; significance from, 11, 13; traumatic stress and, 145
Anderson, C. M., 11
appearance, 105, 106, 196
archeology, 120
armed conflicts, ix, 12
Army Corp of Engineers, 169
art, 42, 47
assimilation: into culture, 76–77; of education, 110
Atwell, N., 219
audience, 119, 136, 137
authority, 46
autobiographical narrative, 51–52

Bain, Alexander, 219
Barenbaum, J., 12–13
basketball, 165, 166, 176
behavior: after natural disaster, 143, 144; risky, 143, 144
bigamy, 156
Bishop, Wendy, 6

St. Bernard Parish, 155
St. Charles Street, 155
State Assessment Survey (SAS), 125, 126
status symbol, 196
"Stella Calling" contest, 155
story telling, 17–18; for adolescents,
119; after traumatic stress, 149, 228;
autobiographical, 51–52; by Chase,
81–82, 84–85; as compensatory
strategy, 100–101, 136; culture in, 49;
emotion in, 133; of families, 65–66;
instruction in, 220; language with,
85, 180; in media, 81–82, 85; by Mr.
Muller, 79; personal, 189; revision of,
149–50; self-awareness through, 104;
as self-expression, 86; visual, 131–34
*A Student-Centered Language Arts
and Reading Curriculum* (Moffett),
219–20
students: engagement of, 79–81; limitations
with, 70, 87, 88; manipulation by,
193–94; needs of, 152, 178, 191, 206,
212, 221; support for, 128
student-writer-author, 227
substance abuse: by adolescents, 106;
in family, 110, 122, 128, 135, 202;
writing about, 150
suicide, 72
summaries, 80
syntax, 88

tattoo, 188, 189
Taylor, Denny, ix
teachers: after traumatic stress,
148, 188, 190, 191, 196–97,
215–16; communication with, 115;
compensatory strategies of, 153, 172,
175, 177–78, 179, 190, 191, 206,
216; connection with, 113, 224; goals
of, 148; in research methodology,
33, *33*, 37–38, 158, 160–61, *161*;
responsibility of, 72, 206, 225, 227;
support for, 191; support from, 152,
232; trust in, 144, 151, 152

Teaching the Universe of Discourse
(Moffett), 219–20
technology, 197–98, 207, 209;
importance of, 215; for visual
learners, 210
Telling Writing (Macrorie), 220
think-aloud protocol, 65, 110
third-person perspective, 54
The Time Machine (Wells), 209
Time magazine, 26n4 205
Tommie: suicide of, 72; writing by,
70–71, 72
traumatic stress: amygdala and, 145;
breakthrough moments with, 183–84,
185; causes of, 141–42; children
after, 142; classroom after, 148,
170–71, 177–79; cognition with, 13,
53–54, 111, 131, 133, 142–43, 145,
147, 152, 224, 226, 230; counseling
after, 170, 202; curriculum for, 53,
221, 232; definition of, 9; effect of,
6–7, 53–54; expression of, 21, 113,
228; integration of, 18, 19, 20, 43,
53, 54, 57, 60, 67, 134, 182; learning
after, x, 151–52, 176, 182, 187, 192,
203, 205, 225, 232; as material, 59;
from relationships, 129–30; revisions
with, 60; story telling after, 149, 228;
symptoms of, 12, 142; teachers after,
148, 188, 190, 191, 196–97, 215–16;
violence after, 144; writing for, 175,
187, 212, 222, 226. *See also* disaster,
natural; Post Traumatic Stress
Disorder
Tremé, 156
trust, 12, 144, 151, 152
tsunami. *See* Indonesian Tsunami
Tyrone, 154, 200; after Hurricane Katrina,
213–14; compensatory strategies of,
197–98, 206–7, 209, 210–11, 212–13;
family of, 193, 195–96; friends of,
193, 194, 201, 202; privileges of, 193,
194, 204; self-awareness of, 214;
writing by, 195, 207–10, 211, 214

About the Author

Deborah M. Alvarez began her teaching career in Kansas as secondary English language arts teacher. After receiving her doctorate from the University of Wisconsin–Madison in composition studies, Deborah now teaches methods and writing courses to future teachers at the University of Delaware while continuing her research in the effects of natural disasters on teacher instruction and adolescent writing.

Breinigsville, PA USA
16 January 2011
253388BV00003B/2/P